The Essential Keto Diet
Cookbook for Beginners 2023

2000+ Days Super Easy, Low Carb & Low Sugar Keto Recipes Book - Help Lose Extra Body Fat | Includes 30-Day Meal Plan

Carrie E. Hughes

Copyright© 2023 By Carrie E. Hughes

All rights reserved worldwide.

No part of this book may be reproduced or transmitted in any form or by any means, electronic or mechanical, including photo- copying, recording or by any information storage and retrieval system, without written permission from the publisher, except for the inclusion of brief quotations in a review.

Warning-Disclaimer

The purpose of this book is to educate and entertain. The author or publisher does not guarantee that anyone following the techniques, suggestions, tips, ideas, or strategies will become successful. The author and publisher shall have neither liability or responsibility to anyone with respect to any loss or damage caused, or alleged to be caused, directly or indirectly by the information contained in this book.

Table of Contents

INTRODUCTION	1

Chapter 1 Keto Diet Essentials — 2

The Power of the Ketogenic Diet	2	Tips for Success on the Keto Journey	10
The Basic Principles of the Ketogenic Diet	4	Conclusion and Invitation	12
Why This Cookbook is Different	6	30 Days Keto Diet Meal Plan	14
Navigating the Cookbook	8		

Chapter 2 Breakfasts — 16

Super Green Smoothie with Coconut and Raspberries	16	Kale Pâté	22
Chocolate Chip Pancake	16	Heart-Healthy Hazelnut-Collagen Shake	22
Creamy Almond Coffee Smoothie	16	Italian Sausage Stacks	22
Blackberry Vanilla Cake	16	Blackberry-Chia Pudding	22
Buffalo Chicken Breakfast Muffins	17	Nutty "Oatmeal"	22
Santa Fe Frittata	17	Sausage, Egg, and Cheese Breakfast Bake	23
Pumpkin Spice Keto Pancakes	17	Meritage Eggs	23
Mushroom Frittata	17	Breakfast Quesadilla	23
Baked Eggs in Avocados	18	Hashed Zucchini & Bacon Breakfast	23
BLT Breakfast Wrap	18	Classic Coffee Cake	24
Mini Spinach Quiche	18	Cauliflower Avocado Toast	24
Pancake for Two	18	Breakfast Burrito Bowls	24
Cheesy Egg and Spinach Nest	18	Cream Cheese Muffins	24
Chocolate Chip Waffle	19	Ricotta Cloud Pancakes with Whipped Cream	25
Yogurt Parfait with Creamy Blueberry Crumble	19	Egg Roll in a Bowl	25
Mug Biscuit	19	Cinnamon Roll Fat Bombs	25
Lemon–Olive Oil Breakfast Cakes with Berry Syrup	19	Parmesan Baked Eggs	25
Bacon Spaghetti Squash Fritters	20	DLK Bulletproof Coffee	26
Rosti with Bacon, Mushrooms, and Green Onions	20	Bacon-Wrapped Western Quiche Tarts	26
Creamy Cinnamon Porridge	20	Broccoli & Colby Cheese Frittata	26
Olivia's Cream Cheese Pancakes	20	Pumpkin Spice Latte Overnight "Oats"	26
Butter Coffee Latte	21	Ham and Vegetable Frittata	26
Pulled Pork Hash	21	Sausage and Cheese Balls	27
Breakfast Bake	21	Cauliflower & Cheese Burgers	27
Greek Yogurt Parfait	21		
Smoked Salmon and Cream Cheese Roll-Ups	21		

Chapter 3 Poultry — 28

- Baked Cheesy Mushroom Chicken 28
- Chicken Thighs with Cilantro 28
- Buffalo Chicken Crust Pizza 28
- Chicken Croquettes with Creole Sauce 29
- Chicken with Parmesan Topping 29
- Buttery Garlic Chicken 29
- Herb and Lemon Whole Chicken 29
- Crunchy Chicken Milanese 30
- "K.F.C." Keto Fried Chicken 30
- Chicken with Lettuce 30
- Chicken with Monterey Jack Cheese 30
- Caprese Chicken Thighs 31
- Parmesan Baked Chicken 31
- Chicken Gumbo 31
- Pesto Chicken 31
- Thanksgiving Turkey Breast 32
- Garlic & Ginger Chicken with Peanut Sauce 32
- Bruschetta and Cheese Stuffed Chicken 32
- Marjoram Chicken Wings with Cream Cheese 32
- Chicken Patties 33
- Fried Chicken Breasts 33
- Chipotle Dry-Rub Wings 33
- Pancetta & Chicken Casserole 33
- Turmeric Chicken Nuggets 34
- Zucchini Spaghetti with Turkey Bolognese Sauce 34
- Pecorino Chicken 34
- Poblano Chicken 34
- Chicken Cordon Bleu 34
- Cheese Stuffed Chicken 35
- Coconut Curry Chicken 35
- Chicken Fajitas with Bell Peppers 35
- Easy Chicken Chili 35
- Buttered Duck Breast 36
- Creamy Stuffed Chicken with Parma Ham 36
- Chicken Skewers with Celery Fries 36

Chapter 4 Beef, Pork, and Lamb — 37

- Braised Short Ribs 37
- Cheesy Southwestern Meat Loaf 37
- Stuffed Pork with Red Cabbage Salad 37
- Ground Beef Stroganoff 38
- Jamaican Pork Oven Roast 38
- Beef Sausage Casserole 38
- Beef Meatballs 38
- Veal Stew 38
- Chili Cheese Pot Pie 39
- Beef Flank Steak with Sage 39
- Garlicky Pork with Bell Peppers 39
- Mojito Lamb Chops 39
- Sloppy Joe Chili 40
- Blue Cheese Steak Salad 40
- Peppercorn Pork with Salsa Verde 40
- Sausage Bagels 41
- Paprika Pork Chops 41
- Simple Liver and Onions 41
- Chorizo and Beef Burger 41
- Pepperoni Low-Carb Tortilla Pizza 41
- Cajun Bacon Pork Loin Fillet 42
- Parmesan Pork Chops and Roasted Asparagus 42
- Beef Shoulder Roast 42
- Swiss-Style Italian Sausage 42
- Beef Back Ribs with Barbecue Glaze 43
- Shoulder Chops with Lemon-Thyme Gravy 43
- Pork Goulash with Cauliflower 43
- Beef Provençal 43
- Sausage and Peppers 44
- Italian Beef Meatloaf 44
- Spaghetti Squash and Ground Pork Stir-Fry with Kale 44
- Paprika Pork Ribs 44
- Cilantro Pork 45
- Rosemary Pork Belly 45
- Easy Zucchini Beef Lasagna 45
- Lamb Koobideh 45
- Grilled Herbed Pork Kebabs 45
- Baked Pork Meatballs in Pasta Sauce 46
- Cottage Pie 46
- Buttery Beef and Spinach 46

Chapter 5 Fish and Seafood — 47

- Cheesy Garlic Salmon 47
- Tilapia Fillets with Arugula 47
- Snapper Scampi 47
- Seared Scallops with Chorizo and Asiago Cheese 47
- Cod Fillets with Cherry Tomatoes 48
- Basil Alfredo Sea Bass 48
- Zoodles in Clam Sauce 48
- Pork Rind Salmon Cakes 48
- Coconut Shrimp with Spicy Dipping Sauce 49
- Oven-Baked Dijon Salmon 49
- Salmon Poke 49
- Halibut in a Butter and Garlic Blanket 49
- Cajun Cod Fillet 50
- Sole Asiago 50
- Lemony Salmon 50
- Shrimp Zoodle Alfredo 50
- Pan-Seared Scallops with Lemon Butter 50
- Sushi 51
- Simply Broiled or Air-Fried Salmon 51
- Pan-Seared Lemon-Garlic Salmon 51
- Garlic Lemon Scallops 51
- Tuna Stuffed Poblano Peppers 52
- Dill Lemon Salmon 52
- Pistachio-Crusted Salmon 52
- Muffin Top Tuna Pops 52
- Parmesan Lobster Tails 52
- Cod with Jalapeño 53
- Coconut Shrimp Curry 53
- Fried Red Snapper 53
- Mackerel and Broccoli Casserole 53
- White Fish with Cauliflower 53
- Sardine Fritter Wraps 54
- Lemon Shrimp Skewers 54
- Shrimp Alfredo 54
- Tuna with Herbs 54
- Caprese Salmon 55
- Baked Tilapia and Parmesan 55
- Tuna Salad Wrap 55
- Shrimp Bake 55

Chapter 6 Snacks and Appetizers — 56

- Creole Pancetta and Cheese Balls 56
- Chinese Spare Ribs 56
- Baked Brie with Pecans 56
- Granola Clusters 56
- Cucumber Salmon Coins 57
- Warm Herbed Olives 57
- Easy Baked Zucchini Chips 57
- Keto Taco Shells 57
- Lemon-Cheese Cauliflower Bites 57
- Easy Peasy Peanut Butter Cookies 58
- Sweet and Spicy Beef Jerky 58
- Cinnamon Sugar Muffins 58
- 90-Second Bread 58
- Smoky "Hummus" and Veggies 59
- Antipasto Skewers 59
- Loaded Bacon and Cheddar Cheese Balls 59
- Fresh Rosemary Keto Bread 59
- Crispy Grilled Kale Leaves 60
- N'Oatmeal Bars 60
- Hushpuppies 60
- Pesto-Stuffed Mushrooms 60
- Cauliflower Fritters with Cheese 61
- Herbed Zucchini Slices 61
- Zucchini Chips 61
- Almond Sesame Crackers 61
- Garlic Meatballs 61
- Keto Asian Dumplings 62
- Fried Cabbage Wedges 62
- Finger Tacos 62
- Parmesan Chicken Balls with Chives 62
- Sweet Pepper Nacho Bites 63
- Lime Brussels Chips 63
- 3-Ingredient Almond Flour Crackers 63
- Ketone Gummies 63
- Olive Pâté 63
- Cayenne Beef Bites 64
- Mac Fatties 64
- Broccoli with Garlic-Herb Cheese Sauce 64
- Herbed Cashew Cheese 64
- Cream Cheese and Berries 65
- Parmesan Crisps 65
- Haystack Cookies 65
- Curried Broccoli Skewers 65
- Red Wine Mushrooms 65
- Lemon-Butter Mushrooms 65
- Garlic Herb Butter 66
- Chicken and Cabbage Salad 66
- Baked Crab Dip 66

- Sausage Balls ... 66
- Greens Chips with Curried Yogurt Sauce ... 66
- Salmon-Stuffed Cucumbers ... 67
- Walnut Herb-Crusted Goat Cheese ... 67
- Macadamia Nut Cream Cheese Log ... 67
- Sarah's Expert Crackers ... 67
- Crab Salad–Stuffed Avocado ... 67
- Cheesy Sausage Balls ... 68
- Bacon-Cheddar Dip Stuffed Mushrooms ... 68
- Buffalo Chicken Meatballs ... 68
- Salami Chips with Buffalo Chicken Dip ... 68
- Keto Trail Mix ... 69
- Burrata Caprese Stack ... 69
- Cheesy Spinach Puffs ... 69
- Roasted Garlic Bulbs ... 69
- Herbed Shrimp ... 69
- Salsa Shrimp-Stuffed Avocados ... 70
- Cucumber Finger Sandwiches ... 70
- Pizza Bites ... 70
- Cheese Stuffed Mushrooms ... 70
- English Cucumber Tea Sandwiches ... 70
- Cauliflower Popcorn ... 71
- Low-Carb Granola Bars ... 71
- Sautéed Asparagus with Lemon-Tahini Sauce ... 71
- Avocado Feta Dip ... 71
- Hot Chard Artichoke Dip ... 72
- Pancetta Pizza Dip ... 72
- Smoked Salmon Cream Cheese Rollups with Arugula and Truffle Oil Drizzle ... 72
- Chocolate Soft-Serve Ice Cream ... 72

Chapter 7 Vegetarian Mains 73

- Three-Cheese Zucchini Boats ... 73
- Crispy Eggplant Rounds ... 73
- Crustless Spinach Cheese Pie ... 73
- Broccoli-Cheese Fritters ... 73
- Cauliflower Steak with Gremolata ... 74
- Eggplant Parmesan ... 74
- Broccoli with Garlic Sauce ... 74
- Zucchini-Ricotta Tart ... 74
- Vegetable Burgers ... 75
- Fettuccine Alfredo (2 Variations) ... 75
- Cauliflower Tikka Masala ... 75
- Pesto Vegetable Skewers ... 75
- Greek Vegetable Briam ... 76
- Buffalo Cauliflower Bites with Blue Cheese ... 76
- Cheesy Broccoli Casserole ... 76
- Sweet Pepper Nachos ... 76
- Green Vegetable Stir-Fry with Tofu ... 77
- Herbed Ricotta–Stuffed Mushrooms ... 77
- Stuffed Eggplant ... 77
- Mediterranean Pan Pizza ... 77
- Vegetarian Chili with Avocado and Sour Cream ... 78
- Zucchini Lasagna ... 78
- Eggplant and Zucchini Bites ... 78
- Parmesan Artichokes ... 78
- Cheesy Garden Veggie Crustless Quiche ... 79
- Zucchini Roll Manicotti ... 79
- Mediterranean Filling Stuffed Portobello Mushrooms ... 79
- Greek Stuffed Eggplant ... 80

Chapter 8 Stews and Soups 81

- Beef and Cauliflower Soup ... 81
- Chicken Enchilada Soup ... 81
- Coconut Curry Broccoli Soup ... 81
- Garlicky Chicken Soup ... 81
- Slow Cooker Beer Soup with Cheddar & Sausage ... 82
- Cioppino Seafood Soup ... 82
- Broccoli Ginger Soup ... 82
- Tuscan Kale Soup ... 82
- Beef and Mushroom Stew ... 83
- Chilled Cilantro and Avocado Soup ... 83
- Broc Obama Cheese Soup ... 83
- Cauliflower Rice and Chicken Thigh Soup ... 83
- Broccoli Cheddar Pancetta Soup ... 84
- Power Green Soup ... 84
- Creamy Mushroom Soup ... 84
- Miso Magic ... 84
- Green Garden Soup ... 85
- Venison and Tomato Stew ... 85
- Chili-Infused Lamb Soup ... 85
- Chicken Zucchini Soup ... 85
- Thai Shrimp and Mushroom Soup ... 86
- Avocado and Serrano Chile Soup ... 86
- Pancetta and Jalapeño Soup ... 86
- Mushroom Pizza Soup ... 86
- Shrimp Chowder ... 87
- Tomato-Basil Parmesan Soup ... 87
- Loaded Fauxtato Soup ... 87
- Cauliflower Soup ... 87
- Chicken Soup ... 88
- Curried Chicken Soup ... 88

Chapter 9 Desserts 89

- Creamy Banana Fat Bombs 89
- Chocolate Cheesecake with Toasted Almond Crust 89
- Strawberry Shortcakes 89
- Birthday Mug Cakes 90
- Ultimate Chocolate Cheesecake 90
- Giant Skillet Cookie for Two 90
- Mini Cheesecake 90
- Strawberry-Lime Ice Pops 91
- Cookies-and-Cream Fat Bomb 91
- Electrolyte Gummies 91
- Pecan Butter Cookies 91
- Fresh Cream-Filled Strawberries 91
- Snickerdoodle Cream Cheesecake 92
- Fudge Pops 92
- Blueberry Fat Bombs 92
- Glazed Pumpkin Bundt Cake 92
- Chocolate Mousse 93
- Blackberry "Cheesecake" Bites 93
- Pumpkin Pie Spice Pots De Crème 93
- Protein Powder Doughnut Holes 93
- Pecan Bars 93
- Crustless Cheesecake Bites 94
- Almond Chai Truffles 94
- Daikon and Almond Cake 94
- Mint–Chocolate Chip Ice Cream 94
- Lime Muffins 95
- Lemon Vanilla Cheesecake 95
- Cheesecake 95
- "Frosty" Chocolate Shake 95
- Keto Macaroons 96
- Zucchini Bread 96
- Coconut Whipped Cream 96
- Strawberry Shake 96

Appendix 1: Measurement Conversion Chart 97

Appendix 2: The Dirty Dozen and Clean Fifteen 98

INTRODUCTION

Imagine a way of eating that allows you to shed excess weight while indulging in mouthwatering, satisfying meals. Picture a lifestyle that not only boosts your energy levels but also sharpens your mental clarity. Welcome to the world of the ketogenic diet—a revolutionary approach to nutrition that has taken the health and wellness community by storm. By manipulating your macronutrient intake, the ketogenic diet shifts your body into a state of ketosis, where it efficiently burns stored fat for fuel. The result? A slimmer waistline, improved body composition, and a host of other benefits that go far beyond mere weight loss. Get ready to embark on a journey that will not only transform your relationship with food but also revolutionize your overall well-being.

In this keto cookbook, we have curated a treasure trove of delectable recipes that will tantalize your taste buds while keeping you firmly on track with your keto goals. This cookbook serves as your passport to a world of culinary delights, where every dish is carefully crafted to be both nutritious and delicious. We understand that taste and variety are key to sticking to any eating plan, which is why our collection of recipes spans a wide range of cuisines, flavors, and meal types. From hearty breakfasts to satisfying lunches, from indulgent dinners to mouthwatering desserts, our comprehensive guide has you covered every step of the way. Say goodbye to boring, restrictive meals and say hello to a vibrant and flavorful keto lifestyle.

As the author of this cookbook, I bring to the table not only a passion for flavorful cooking but also a deep understanding of the ketogenic diet. My journey with the ketogenic lifestyle began years ago when I sought a sustainable and enjoyable way to achieve my own health and wellness goals. Through extensive research, experimentation, and culinary creativity, I discovered the art of crafting delicious meals that adhere to the principles of ketosis. Today, as an experienced practitioner and advocate of the ketogenic lifestyle, I am excited to share my knowledge, expertise, and favorite recipes with you. Rest assured, each recipe in this cookbook has been meticulously tested and refined to ensure both taste and nutritional integrity. Join me on this culinary adventure and unlock the secrets to a healthier, happier you.

By using attention-grabbing statements, introducing the cookbook as a comprehensive guide, and establishing the author's expertise and credibility, the introduction sets the stage for an exciting and informative journey through the world of ketogenic cuisine.

Chapter 1 Keto Diet Essentials

The Power of the Ketogenic Diet

The ketogenic diet operates on a simple yet powerful principle: by drastically reducing carbohydrate intake and increasing healthy fats, the body shifts from using glucose as its primary fuel source to relying on ketones, which are produced from fat metabolism. This metabolic shift puts the body into a state called ketosis. In ketosis, the body becomes incredibly efficient at burning stored fat for energy, leading to significant weight loss and improved body composition. When carbohydrates are restricted, insulin levels remain low, allowing stored fat to be released and burned for energy. As a result, stubborn fat deposits, particularly around the waist and abdomen, can be targeted and reduced.

The science behind ketosis is rooted in our evolutionary biology. Our ancestors evolved to adapt to periods of food scarcity, during which the body would rely on fat stores for survival. In the absence of dietary carbohydrates, the liver converts fatty acids into ketones, which are then used as an alternative fuel source. This metabolic adaptation not only promotes fat burning but also supports stable blood sugar levels, reduces inflammation, and enhances mitochondrial function. Mitochondria, the powerhouses of our cells, are responsible for generating energy. Ketones provide a highly efficient and clean source of energy for mitochondria, resulting in improved cellular function and overall vitality.

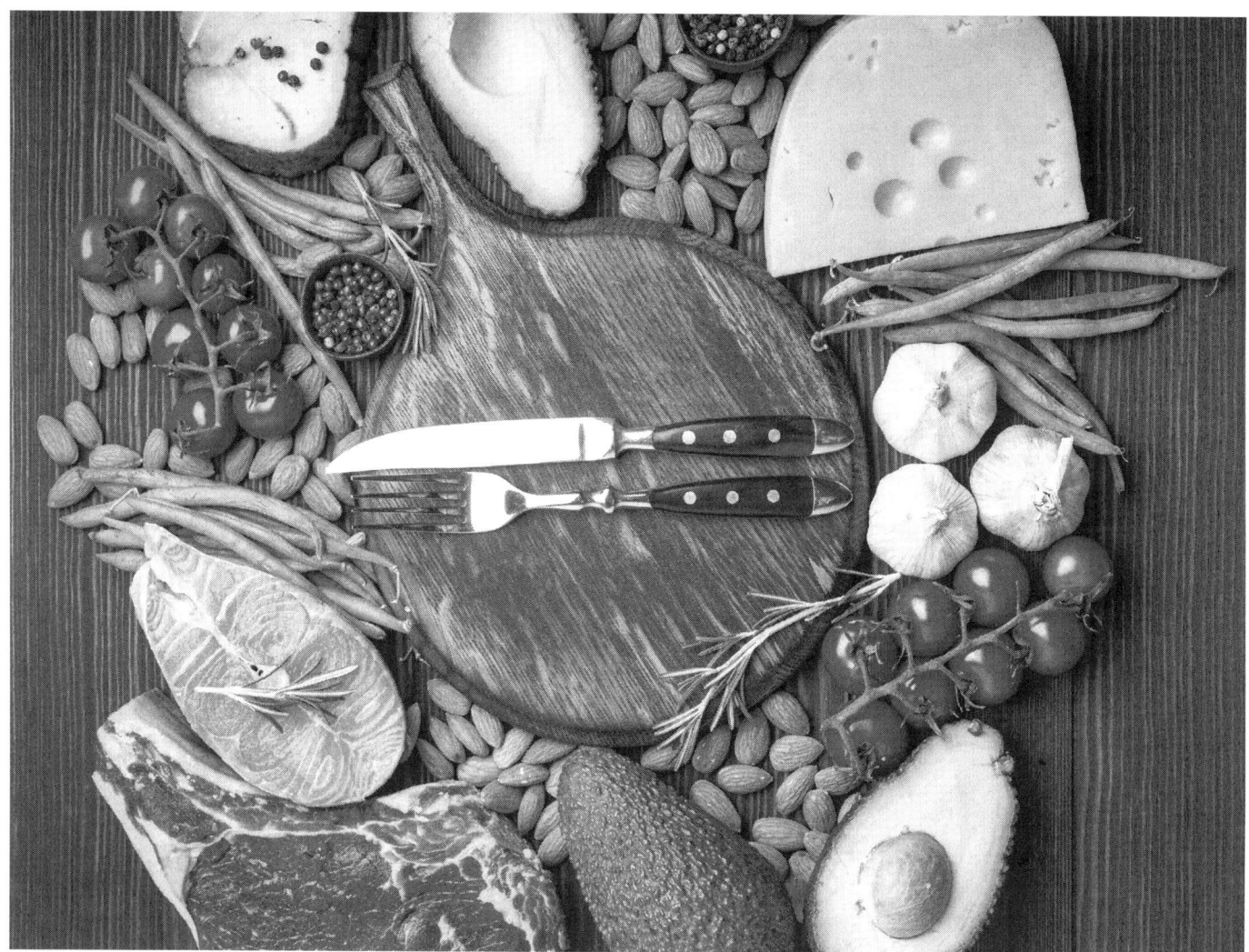

Beyond weight loss, the ketogenic diet has been associated with a wide range of health benefits. Many individuals report experiencing heightened energy levels and improved physical performance due to the stable and sustained energy provided by ketones. By reducing carbohydrate intake, the ketogenic diet can also help regulate blood sugar levels, making it particularly beneficial for individuals with diabetes or insulin resistance. The diet promotes greater insulin sensitivity, allowing the body to efficiently utilize glucose and maintain stable blood sugar levels. Additionally, the ketogenic diet has shown promise in managing epilepsy, reducing seizures in those with drug-resistant forms of the condition. Emerging research suggests that the ketogenic diet may have neuroprotective properties, potentially benefiting conditions like Alzheimer's disease and Parkinson's disease by providing an alternative energy source for the brain and reducing oxidative stress.

The power of the ketogenic diet lies in its ability to reprogram the body's metabolism and tap into its innate fat-burning potential. By adopting a low-carbohydrate, high-fat dietary approach, individuals can experience not only significant weight loss but also a myriad of health benefits. The ketogenic diet offers the potential for improved energy levels, enhanced mental clarity, better blood sugar control, and even neuroprotective effects. Embracing the ketogenic lifestyle allows you to harness the remarkable power of your own body, optimizing your well-being and unlocking a path towards sustainable health.

The Basic Principles of the Ketogenic Diet

The ketogenic diet, often referred to as the keto diet, is a low-carbohydrate, high-fat eating plan that has gained significant popularity in recent years. Its primary goal is to shift the body into a metabolic state called ketosis, where it becomes highly efficient at burning fat for fuel.

The fundamental principles of the ketogenic diet are as follows:

♦ Carbohydrate Restriction:

One of the key principles of the ketogenic diet is the significant restriction of carbohydrate intake. Carbohydrates are the body's primary source of energy, and when consumed in excess, they can lead to the production of glucose and subsequent insulin release. By reducing carbohydrate consumption to a minimal level, typically around 20-50 grams per day, the body is forced to find an alternative fuel source.

♦ Increased Fat Intake:

To compensate for the reduction in carbohydrates, the ketogenic diet emphasizes consuming high amounts of healthy fats. These include sources such as avocados, nuts and seeds, olive oil, coconut oil, and fatty fish. The increased fat intake provides the body with an alternative energy source, as fats are broken down into fatty acids and then converted into ketones by the liver. Ketones can be utilized by the body and the brain as an efficient and sustainable energy source.

- ♦ Moderate Protein Consumption:

While the focus of the ketogenic diet is on reducing carbohydrates and increasing fats, it also includes a moderate intake of protein. Adequate protein is essential for supporting muscle health, tissue repair, and various other physiological functions. However, excessive protein intake can potentially hinder the body's ability to enter and maintain a state of ketosis. The recommended protein intake on the ketogenic diet typically ranges from 0.6 to 1 gram per pound of lean body mass.

- ♦ Ketosis:

The ultimate aim of the ketogenic diet is to induce and maintain a state of ketosis. Ketosis occurs when the body has depleted its carbohydrate stores and begins to rely primarily on fat for energy. In this state, ketones are produced in the liver from fatty acids, which are then used by the body and the brain as an alternative energy source. Achieving ketosis typically requires several days to a couple of weeks of consistently following the diet's principles.

It's important to note that the ketogenic diet is highly individualized, and the ideal macronutrient ratios may vary from person to person based on factors such as activity level, metabolic rate, and personal health goals. However, a common guideline is to aim for a daily intake of approximately 70-75% of calories from fats, 20-25% from protein, and 5-10% from carbohydrates.

By following these basic principles, individuals on the ketogenic diet can effectively transition their bodies into a fat-burning mode and potentially experience numerous health benefits. These may include weight loss, improved insulin sensitivity, increased energy levels, enhanced mental clarity, reduced inflammation, and even potential therapeutic benefits for certain health conditions.

As you explore the recipes in this cookbook, you will find delicious and creative ways to adhere to these principles, making your ketogenic journey both enjoyable and satisfying. The recipes are designed to be rich in healthy fats, moderate in protein, and low in carbohydrates, ensuring that you stay within the boundaries of the ketogenic diet while still indulging in flavorful meals and treats.

Whether you're new to the ketogenic lifestyle or have been following it for some time, this cookbook is here to inspire and guide you on your journey to better health and well-being. So, get ready to embark on a delicious adventure, discover new flavors, and experience the transformative power of the ketogenic diet!

Why This Cookbook is Different

This cookbook stands out from others in the market due to its unique approach and features that cater to the needs and preferences of those following a ketogenic lifestyle.

♦ Unleashing Culinary Creativity:

Unlike many other cookbooks that may rely on repetitive and uninspiring recipes, this cookbook encourages readers to unleash their culinary creativity and explore a wide range of flavors, textures, and ingredients. From decadent comfort foods to vibrant and refreshing dishes, the cookbook provides a diverse selection that keeps keto eating exciting and enjoyable.

♦ Emphasizing Flavor and Variety:

This cookbook understands that taste is paramount in sustaining a healthy eating plan. It goes beyond the notion that keto meals are limited to a few repetitive options. The cookbook offers a wealth of flavorful recipes that span various cuisines, ensuring a diverse and satisfying culinary experience. Readers can explore mouthwatering dishes inspired by Mediterranean, Asian, Mexican, and other global cuisines, all while staying true to the principles of the ketogenic diet.

♦ Practicality and Adaptability:

This cookbook recognizes that busy lifestyles and varying dietary preferences require flexibility. It provides practical guidance on meal planning, prepping, and customization, allowing readers to adapt the recipes to their specific needs. Whether you're a busy professional, a parent juggling multiple responsibilities, or someone with dietary restrictions, this cookbook offers options and tips to make keto cooking practical and accessible.

♦ Education and Empowerment:

This cookbook goes beyond being a mere compilation of recipes. It strives to educate and empower readers with a deep understanding of the ketogenic diet. The cookbook includes valuable information on the science behind ketosis, macronutrient ratios, and how to maintain a well-rounded and balanced keto lifestyle. By providing this knowledge, readers are empowered to make informed decisions, customize their meals, and confidently navigate their keto journey.

♦ A Holistic Approach:

This cookbook recognizes that the ketogenic diet is not solely about weight loss; it encompasses overall health and well-being. It offers a holistic approach by including recipes that prioritize nutrient-dense ingredients, highlight the benefits of whole foods, and promote long-term sustainable eating habits. Readers will find recipes that support gut health, provide essential micronutrients, and prioritize high-quality fats and proteins.

This cookbook sets itself apart from others by offering a unique blend of culinary creativity, flavor, practicality, education, and a holistic approach to keto living. It is a comprehensive resource that caters to the diverse needs and tastes of those embracing a ketogenic lifestyle, making the journey not only effective but also enjoyable and sustainable.

Navigating the Cookbook

This cookbook is designed to make your keto journey seamless and enjoyable. By providing clear guidance and intuitive organization, it aims to empower you to create delicious and nourishing meals that align with your ketogenic lifestyle.

♦ A. Introduction and Getting Started:

The cookbook begins with an informative introduction that sets the stage for your keto experience. It offers an overview of the ketogenic diet, explaining its principles and benefits. Additionally, you'll find practical tips on how to transition into a ketogenic lifestyle, including guidance on pantry essentials, meal planning, and understanding macronutrients.

♦ B. Recipe Categories and Chapters:

The cookbook is divided into thoughtfully curated recipe categories or chapters. Each chapter focuses on a specific aspect of your keto journey, such as breakfast and brunch, appetizers and snacks, main dishes, desserts, and more. Within these chapters, you'll discover an array of tantalizing recipes tailored to your taste buds and dietary needs.

♦ C. Recipe Layout and Instructions:

Each recipe is presented in a clear and user-friendly format. You'll find an enticing photograph of the final dish, followed by a concise list of ingredients, ensuring you have everything you need at your fingertips. The step-by-step instructions are easy to follow, providing guidance on cooking techniques, times, and tips for success. Furthermore, the recipes indicate serving sizes, nutritional information, and any dietary modifications or variations for added flexibility.

♦ D. Flavorful and Nutrient-Dense Ingredients:

This cookbook celebrates the use of flavorful and nutrient-dense ingredients that form the foundation of a satisfying keto diet. You'll discover a variety of fresh vegetables, high-quality proteins, healthy fats, herbs, and spices that combine to create mouthwatering meals. The cookbook encourages you to explore new flavors and experiment with different ingredient combinations to keep your culinary experience exciting and diverse.

♦ E. Special Dietary Considerations:

Recognizing that dietary needs may vary, the cookbook addresses common special considerations. Whether you're looking for dairy-free, gluten-free, or vegetarian options, you'll find recipe variations and substitutions that cater to your specific requirements. The cookbook aims to be inclusive, ensuring that everyone can enjoy the benefits of a ketogenic lifestyle.

♦ F. Tips, Tricks, and Additional Resources:

Throughout the cookbook, you'll find valuable tips, tricks, and suggestions to enhance your cooking experience. From ingredient substitutions to time-saving techniques, these insights are designed to make your keto journey smoother. Additionally, the cookbook may include references to external resources, such as online communities, reputable websites, and recommended reading, to further support your understanding and exploration of the ketogenic lifestyle.

By navigating this cookbook, you'll embark on a culinary adventure that brings the principles of the ketogenic diet to life. The intuitive layout, detailed instructions, and diverse recipe collection will inspire you to create nourishing and delicious meals that fit seamlessly into your keto lifestyle. Whether you're a seasoned keto enthusiast or just starting your journey, this cookbook is your trusted companion for success in the kitchen.

Tips for Success on the Keto Journey

Embarking on a ketogenic lifestyle can be both exciting and challenging. To ensure a successful and sustainable keto journey, consider the following tips:

♦ Educate Yourself:

Take the time to educate yourself about the ketogenic diet and its principles. Understand the macronutrient ratios, learn about food sources that are high in healthy fats and low in carbohydrates, and familiarize yourself with the potential benefits and challenges of the diet. By having a solid foundation of knowledge, you'll be better equipped to make informed choices and navigate potential pitfalls.

♦ Plan and Prep Ahead:

Planning and preparation are key to maintaining a keto lifestyle. Take the time to plan your meals and snacks in advance, ensuring they align with your dietary goals. Consider batch cooking or meal prepping on weekends to save time during busy weekdays. Having keto-friendly meals and snacks readily available will help you stay on track and avoid impulse food choices.

- ♦ Embrace Whole Foods:

Prioritize whole, unprocessed foods on your keto journey. Opt for nutrient-dense choices such as lean proteins, vegetables, healthy fats, and nuts. Avoid highly processed and sugary foods that can derail your progress. By focusing on whole foods, you'll nourish your body with essential nutrients and support your overall well-being.

- ♦ Stay Hydrated:

Adequate hydration is crucial for overall health and well-being, especially on a ketogenic diet. Ensure you drink plenty of water throughout the day to stay properly hydrated. Hydration helps regulate body functions, supports digestion, and can assist in managing keto flu symptoms that may arise during the initial adaptation phase.

- ♦ Listen to Your Body:

Pay attention to your body's signals and adjust your keto journey accordingly. Each individual's response to the ketogenic diet may vary, so be mindful of how certain foods and macronutrient ratios affect your energy levels, satiety, and overall well-being. Tweak your diet as needed to find what works best for you.

- ♦ Don't Be Afraid of Healthy Fats:

Embrace healthy fats as a cornerstone of your keto diet. Avocado, coconut oil, olive oil, nuts, and seeds are excellent sources of healthy fats that provide satiety and essential nutrients. Incorporating these fats into your meals will not only enhance flavor but also help you feel satisfied and support ketosis.

- ♦ Practice Mindful Eating:

Cultivate a mindful eating practice by being present and attentive during meals. Slow down, savor each bite, and pay attention to your body's hunger and fullness cues. Mindful eating can help prevent overeating and promote a healthier relationship with food.

♦ Seek Support and Accountability:

Surround yourself with a supportive community or seek accountability partners who are also on a keto journey. Connecting with like-minded individuals can provide motivation, inspiration, and a space to share challenges and successes. Online forums, social media groups, or local keto meetups are great places to find support and encouragement.

Remember, the keto journey is unique to each individual, and it may take time to find the approach that works best for you. Be patient with yourself, celebrate your successes, and embrace the learning process. With these tips for success, you'll be well-equipped to navigate the keto journey with confidence and achieve your health and wellness goals.

Conclusion and Invitation

Congratulations! By exploring the contents of this cookbook and gaining valuable insights into the ketogenic diet, you have taken a significant step towards improving your health and transforming your relationship with food. As you embark on your keto journey, remember that it is a lifestyle change rather than a short-term fix. It is an opportunity to prioritize your well-being, nourish your body with wholesome ingredients, and discover a world of flavorful and satisfying meals.

This cookbook has been carefully crafted to support and guide you throughout your keto journey. It offers a diverse collection of delicious recipes, practical tips, and educational resources to empower you in the kitchen and on your path to a healthier you. It is more than just a cookbook; it is a companion that will inspire and motivate you to make positive changes in your life.

As you flip through the pages of this cookbook, let your imagination run wild. Experiment with different flavors, adapt the recipes to your liking, and discover your own keto favorites. Embrace the joy of cooking and savor the satisfaction of nourishing your body with wholesome, keto-friendly meals.

We invite you to embark on this exciting journey with us. Together, let's explore the incredible world of ketogenic cuisine, where flavor, health, and enjoyment converge. Whether you're a keto enthusiast, a curious beginner, or someone seeking a fresh approach to healthy eating, this cookbook is here to guide and support you every step of the way.

Get ready to experience the power of the ketogenic diet and unlock a new world of culinary possibilities. Let this cookbook be your trusted companion as you embrace a healthier, more vibrant lifestyle. So, gather your ingredients, fire up your stove, and let's begin this delicious adventure together!

Welcome to the world of keto cuisine.

30 Days Keto Diet Meal Plan

DAYS	BREAKFAST	LUNCH	DINNER	SNACK/DESSERT
1	Mug Biscuit	Three-Cheese Zucchini Boats	Pork Goulash with Cauliflower	Mint–Chocolate Chip Ice Cream
2	Chocolate Chip Pancake	Crispy Eggplant Rounds	Ground Beef Stroganoff	Creamy Banana Fat Bombs
3	Baked Eggs in Avocados	Zucchini-Ricotta Tart	Baked Cheesy Mushroom Chicken	Chocolate Cheesecake with Toasted Almond Crust
4	Nutty "Oatmeal"	Greek Stuffed Eggplant	Cioppino Seafood Soup	Strawberry-Lime Ice Pops
5	Heart-Healthy Hazelnut-Collagen Shake	Mediterranean Pan Pizza	Chicken Enchilada Soup	Cookies-and-Cream Fat Bomb
6	Creamy Almond Coffee Smoothie	Vegetable Burgers	Tuscan Kale Soup	Electrolyte Gummies
7	Blackberry-Chia Pudding	Fettuccine Alfredo (2 Variations)	Venison and Tomato Stew	Pecan Butter Cookies
8	Classic Coffee Cake	Crustless Spinach Cheese Pie	Avocado and Serrano Chile Soup	Chocolate Mousse
9	Olivia's Cream Cheese Pancakes	Broccoli with Garlic Sauce	Slow Cooker Beer Soup with Cheddar & Sausage	Ultimate Chocolate Cheesecake
10	Chocolate Chip Waffle	Broccoli-Cheese Fritters	Garlicky Chicken Soup	Birthday Mug Cakes
11	Creamy Cinnamon Porridge	Sautéed Spinach and Tomatoes	Creamy Mushroom Soup	Mini Cheesecake
12	Cauliflower Avocado Toast	Cauliflower Steak with Gremolata	Pancetta and Jalapeño Soup	Giant Skillet Cookie for Two
13	Blackberry Vanilla Cake	Herbed Ricotta–Stuffed Mushrooms	Miso Magic	Giant Skillet Cookie for Two
14	BLT Breakfast Wrap	Vegetarian Chili with Avocado and Sour Cream	Green Garden Soup	Coconut Whipped Cream
15	Mini Spinach Quiche	Zucchini Lasagna	Mushroom Pizza Soup	Blackberry "Cheesecake" Bites
16	Pancake for Two	Parmesan Artichokes	Coconut Curry Broccoli Soup	Almond Chai Truffles
17	Cheesy Egg and Spinach Nest	Eggplant and Zucchini Bites	Broccoli Ginger Soup	Strawberry Shortcakes
18	Kale Pâté	Eggplant Parmesan	Power Green Soup	Keto Macaroons

DAYS	BREAKFAST	LUNCH	DINNER	SNACK/DESSERT
19	Italian Sausage Stacks	Cheesy Garden Veggie Crustless Quiche	Chicken Zucchini Soup	Crustless Cheesecake Bites
20	Breakfast Burrito Bowls	Sweet Pepper Nachos	Chicken Soup	Keto Macaroons
21	Pulled Pork Hash	Pesto Vegetable Skewers	Broccoli Cheddar Pancetta Soup	Cheesecake
22	Butter Coffee Latte	Cauliflower Tikka Masala	Loaded Fauxtato Soup	Pecan Bars
23	Breakfast Bake	Stuffed Eggplant	Thai Shrimp and Mushroom Soup	Daikon and Almond Cake
24	Greek Yogurt Parfait	Zucchini Roll Manicotti	Chili-Infused Lamb Soup	Zucchini Bread
25	DLK Bulletproof Coffee	Greek Vegetable Briam	Tomato-Basil Parmesan Soup	"Frosty" Chocolate Shake
26	Pumpkin Spice Keto Pancakes	Buffalo Cauliflower Bites with Blue Cheese	Cauliflower Soup	Hot Chard Artichoke Dip
27	Buffalo Chicken Breakfast Muffins	Cheesy Broccoli Casserole	Curried Chicken Soup	Chinese Spare Ribs
28	Santa Fe Frittata	Green Vegetable Stir-Fry with Tofu	Broc Obama Cheese Soup	Herbed Cashew Cheese
29	Mushroom Frittata	Tilapia Fillets with Arugula	Beef and Mushroom Stew	Granola Clusters
30	Cream Cheese Muffins	Snapper Scampi	Cauliflower Rice and Chicken Thigh Soup	Cinnamon Sugar Muffins

Chapter 2 Breakfasts

Super Green Smoothie with Coconut and Raspberries

Prep time: 10 minutes | Cook time: 0 minutes | Serves 2

2 cups spinach
2 cups unsweetened almond milk
1 cup coconut water
2 scoops (25–28 grams) vanilla protein powder
½ cup fresh parsley
½ cup raspberries
2 tablespoons almond butter
2 tablespoons coconut oil
6 ice cubes

1. Blend the smoothie. Put the spinach, almond milk, coconut water, protein powder, parsley, raspberries, almond butter, coconut oil, and ice in a blender and blend until smooth and creamy. 2. Serve. Pour into two tall glasses and serve.

Per Serving:
calories: 401 | fat: 27g | protein: 28g | carbs: 16g | net carbs: 8g | fiber: 8g

Creamy Almond Coffee Smoothie

Prep time: 5 minutes | Cook time: 0 minutes | Serves 2

2 cups unsweetened strong-brewed coffee
1 cup unsweetened almond milk
1 cup unsweetened coconut milk
2 tablespoons chia seeds
2 tablespoons flaxseed meal
2 tablespoons coconut oil
⅛ teaspoon ground cinnamon
Monk fruit sweetener, granulated, to taste

1. Make coffee ice cubes. Pour the coffee into an ice cube tray and freeze for 4 hours minimum. 2. Blend the smoothie. Put all of the coffee ice cubes (2 cups worth), almond milk, coconut milk, chia seeds, flaxseed meal, coconut oil, and cinnamon in a blender and blend until smooth and creamy. 3. Add a sweetener. Add in as much (or as little) sweetener as you like and blend again. 4. Serve. Pour into two tall glasses and serve immediately.

Per Serving:
calories: 444 | fat: 44g | protein: 6g | carbs: 6g | net carbs: 2g | fiber: 4g

Chocolate Chip Pancake

Prep time: 5 minutes | Cook time: 37 minutes | Serves 5 to 6

4 tablespoons salted grass-fed butter, softened
2 cups blanched almond flour
½ cup Swerve, or more to taste
1 ¼ cups full-fat coconut milk
¼ cup sugar-free chocolate chips
¼ cup organic coconut flour
2 eggs
1 tablespoon chopped walnuts
¼ teaspoon baking soda
½ teaspoon salt
½ cup dark berries, for serving (optional)

1. Grease the bottom and sides of your Instant Pot with the butter. Make sure you coat it very liberally. 2. In a large bowl, mix together the almond flour, Swerve, milk, chocolate chips, coconut flour, eggs, walnuts, baking soda, and salt. Add this mixture to the Instant Pot. Close the lid, set the pressure release to Sealing, and select Multigrain. Set the Instant Pot to 37 minutes on Low Pressure, and let cook. 3. Switch the pressure release to Venting and open the Instant Pot. Confirm your pancake is cooked, then carefully remove it using a spatula. Serve with the berries (if desired), and enjoy!

Per Serving:
calories: 369 | fat: 31g | protein: 7g | carbs: 16g | net carbs: 9g | fiber: 7g

Blackberry Vanilla Cake

Prep time: 10 minutes | Cook time: 25 minutes | Serves 8

1 cup almond flour
2 eggs
½ cup erythritol
2 teaspoons vanilla extract
1 cup blackberries
4 tablespoons melted butter
¼ cup heavy cream
½ teaspoon baking powder
1 cup water

1. In large bowl, mix all ingredients except water. Pour into 7-inch round cake pan or divide into two 4-inch pans, if needed. Cover with foil. 2. Pour water into Instant Pot and place steam rack in bottom. Place pan on steam rack and click lid closed. Press the Cake button and press the Adjust button to set heat to Less. Set time for 25 minutes. 3. When timer beeps, allow a 15-minute natural release then quick-release the remaining pressure. Let cool completely.

Per Serving:
calories: 174 | fat: 15g | protein: 10g | carbs: 17g | net carbs: 15g | fiber: 2g

Buffalo Chicken Breakfast Muffins

Prep time: 7 minutes | Cook time: 13 to 16 minutes | Serves 10

6 ounces (170 g) shredded cooked chicken
3 ounces (85 g) blue cheese, crumbled
2 tablespoons unsalted butter, melted
⅓ cup Buffalo hot sauce, such as Frank's RedHot
1 teaspoon minced garlic
6 large eggs
Sea salt and freshly ground black pepper, to taste
Avocado oil spray

1. In a large bowl, stir together the chicken, blue cheese, melted butter, hot sauce, and garlic. 2. In a medium bowl or large liquid measuring cup, beat the eggs. Season with salt and pepper. 3. Spray 10 silicone muffin cups with oil. Divide the chicken mixture among the cups, and pour the egg mixture over top. 4. Place the cups in the air fryer and set to 300°F (149°C). Bake for 13 to 16 minutes, until the muffins are set and cooked through. (Depending on the size of your air fryer, you may need to cook the muffins in batches.)

Per Serving:

calories: 129 | fat: 9g | protein: 10g | carbs: 1g | net carbs: 1g | fiber: 0g

Santa Fe Frittata

Prep time: 10 minutes | Cook time: 30 minutes | Serves 4

1 to 2 tablespoons olive oil
½ onion, diced
2 garlic cloves, minced
6 ounces (170 g) ground pork sausage
½ red bell pepper, diced
½ green bell pepper, diced
Salt and freshly ground black pepper, to taste
6 eggs
½ cup shredded pepper jack cheese
Sliced scallion, for garnish
Salsa, for garnish
Sour cream, for garnish
Fresh cilantro leaves, for garnish

1. Preheat the oven to 350°F (180°C). 2. In a cast-iron skillet over medium heat, heat the olive oil. 3. Add the onion and garlic. Sauté for 5 to 7 minutes until the onion is softened and translucent. 4. Add the sausage. Cook for 5 to 7 minutes or until browned, stirring to break up the meat. 5. Add the red and green bell peppers and stir gently. Season with salt and pepper. 6. In a large bowl, whisk the eggs. Arrange the onion, sausage, and pepper mixture in the skillet so the ingredients are evenly distributed. Slowly pour the eggs over the top. Increase the heat to medium high. Season with salt and pepper and cook for 3 to 4 minutes until the edges start to pull away from the skillet. 7. Top the frittata with cheese and transfer to the oven. Cook for 15 to 20 minutes until the top is no longer runny. Remove from the oven, cool slightly, and serve garnished with scallion, salsa, sour cream, and a few cilantro leaves. 8. Refrigerate leftovers in an airtight container for up to 3 days.

Per Serving:

calories: 493 | fat: 41g | protein: 27g | carbs: 4g | net carbs: 3g | fiber: 1g

Pumpkin Spice Keto Pancakes

Prep time: 15 minutes | Cook time: 40 minutes | Makes 12 to 14 pancakes

6 large eggs
¾ cup canned pumpkin
¼ cup plus 2 tablespoons coconut flour
2 teaspoons pumpkin pie spice
1 teaspoon pure vanilla extract
1 teaspoon baking soda
1 teaspoon ground cinnamon, plus extra for garnish
2 pinches of sea salt
10 to 20 drops stevia extract
4 tablespoons ghee or butter, divided, plus more for serving

1. Place all the ingredients except the ghee in a food processor and pulse to combine. Alternatively, place all the ingredients in a medium-sized mixing bowl and whisk vigorously. Allow the batter to sit on the countertop for about 10 minutes, until it thickens a bit. 2. Melt 1 tablespoon of the ghee in a large skillet over medium-low heat. Pour it into the batter and stir to combine. 3. Add 1 tablespoon of the ghee to the skillet and return it to the heat. Spoon 3 to 4 tablespoons of batter into the skillet to make 3-inch pancakes. Cook until bubbles begin to appear on the tops of the pancakes, 2 to 3 minutes. Flip the pancakes over and cook for another 2 to 3 minutes, until the bottom is golden brown. Repeat with the remaining batter, adding 1 tablespoon of ghee to the skillet between batches. 4. Serve with ghee and a sprinkle of cinnamon.

Per Serving:

calories: 417 | fat: 27g | protein: 19g | carbs: 24g | net carbs: 11g | fiber: 13g

Mushroom Frittata

Prep time: 10 minutes | Cook time: 15 minutes | Serves 6

2 tablespoons olive oil
1 cup sliced fresh mushrooms
1 cup shredded spinach
6 bacon slices, cooked and chopped
10 large eggs, beaten
½ cup crumbled goat cheese
Sea salt
Freshly ground black pepper

1. Preheat the oven to 350°F. 2. Place a large ovenproof skillet over medium-high heat and add the olive oil. 3. Sauté the mushrooms until lightly browned, about 3 minutes. 4. Add the spinach and bacon and sauté until the greens are wilted, about 1 minute. 5. Add the eggs and cook, lifting the edges of the frittata with a spatula so uncooked egg flows underneath, for 3 to 4 minutes. 6. Sprinkle the top with the crumbled goat cheese and season lightly with salt and pepper. 7. Bake until set and lightly browned, about 15 minutes. 8. Remove the frittata from the oven, and let it stand for 5 minutes. 9. Cut into 6 wedges and serve immediately.

Per Serving:

calories: 379 | fat: 27g | protein: 16g | carbs: 1g | net carbs: 1g | fiber: 0g

Baked Eggs in Avocados

Prep time: 10 minutes | Cook time: 10 minutes | Serves 4

2 large avocados, halved and pitted
4 small eggs
Salt and black pepper to season
Chopped parsley to garnish

1. Preheat the oven to 400ºF. 2. Crack each egg into each avocado half and place them on a greased baking sheet. Bake the filled avocados in the oven for 8 or 10 minutes or until eggs are cooked. 3. Season with salt and pepper, and garnish with parsley.

Per Serving:
calories: 221 | fat: 18g | protein: 7g | carbs: 9g | net carbs: 3g | fiber: 6g

BLT Breakfast Wrap

Prep time: 5 minutes | Cook time: 10 minutes | Serves 4

8 ounces (227 g) reduced-sodium bacon
8 tablespoons mayonnaise
8 large romaine lettuce leaves
4 Roma tomatoes, sliced
Salt and freshly ground black pepper, to taste

1. Arrange the bacon in a single layer in the air fryer basket. (It's OK if the bacon sits a bit on the sides.) Set the air fryer to 350ºF (177ºC) and air fry for 10 minutes. Check for crispiness and air fry for 2 to 3 minutes longer if needed. Cook in batches, if necessary, and drain the grease in between batches. 2. Spread 1 tablespoon of mayonnaise on each of the lettuce leaves and top with the tomatoes and cooked bacon. Season to taste with salt and freshly ground black pepper. Roll the lettuce leaves as you would a burrito, securing with a toothpick if desired.

Per Serving:
calories: 343 | fat: 32g | protein: 10g | carbs: 5g | net carbs: 4g | fiber: 1g

Mini Spinach Quiche

Prep time: 5 minutes | Cook time: 15 minutes | Serves 1

2 eggs
1 tablespoon heavy cream
1 tablespoon diced green pepper
1 tablespoon diced red onion
¼ cup chopped fresh spinach
½ teaspoon salt
¼ teaspoon pepper
1 cup water

1. In medium bowl whisk together all ingredients except water. Pour into 4-inch ramekin. Generally, if the ramekin is oven-safe, it is also safe to use in pressure cooking. 2. Pour water into Instant Pot. Place steam rack into pot. Carefully place ramekin onto steam rack. Click lid closed. Press the Manual button and set time for 15 minutes. When timer beeps, quick-release the pressure. Serve warm.

Per Serving:
calories: 201 | fat: 14g | protein: 13g | carbs: 3g | net carbs: 2g | fiber: 1g

Pancake for Two

Prep time: 5 minutes | Cook time: 30 minutes | Serves 2

1 cup blanched finely ground almond flour
2 tablespoons granular erythritol
1 tablespoon salted butter, melted
1 large egg
⅓ cup unsweetened almond milk
½ teaspoon vanilla extract

1. In a large bowl, mix all ingredients together, then pour half the batter into an ungreased round nonstick baking dish. 2. Place dish into air fryer basket. Adjust the temperature to 320ºF (160ºC) and bake for 15 minutes. The pancake will be golden brown on top and firm, and a toothpick inserted in the center will come out clean when done. Repeat with remaining batter. 3. Slice in half in dish and serve warm.

Per Serving:
calories: 267 | fat: 24g | protein: 11g | carbs: 7g | net carbs: 2g | fiber: 5g

Cheesy Egg and Spinach Nest

Prep time: 5 minutes | Cook time: 10 minutes | Serves 1

1 tablespoon olive oil
2 large eggs
Pink Himalayan salt
Freshly ground black pepper
½ cup shredded mozzarella cheese
½ avocado, diced
¼ cup chopped fresh spinach
1 tablespoon grated Parmesan cheese

1. In a medium skillet over medium-high heat, heat the olive oil. 2. Crack the eggs into the skillet right next to each other. 3. Season the eggs with pink Himalayan salt and pepper. 4. When the egg whites start to set, after about 2 minutes, sprinkle the mozzarella cheese around the entire perimeter of the eggs. 5. Add the diced avocado and chopped spinach to the cheese "nest." 6. Sprinkle the Parmesan cheese over the eggs and the nest. 7. Cook until the edges of the mozzarella cheese just begin to brown and get crispy, 7 to 10 minutes. 8. Transfer to a warm plate and enjoy hot.

Per Serving:
calories: 563 | fat: 46g | protein: 31g | carbs: 9g | net carbs: 4g | fiber: 5g

Chocolate Chip Waffle

Prep time: 5 minutes | Cook time: 5 minutes | Serves 1

⅓ cup blanched almond flour
½ tablespoon coconut flour
¼ teaspoon baking powder
2 large eggs
¼ teaspoon vanilla extract
4 drops liquid stevia
1 tablespoon stevia-sweetened chocolate chips

For Topping (Optional)
Swerve confectioners'-style sweetener
Sugar-free syrup
Salted butter

1. Preheat a waffle maker to medium-high heat. 2. Place all the ingredients except the chocolate chips in a large bowl and blend until smooth. Fold in the chocolate chips. 3. Spray the hot waffle maker with nonstick cooking spray. 4. Pour the batter into the hot waffle iron and cook for 3 to 5 minutes, until light golden brown. 5. Serve dusted with Swerve confectioners'-style sweetener and topped with sugar-free syrup and butter, if desired.

Per Serving:

1 waffle: calories: 398 | fat: 31g | protein: 23g | carbs: 14g | net carbs: 6g | fiber: 8g

Yogurt Parfait with Creamy Blueberry Crumble

Prep time: 10 minutes | Cook time: 25 minutes | Serves 4

6 tablespoons cold unsalted butter, divided
¼ cup almond flour
¼ cup ground flaxseed
¼ cup slivered almonds
¼ cup chopped roasted unsalted walnuts
1 cup fresh or frozen blueberries
2 to 4 tablespoons granulated sugar-free sweetener
Zest of 1 lemon
1 teaspoon vanilla extract
½ teaspoon ground ginger or cinnamon
½ cup heavy cream
2 cups plain full-fat Greek yogurt

1. Preheat the oven to 350°F (180°C) and generously coat the bottom and sides of an 8-inch square glass baking dish or 8-inch pie pan with 2 tablespoons of butter. 2. In a medium bowl, cut the remaining 4 tablespoons of butter into very small pieces. Add the almond flour, flaxseed, almonds, and walnuts and mix until crumbly. Set aside. 3. In a separate bowl, combine the blueberries, sweetener, lemon zest, vanilla extract, and ginger or cinnamon. Toss to coat the blueberries well. 4. Add the blueberry mixture to the prepared baking dish (they won't quite cover the bottom), and pour the heavy cream over the blueberry mixture. 5. Top the blueberry mixture evenly with the flour-and-nut mixture, and bake for 20 to 25 minutes, until golden brown. Let rest for 10 minutes before serving to allow the mixture to thicken. 6. To serve, top one-quarter of the warm crumble mixture with ½ cup of Greek yogurt.

Per Serving:

calories: 500 | fat: 45g | protein: 10g | carbs: 18g | net carbs: 13g | fiber: 5g

Mug Biscuit

Prep time: 2 minutes | Cook time: 2 minutes | Serves 4

¼ cup (28 g) blanched almond flour
1 tablespoon coconut flour
½ teaspoon baking powder
¼ teaspoon finely ground sea salt
1 large egg
1 tablespoon softened coconut oil or ghee, plus more for serving if desired
1 teaspoon apple cider vinegar

1. Place all the ingredients in a microwave-safe mug with a base at least 2 inches (5 cm) in diameter. Mix until fully incorporated, then flatten with the back of a spoon. 2. Place the mug in the microwave and cook on high for 1 minute 30 seconds. 3. Remove the mug from the microwave and insert a toothpick. It should come out clean. If batter is clinging to the toothpick, microwave the biscuit for an additional 15 to 30 seconds. 4. Flip the mug over a clean plate and shake it a bit until the biscuit releases from the mug. If desired, slather the biscuit with the fat of your choice while still warm.

Per Serving:

calories: 399 | fat: 34g | protein: 14g | carbs: 11g | net carbs: 5g | fiber: 6g

Lemon–Olive Oil Breakfast Cakes with Berry Syrup

Prep time: 5 minutes | Cook time: 10 minutes | Serves 4

For the Pancakes:
1 cup almond flour
1 teaspoon baking powder
¼ teaspoon salt
6 tablespoon extra-virgin olive oil, divided
2 large eggs
Zest and juice of 1 lemon
½ teaspoon almond or vanilla extract

For the Berry Sauce:
1 cup frozen mixed berries
1 tablespoon water or lemon juice, plus more if needed
½ teaspoon vanilla extract

Make the Pancakes: 1. In a large bowl, combine the almond flour, baking powder, and salt and whisk to break up any clumps. 2. Add the 4 tablespoons olive oil, eggs, lemon zest and juice, and almond extract and whisk to combine well. 3. In a large skillet, heat 1 tablespoon of olive oil and spoon about 2 tablespoons of batter for each of 4 pancakes. Cook until bubbles begin to form, 4 to 5 minutes, and flip. Cook another 2 to 3 minutes on second side. Repeat with remaining 1 tablespoon olive oil and batter. Make the Berry Sauce 1. In a small saucepan, heat the frozen berries, water, and vanilla extract over medium-high for 3 to 4 minutes, until bubbly, adding more water if mixture is too thick. Using the back of a spoon or fork, mash the berries and whisk until smooth.

Per Serving:

calories: 508 | fat: 49g | protein: 12g | carbs: 13g | net carbs: 11g | fiber: 2g

Bacon Spaghetti Squash Fritters

Prep time: 20 minutes | Cook time: 15 minutes | Serves 4

½ cooked spaghetti squash
2 tablespoons cream cheese
½ cup shredded whole-milk Mozzarella cheese
1 egg
½ teaspoon salt
¼ teaspoon pepper
1 stalk green onion, sliced
4 slices cooked bacon, crumbled
2 tablespoons coconut oil

1. Remove seeds from cooked squash and use fork to scrape strands out of shell. Place strands into cheesecloth or kitchen towel and squeeze to remove as much excess moisture as possible. 2. Place cream cheese and Mozzarella in small bowl and microwave for 45 seconds to melt together. Mix with spoon and place in large bowl. Add all ingredients except coconut oil to bowl. Mixture will be wet like batter. 3. Press the Sauté button and then press the Adjust button to set heat to Less. Add coconut oil to Instant Pot. When fully preheated, add 2 to 3 tablespoons of batter to pot to make a fritter. Let fry until firm and completely cooked through.

Per Serving:

calories: 202 | fat: 16g | protein: 9g | carbs: 2g | net carbs: 1g | fiber: 1g

Rosti with Bacon, Mushrooms, and Green Onions

Prep time: 10 minutes | Cook time: 25 minutes | Serves 2

2 slices bacon, diced
2 tablespoons coconut oil or lard
1 cup mushrooms, thinly sliced
¼ cup chopped green onions, plus more for garnish (optional)
¼ teaspoon minced garlic
1 cup shredded cabbage
1 large egg
½ teaspoon fine sea salt
⅛ teaspoon freshly ground black pepper

1. Place the bacon in a large skillet over medium heat and fry until cooked and crispy. Reserve a little bit of the cooked bacon for garnish, if desired. Add the coconut oil, mushrooms, green onions, and garlic. Sauté for 5 minutes, or until the mushrooms are golden. 2. In a large bowl, mix the shredded cabbage, egg, salt, and pepper. Transfer to the skillet with the bacon mixture. Spread out the cabbage mixture in the pan and press it down to form a large pancake. Cook over medium heat until the bottom is crispy and golden brown, about 5 minutes. Flip with a large spatula and cook for another 10 minutes, or until the cabbage softens. 3. Remove from the heat and serve. Store extras in an airtight container in the fridge for up to 4 days. To reheat, fry in a skillet with a tablespoon of Paleo fat or coconut oil on both sides until crispy, about 3 minutes a side. Garnish with green onions and/or reserved bacon, if desired.

Per Serving:

calories: 275 | fat: 24g | protein: 10g | carbs: 5g | net carbs: 3g | fiber: 2g

Creamy Cinnamon Porridge

Prep time: 10 minutes | Cook time: 10 minutes | Serves 2

¼ cup coconut milk
¾ cup unsweetened almond milk or water
¼ cup almond butter or hazelnut butter
1 tablespoon virgin coconut oil
2 tablespoons chia seeds
1 tablespoon flax meal
1 teaspoon cinnamon
¼ cup macadamia nuts
¼ cup hazelnuts
4 Brazil nuts
Optional: low-carb sweetener, to taste
¼ cup unsweetened large coconut flakes
1 tablespoon cacao nibs

1. In a small saucepan, mix the coconut milk and almond milk and heat over medium heat. Once hot (not boiling), take off the heat. Add the almond butter and coconut oil. Stir until well combined. If needed, use an immersion blender and process until smooth. 2. Add the chia seeds, flax meal, and cinnamon, and leave to rest for 5 to 10 minutes. Roughly chop the macadamias, hazelnuts, and Brazil nuts and stir in. Add sweetener, if using, and stir. Transfer to serving bowls. In a small skillet, dry-roast the coconut flakes over medium-high heat for 1 to 2 minutes, until lightly toasted and fragrant. Top the porridge with the toasted coconut flakes and cacao nibs (or you can use chopped 100% chocolate). Serve immediately or store in the fridge for up to 3 days.

Per Serving:

calories: 852 | fat: 78g | protein: 17g | carbs: 23g | net carbs: 10g | fiber: 13g

Olivia's Cream Cheese Pancakes

Prep time: 15 minutes | Cook time: 15 minutes | Serves 3

2 medium eggs
2 ounces cream cheese
½ teaspoon vanilla extract
¼ cup blanched almond flour
1 teaspoon Swerve
confectioners'-style sweetener
¼ teaspoon baking powder
Salted butter, for serving
Sugar-free syrup, for serving

1 Combine the eggs, cream cheese, vanilla, almond flour, sweetener, and baking powder in a blender and blend on medium-high speed until smooth. Use a fork to pop the large bubbles on the top of the batter. 2 Coat a medium-sized skillet with coconut oil spray or ghee and place over medium heat. Once hot, pour one-third of the batter into the pan. Flip the pancake when the sides are firm and bubbles appear evenly throughout, 1 to 3 minutes, then cook for another 1 to 3 minutes on the second side. 3 Repeat with the remaining batter to make a total of 3 pancakes. 4 Serve topped with butter and sugar-free syrup.

Per Serving:

calories: 487 | fat: 40g | protein: 21g | carbs: 12g | net carbs: 6g | fiber: 6g

Butter Coffee Latte

Prep time: 5 minutes | Cook time: 0 minutes | Serves 1

- 1 cup (8 ounces / 227 g) brewed coffee
- ½ tablespoon unsalted butter
- ½ tablespoon MCT oil
- 3 tablespoons unsweetened vanilla almond milk

1. In a blender, combine coffee, butter, MCT oil, and almond milk and blend until frothy. (Do not just stir the ingredients together. This will make your coffee oily, not frothy-yuck.) 2. Pour into a mug to serve.

Per Serving:
calories: 119 | fat: 13g | protein: 0g | carbs: 0g | net carbs: 0g | fiber: 0g

Pulled Pork Hash

Prep time: 10 minutes | Cook time: 15 minutes | Serves 4

- 4 eggs
- 10 ounces (283 g) pulled pork, shredded
- 1 teaspoon coconut oil
- 1 teaspoon red pepper
- 1 teaspoon chopped fresh cilantro
- 1 tomato, chopped
- ¼ cup water

1. Melt the coconut oil in the instant pot on Sauté mode. 2. Then add pulled pork, red pepper, cilantro, water, and chopped tomato. 3. Cook the ingredients for 5 minutes. 4. Then stir it well with the help of the spatula and crack the eggs over it. 5. Close the lid. 6. Cook the meal on Manual mode (High Pressure) for 7 minutes. Then make a quick pressure release.

Per Serving:
calories: 275 | fat: 18g | protein: 22g | carbs: 6g | net carbs: 5g | fiber: 1g

Breakfast Bake

Prep time: 10 minutes | Cook time: 50 minutes | Serves 8

- 1 tablespoon olive oil, plus extra for greasing the casserole dish
- 1 pound preservative-free or homemade sausage
- 8 large eggs
- 2 cups cooked spaghetti squash
- 1 tablespoon chopped fresh oregano
- Sea salt
- Freshly ground black pepper
- ½ cup shredded Cheddar cheese

1. Preheat the oven to 375°F. Lightly grease a 9-by-13-inch casserole dish with olive oil and set aside. 2. Place a large ovenproof skillet over medium-high heat and add the olive oil. 3. Brown the sausage until cooked through, about 5 minutes. While the sausage is cooking, whisk together the eggs, squash, and oregano in a medium bowl. Season lightly with salt and pepper and set aside. 4. Add the cooked sausage to the egg mixture, stir until just combined, and pour the mixture into the casserole dish. 5. Sprinkle the top of the casserole with the cheese and cover the casserole loosely with aluminum foil. 6. Bake the casserole for 30 minutes, and then remove the foil and bake for an additional 15 minutes. 7. Let the casserole stand for 10 minutes before serving.

Per Serving:
calories: 303 | fat: 24g | protein: 17g | carbs: 4g | net carbs: 3g | fiber: 1g

Greek Yogurt Parfait

Prep time: 5 minutes | Cook time: 0 minutes | Serves 1

- ½ cup plain whole-milk Greek yogurt
- 2 tablespoons heavy whipping cream
- ¼ cup frozen berries, thawed with juices
- ½ teaspoon vanilla or almond extract (optional)
- ¼ teaspoon ground cinnamon (optional)
- 1 tablespoon ground flaxseed
- 2 tablespoons chopped nuts (walnuts or pecans)

1. In a small bowl or glass, combine the yogurt, heavy whipping cream, thawed berries in their juice, vanilla or almond extract (if using), cinnamon (if using), and flaxseed and stir well until smooth. Top with chopped nuts and enjoy.

Per Serving:
calories: 401 | fat: 32g | protein: 15g | carbs: 16g | net carbs: 11g | fiber: 5g

Smoked Salmon and Cream Cheese Roll-Ups

Prep time: 25 minutes | Cook time: 0 minutes | Serves 2

- 4 ounces cream cheese, at room temperature
- 1 teaspoon grated lemon zest
- 1 teaspoon Dijon mustard
- 2 tablespoons chopped scallions, white and green parts
- Pink Himalayan salt
- Freshly ground black pepper
- 1 (4-ounce) package cold-smoked salmon (about 12 slices)

1. Put the cream cheese, lemon zest, mustard, and scallions in a food processor (or blender), and season with pink Himalayan salt and pepper. Process until fully mixed and smooth. 2. Spread the cream-cheese mixture on each slice of smoked salmon, and roll it up. Place the rolls on a plate seam-side down. 3. Serve immediately or refrigerate, covered in plastic wrap or in a lidded container, for up to 3 days.

Per Serving:
calories: 268 | fat: 22g | protein: 14g | carbs: 4g | net carbs: 3g | fiber: 1g

Kale Pâté

Prep time: 10 minutes | Cook time: 0 minutes | Makes 2 cups

2 tablespoons refined avocado oil, for the pan
4 cups (190 g) chopped kale
½ cup (75 g) sesame seeds
½ cup (120 ml) refined avocado oil or extra-virgin olive oil
8 green onions, green parts only, roughly chopped
3 tablespoons apple cider vinegar
1¼ teaspoons finely ground gray sea salt

1. Place 2 tablespoons of avocado oil and the chopped kale in a large frying pan over medium heat. Cover and cook until the kale is slightly crispy, stirring occasionally, 3 to 6 minutes. 2. Meanwhile, place the remaining ingredients in a blender or food processor.

Per Serving:
calories: 228 | fat: 22g | protein: 3g | carbs: 6g | net carbs: 4g | fiber: 2g

Heart-Healthy Hazelnut-Collagen Shake

Prep time: 5 minutes | Cook time: 0 minutes | Serves 1

1½ cups unsweetened almond milk
2 tablespoons hazelnut butter
2 tablespoons grass-fed collagen powder
½ to 1 teaspoon cinnamon
⅛ teaspoon LoSalt or pink Himalayan salt
⅛ teaspoon sugar-free almond extract
1 tablespoon macadamia oil or hazelnut oil

1. Place all of the ingredients in a blender and pulse until smooth and frothy. Serve immediately.

Per Serving:
calories: 345 | fat: 32g | protein: 13g | carbs: 8g | net carbs: 3g | fiber: 5g

Italian Sausage Stacks

Prep time: 10 minutes | Cook time: 10 minutes | Serves 6

6 Italian sausage patties
4 tablespoons olive oil
2 ripe avocados, pitted
2 teaspoons fresh lime juice
Salt and black pepper to taste
6 fresh eggs
Red pepper flakes to garnish

1. In a skillet, warm the oil over medium heat and fry the sausage patties about 8 minutes until lightly browned and firm. Remove the patties to a plate. 2. Spoon the avocado into a bowl, mash with the lime juice, and season with salt and black pepper. Spread the mash on the sausages. 3. Boil 3 cups of water in a wide pan over high heat, and reduce to simmer (don't boil). 4. Crack each egg into a small bowl and gently put the egg into the simmering water; poach for 2 to 3 minutes. Use a perforated spoon to remove from the water on a paper towel to dry. Repeat with the other 5 eggs. Top each stack with a poached egg, sprinkle with chili flakes, salt, black pepper, and chives. Serve with turnip wedges.

Per Serving:
calories: 537 | fat: 45g | protein: 22g | carbs: 12g | net carbs: 7g | fiber: 8g

Blackberry-Chia Pudding

Prep time: 10 minutes | Cook time: 0 minutes | Serves 2

1 cup unsweetened full-fat coconut milk
1 teaspoon liquid stevia 1 teaspoon vanilla extract
½ cup blackberries, fresh or frozen (no sugar added if frozen)
¼ cup chia seeds

1. In a food processor (or blender), process the coconut milk, stevia, and vanilla until the mixture starts to thicken. 2. Add the blackberries, and process until thoroughly mixed and purple. Fold in the chia seeds. 3. Divide the mixture between two small cups with lids, and refrigerate overnight or up to 3 days before serving.

Per Serving:
calories: 437 | fat: 38g | protein: 8g | carbs: 23g | net carbs: 8g | fiber: 15g

Nutty "Oatmeal"

Prep time: 5 minutes | Cook time: 4 minutes | Serves 4

2 tablespoons coconut oil
1 cup full-fat coconut milk
1 cup heavy whipping cream
½ cup macadamia nuts
½ cup chopped pecans
⅓ cup Swerve, or more to taste
¼ cup unsweetened coconut flakes
2 tablespoons chopped hazelnuts
2 tablespoons chia seeds
½ teaspoon ground cinnamon

1. Before you get started, soak the chia seeds for about 5 to 10 minutes (can be up to 20, if desired) in 1 cup of filtered water. After soaking, set the Instant Pot to Sauté and add the coconut oil. Once melted, pour in the milk, whipping cream, and 1 cup of filtered water. Then add the macadamia nuts, pecans, Swerve, coconut flakes, hazelnuts, chia seeds, and cinnamon. Mix thoroughly inside the Instant Pot. 2. Close the lid, set the pressure release to Sealing, and hit Cancel to stop the current program. Select Manual, set the Instant Pot to 4 minutes on High Pressure, and let cook. 3. Once cooked, carefully switch the pressure release to Venting. 4. Open the Instant Pot, serve, and enjoy!

Per Serving:
calories: 506 | fat: 53g | protein: 6g | carbs: 11g | net carbs: 5g | fiber: 6g

Sausage, Egg, and Cheese Breakfast Bake

Prep time: 15 minutes | Cook time: 35 minutes | Serves 6

1 tablespoon unsalted butter
⅓ cup chopped yellow onions
1 pound bulk breakfast sausage
8 large eggs
⅓ cup heavy whipping cream
1 clove garlic, pressed
1 teaspoon salt
½ teaspoon ground black pepper
1 cup shredded cheddar cheese

1. Preheat the oven to 350°F. Lightly coat an 8-inch deep-dish pie dish or baking dish with coconut oil or nonstick cooking spray. 2. Heat the butter in a large skillet over medium heat. Add the onions and sauté until soft, 3 to 4 minutes. 3. Add the sausage and cook until evenly browned, 4 to 5 minutes. Drain and set aside. 4. In a large bowl, whisk the eggs, cream, garlic, salt, and pepper. 5. Spread the sausage evenly on the bottom of the prepared dish and top with the cheese. Pour the egg mixture over the cheese. 6. Bake for 35 minutes, until the eggs are set and the top is lightly golden brown. 7. Allow to cool for 3 to 5 minutes before serving. Leftovers can be covered and stored in the refrigerator for up to 4 days.

Per Serving:

calories: 394 | fat: 33g | protein: 22g | carbs: 3g | net carbs: 3g | fiber: 0g

Meritage Eggs

Prep time: 5 minutes | Cook time: 8 minutes | Serves 2

2 teaspoons unsalted butter (or coconut oil for dairy-free), for greasing the ramekins
4 large eggs
2 teaspoons chopped fresh thyme
½ teaspoon fine sea salt
¼ teaspoon ground black pepper
2 tablespoons heavy cream (or unsweetened, unflavored almond milk for dairy-free)
3 tablespoons finely grated Parmesan cheese (or Kite Hill brand chive cream cheese style spread, softened, for dairy-free)
Fresh thyme leaves, for garnish (optional)

1. Preheat the air fryer to 400°F (204°C). Grease two (4 ounces / 113 g) ramekins with the butter. 2. Crack 2 eggs into each ramekin and divide the thyme, salt, and pepper between the ramekins. Pour 1 tablespoon of the heavy cream into each ramekin. Sprinkle each ramekin with 1½ tablespoons of the Parmesan cheese. 3. Place the ramekins in the air fryer and bake for 8 minutes for soft-cooked yolks (longer if you desire a harder yolk). 4. Garnish with a sprinkle of ground black pepper and thyme leaves, if desired. Best served fresh.

Per Serving:

calories: 326 | fat: 27g | protein: 18g | carbs: 1g | net carbs: 1g | fiber: 0g

Breakfast Quesadilla

Prep time: 5 minutes | Cook time: 20 minutes | Serves 2

2 bacon slices
2 large eggs
Pink Himalayan salt
Freshly ground black pepper
1 tablespoon olive oil
2 low-carbohydrate tortillas
1 cup shredded Mexican blend cheese, divided
½ avocado, thinly sliced

1. In a medium skillet over medium-high heat, cook the bacon on both sides until crispy, about 8 minutes. Transfer the bacon to a paper towel–lined plate to drain and cool for 5 minutes. Transfer to a cutting board, and chop the bacon. 2. Turn the heat down to medium, and crack the eggs onto the hot skillet with the bacon grease. Season with pink Himalayan salt and pepper. 3. Cook the eggs for 3 to 4 minutes, until the egg whites are set. If you want the yolks to set, you can cook them longer. Transfer the cooked eggs to a plate. 4. Pour the olive oil into the hot skillet. Place the first tortilla in the pan. 5. Add ½ cup of cheese, place slices of avocado on the cheese in a circle, top with both fried eggs, the chopped bacon, and the remaining ½ cup of cheese, and cover with the second tortilla. 6. Once the cheese starts melting and the bottom of the tortilla is golden, after about 3 minutes, flip the quesadilla. Cook for about 2 minutes on the second side, until the bottom is golden. 7. Cut the quesadilla into slices with a pizza cutter or a chef's knife and serve.

Per Serving:

calories: 569 | fat: 41g | protein: 27g | carbs: 27g | net carbs: 9g | fiber: 18g

Hashed Zucchini & Bacon Breakfast

Prep time: 10 minutes | Cook time: 15 minutes | Serves 1

1 medium zucchini, diced
2 bacon slices
1 egg
1 tablespoon coconut oil
½ small onion, chopped
1 tablespoon chopped parsley
¼ teaspoon salt

1. Place the bacon in a skillet and cook for a few minutes, until crispy. Remove and set aside. 2. Warm the coconut oil and cook the onion until soft, for about 3-4 minutes, occasionally stirring. Add the zucchini, and cook for 10 more minutes until zucchini is brown and tender, but not mushy. Transfer to a plate and season with salt. 3. Crack the egg into the same skillet and fry over medium heat. Top the zucchini mixture with the bacon slices and a fried egg. Serve hot, sprinkled with parsley.

Per Serving:

calories: 440 | fat: 39g | protein: 15g | carbs: 10g | net carbs: 7g | fiber: 3g

Classic Coffee Cake

Prep time: 5 minutes | Cook time: 40 minutes | Serves 5 to 6

Base:
2 eggs
2 tablespoons salted grass-fed butter, softened
1 cup blanched almond flour
1 cup chopped pecans
¼ cup sour cream, at room temperature
¼ cup full-fat cream cheese, softened
½ teaspoon salt
½ teaspoon ground cinnamon
½ teaspoon ground nutmeg
¼ teaspoon baking soda
Topping:
1 cup sugar-free chocolate chips
1 cup chopped pecans
½ cup Swerve, or more to taste
½ cup heavy whipping cream

1. Pour 1 cup of filtered water into the inner pot of the Instant Pot, then insert the trivet. Using an electric mixer, combine the eggs, butter, flour, pecans, sour cream, cream cheese, salt, cinnamon, nutmeg, and baking soda. Mix thoroughly. Transfer this mixture into a well-greased, Instant Pot-friendly pan (or dish). 2. Using a sling if desired, place the pan onto the trivet, and cover loosely with aluminum foil. Close the lid, set the pressure release to Sealing, and select Manual. Set the Instant Pot to 40 minutes on High Pressure and let cook. 3. While cooking, in a large bowl, mix the chocolate chips, pecans, Swerve, and whipping cream thoroughly. Set aside. 4. Once cooked, let the pressure naturally disperse from the Instant Pot for about 10 minutes, then carefully switch the pressure release to Venting. 5. Open the Instant Pot and remove the pan. Evenly sprinkle the topping mixture over the cake. Let cool, serve, and enjoy!

Per Serving:

calories: 267 | fat: 23g | protein: 7g | carbs: 9g | net carbs: 7g | fiber: 2g

Cauliflower Avocado Toast

Prep time: 15 minutes | Cook time: 8 minutes | Serves 2

1 (12 ounces / 340 g) steamer bag cauliflower
1 large egg
½ cup shredded Mozzarella cheese
1 ripe medium avocado
½ teaspoon garlic powder
¼ teaspoon ground black pepper

1. Cook cauliflower according to package instructions. Remove from bag and place into cheesecloth or clean towel to remove excess moisture. 2. Place cauliflower into a large bowl and mix in egg and Mozzarella. Cut a piece of parchment to fit your air fryer basket. Separate the cauliflower mixture into two, and place it on the parchment in two mounds. Press out the cauliflower mounds into a ¼-inch-thick rectangle. Place the parchment into the air fryer basket. 3. Adjust the temperature to 400°F (204°C) and set the timer for 8 minutes. 4. Flip the cauliflower halfway through the cooking time. 5. When the timer beeps, remove the parchment and allow the cauliflower to cool 5 minutes. 6. Cut open the avocado and remove the pit. Scoop out the inside, place it in a medium bowl, and mash it with garlic powder and pepper. Spread onto the cauliflower. Serve immediately.

Per Serving:

calories: 305 | fat: 23g | protein: 16g | carbs: 13g | net carbs: 7g | fiber: 6g

Breakfast Burrito Bowls

Prep time: 10 minutes | Cook time: 15 minutes | Serves 4

6 eggs
3 tablespoons melted butter
1 teaspoon salt
¼ teaspoon pepper
½ pound (227 g) cooked breakfast sausage
½ cup shredded sharp Cheddar cheese
½ cup salsa
½ cup sour cream
1 avocado, cubed
¼ cup diced green onion

1. In large bowl, mix eggs, melted butter, salt, and pepper. Press the Sauté button and then press the Adjust button to set the heat to Less. 2. Add eggs to Instant Pot and cook for 5 to 7 minutes while gently moving with rubber spatula. When eggs begin to firm up, add cooked breakfast sausage and cheese and continue to cook until eggs are fully cooked. Press the Cancel button. 3. Divide eggs into four bowls and top with salsa, sour cream, avocado, and green onion.

Per Serving:

calories: 613 | fat: 50g | protein: 23g | carbs: 10g | net carbs: 6g | fiber: 4g

Cream Cheese Muffins

Prep time: 10 minutes | Cook time: 10 minutes | Makes 6 muffins

4 tablespoons melted butter, plus more for the muffin tin
1 cup almond flour
¾ tablespoon baking powder
2 large eggs, lightly beaten
2 ounces cream cheese mixed with 2 tablespoons heavy (whipping) cream
Handful shredded Mexican blend cheese

1. Preheat the oven to 400°F. Coat six cups of a muffin tin with butter. 2. In a small bowl, mix together the almond flour and baking powder. 3. In a medium bowl, mix together the eggs, cream cheese–heavy cream mixture, shredded cheese, and 4 tablespoons of the melted butter. 4. Pour the flour mixture into the egg mixture, and beat with a hand mixer until thoroughly mixed. 5. Pour the batter into the prepared muffin cups. 6. Bake for 12 minutes, or until golden brown on top, and serve.

Per Serving:

calories: 247 | fat: 23g | protein: 8g | carbs: 4g | net carbs: 4g | fiber: 2g

Ricotta Cloud Pancakes with Whipped Cream

Prep time: 5 minutes | Cook time: 5 minutes | Serves 4

1 cup almond flour
1 teaspoon baking powder
2½ tablespoons swerve
⅓ teaspoon salt
1¼ cups ricotta cheese
⅓ cup coconut milk
2 large eggs
1 cup heavy whipping cream

1. In a medium bowl, whisk the almond flour, baking powder, swerve, and salt. Set aside. 2. Crack the eggs into the blender and process on medium speed for 30 seconds. Add the ricotta cheese, continue processing it, and gradually pour the coconut milk in while you keep on blending. In about 90 seconds, the mixture will be creamy and smooth. Pour it into the dry ingredients and whisk to combine. 3. Set a skillet over medium heat and let it heat for a minute. Then, fetch a soup spoonful of mixture into the skillet and cook it for 1 minute. 4. Flip the pancake and cook further for 1 minute. Remove onto a plate and repeat the cooking process until the batter is exhausted. Serve the pancakes with whipping cream.

Per Serving:

calories: 712 | fat: 64g | protein: 26g | carbs: 13g | net carbs: 10g | fiber: 3g

Egg Roll in a Bowl

Prep time: 10 minutes | Cook time: 10 minutes | Serves 2

2 large eggs
2 tablespoons sesame oil, divided
2 tablespoons soy sauce, divided
2 tablespoons extra-virgin olive oil
6 ounces (170 g) ground pork
1 tablespoon chopped fresh ginger (or 1 teaspoon ground ginger)
2 cloves garlic, minced
2 cups finely chopped cabbage
(or bagged coleslaw mix; no dressing)
2 ribs celery, diced
½ small red bell pepper, diced
2 tablespoons lime juice, divided
2 scallions, minced (green and white parts)
2 tablespoons mayonnaise
1 teaspoon sriracha or other hot sauce
½ teaspoon garlic powder

1. In a small bowl, beat together the eggs, 1 tablespoon of sesame oil, and 1 tablespoon of soy sauce and set aside. 2. Heat the olive oil in a large skillet over medium heat. Sauté the ground pork, breaking it apart, until browned and no longer pink, 4 to 5 minutes. Add the ginger and garlic and sauté for an additional 30 seconds. 3. Add the cabbage, celery, and bell pepper and sauté, stirring constantly, until the vegetables are wilted and fragrant, another 2 to 3 minutes. 4. Push the vegetables and pork to one side of the skillet and add the egg mixture to the other side. Reduce heat to low and scramble the egg until cooked through, 1 to 2 minutes. Remove the skillet from the heat and mix the egg into the pork and cabbage. 5. In a small bowl, whisk together the remaining 1 tablespoon of sesame oil, the remaining 1 tablespoon of soy sauce, 1 tablespoon of lime juice, and the scallions. Pour over the cooked pork mixture and stir to combine well, reserving the bowl. 6. In the same small bowl, combine the remaining 1 tablespoon of lime juice, the mayonnaise, sriracha, and garlic powder. 7. Divide the pork mixture evenly between two bowls and drizzle each with half of the spicy mayo. Serve warm.

Per Serving:

calories: 695 | fat: 61g | protein: 25g | carbs: 16g | net carbs: 10g | fiber: 4g

Cinnamon Roll Fat Bombs

Prep time: 5 minutes | Cook time: 5 minutes | Serves 5 to 6

2 tablespoons coconut oil
2 cups raw coconut butter
1 cup sugar-free chocolate chips
1 cup heavy whipping cream
½ cup Swerve, or more to taste
½ teaspoon ground cinnamon, or more to taste
½ teaspoon vanilla extract

1. Set the Instant Pot to Sauté and melt the oil. 2. Add the butter, chocolate chips, whipping cream, Swerve, cinnamon, and vanilla to the Instant Pot and cook. Stir occasionally until the mixture reaches a smooth consistency. 3. Pour mixture into a silicone mini-muffin mold. 4. Freeze until firm. Serve, and enjoy!

Per Serving:

calories: 372 | fat: 32g | protein: 4g | carbs: 15g | net carbs: 8g | fiber: 7g

Parmesan Baked Eggs

Prep time: 5 minutes | Cook time: 10 minutes | Serves 1

1 tablespoon butter, cut into small pieces
2 tablespoons keto-friendly low-carb Marinara sauce
3 eggs
2 tablespoons grated Parmesan cheese
¼ teaspoon Italian seasoning
1 cup water

1. Place the butter pieces on the bottom of the oven-safe bowl. Spread the marinara sauce over the butter. Crack the eggs on top of the marinara sauce and top with the cheese and Italian seasoning. 2. Cover the bowl with aluminum foil. Pour the water and insert the trivet in the Instant Pot. Put the bowl on the trivet. 3. Set the lid in place. Select the Manual mode and set the cooking time for 10 minutes on Low Pressure. When the timer goes off, do a quick pressure release. Carefully open the lid. 4. Let the eggs cool for 5 minutes before serving.

Per Serving:

calories: 375 | fat: 30g | protein: 23g | carbs: 2g | net carbs: 2g | fiber: 0g

DLK Bulletproof Coffee

Prep time: 2 minutes | Cook time: 0 minutes | Serves 1

1 tablespoon MCT oil
8 ounces hot brewed coffee

1 Add MCT oil to coffee and blend using a hand immersion blender until froth whips up. This will help prevent the dreaded MCT oil "lip gloss." 2 Serve.

Per Serving:
calories: 120 | fat: 14g | protein: 0g | carbs: 0g | net carbs: 0g | fiber: 0g

Bacon-Wrapped Western Quiche Tarts

Prep time: 10 minutes | Cook time: 20 minutes | Makes 12 quiche tarts

12 bacon slices
8 eggs
⅓ cup heavy (whipping) cream
1 cup shredded Cheddar cheese
¼ cup finely diced red bell pepper
¼ cup finely diced green bell pepper
¼ cup finely diced yellow onion

1. Preheat the oven to 375°F (190°C). 2. Line each cup of a 12-cup muffin tin with a slice of bacon around the edges and then bake for about 10 minutes until browned but not crisp. 3. In a large bowl, whisk together the eggs and cream. Add the Cheddar, red and green bell peppers, and onion and mix well. 4. Pour the egg mixture into the bacon-lined muffin cups, filling each about three-quarters full. 5. Bake for about 20 minutes until the muffins are golden brown and fully cooked. They should be spongy but not soft in the middle. Use a spoon to lift them from the pan. 6. Store in an airtight container in the refrigerator for up to 1 week.

Per Serving:
1 quiche tart: calories: 154 | fat: 12g | protein: 10g | carbs: 2g | net carbs: 2g | fiber: 0g

Broccoli & Colby Cheese Frittata

Prep time: 15 minutes | Cook time: 20 minutes | Serves 4

3 tablespoons olive oil
½ cup onions, chopped
1 cup broccoli, chopped
8 eggs, beaten
½ teaspoon jalapeño pepper, minced
Salt and red pepper, to taste
¾ cup colby cheese, grated
¼ cup fresh cilantro, to serve

1 Set an ovenproof frying pan over medium heat and warm the oil. Add onions and sauté until caramelized. Place in the broccoli and cook until tender. Add in jalapeno pepper and eggs; season with red pepper and salt. Cook until the eggs are set. 2 Scatter colby cheese over the frittata. Set oven to 370°F and cook for approximately 12 minutes, until frittata is set in the middle. Slice into wedges and decorate with fresh cilantro before serving.

Per Serving:
calories: 426 | fat: 34g | protein: 23g | carbs: 8g | net carbs: 6g | fiber: 2g

Pumpkin Spice Latte Overnight "Oats"

Prep time: 5 minutes | Cook time: 0 minutes | Serves 2

½ cup (75 g) hulled hemp seeds
⅓ cup (80 ml) milk (nondairy or regular), plus more for serving
⅓ cup (80 ml) brewed coffee (decaf or regular)
2 tablespoons canned pumpkin puree
1 tablespoon chia seeds
2 teaspoons erythritol, or 3 drops liquid stevia
½ teaspoon vanilla extract
½ teaspoon ground cinnamon
¼ teaspoon ground nutmeg
⅛ teaspoon ground cloves
Pinch of finely ground sea salt
Toppings (Optional):
Chopped raw or roasted pecans
Ground cinnamon
Additional hulled hemp seeds
Toasted unsweetened shredded coconut

1. Place all the ingredients in a 12-ounce (350-ml) or larger container with a lid and stir until combined. Cover and set in the fridge to soak overnight, or for at least 8 hours. 2. The following day, add more milk until the desired consistency is reached. Divide between 2 small bowls, top as desired, and enjoy.

Per Serving:
calories: 337 | fat: 26g | protein: 15g | carbs: 9g | net carbs: 2g | fiber: 7g

Ham and Vegetable Frittata

Prep time: 10 minutes | Cook time: 27 minutes | Serves 4

2 tablespoons butter, at room temperature
½ cup green onions, chopped
2 garlic cloves, minced
1 jalapeño pepper, chopped
1 carrot, chopped
8 ham slices
8 eggs, whisked
Salt and black pepper, to taste
½ teaspoon dried thyme

1. Set a pan over medium heat and warm the butter. Stir in green onions and sauté for 4 minutes. 2. Place in garlic and cook for 1 minute. Stir in carrot and jalapeño pepper, and cook for 4 more minutes. Remove the mixture to a lightly greased baking pan, with cooking spray, and top with ham slices. 3. Place in the eggs over vegetables and ham; add thyme, black pepper, and salt for seasoning. Bake in the oven for about 18 minutes at 360°F. Serve warm alongside a dollop of full-fat natural yogurt.

Per Serving:
calories: 239 | fat: 16g | protein: 19g | carbs: 5g | net carbs: 4g | fiber: 1g

Sausage and Cheese Balls

Prep time: 10 minutes | Cook time: 12 minutes | Makes 16 balls

1 pound (454 g) pork breakfast sausage
½ cup shredded Cheddar cheese

1 ounce (28 g) full-fat cream cheese, softened
1 large egg

1. Mix all ingredients in a large bowl. Form into sixteen (1-inch) balls. Place the balls into the air fryer basket. 2. Adjust the temperature to 400°F (204°C) and air fry for 12 minutes. 3. Shake the basket two or three times during cooking. Sausage balls will be browned on the outside and have an internal temperature of at least 145°F (63°C) when completely cooked. 4. Serve warm.

Per Serving:
(1 balls) calories: 83 | fat: 7g | protein: 4g | carbs: 1g | net carbs: 1g | fiber: 0g

Cauliflower & Cheese Burgers

Prep time: 10 minutes | Cook time: 35 minutes | Serves 6

1½ tablespoons olive oil
1 onion, chopped
1 garlic clove, minced
1 pound cauliflower, grated
6 tablespoons coconut flour

½ cup gruyere cheese, shredded
1 cup Parmesan cheese
2 eggs, beaten
½ teaspoon dried rosemary
Sea salt and ground black pepper, to taste

1. Set a cast iron skillet over medium heat and warm oil. Add in garlic and onion and cook until soft, about 3 minutes. Stir in grated cauliflower and cook for a minute; allow cooling and set aside. 2. To the cooled cauliflower, add the rest of the ingredients; form balls from the mixture, then, press each ball to form burger patty. 3. Set oven to 400°F and bake the burgers for 20 minutes. Flip and bake for another 10 minutes or until the top becomes golden brown.

Per Serving:
calories: 260 | fat: 18g | protein: 16g | carbs: 11g | net carbs: 7g | fiber: 4g

Chapter 3 Poultry

Baked Cheesy Mushroom Chicken

Prep time: 5 minutes | Cook time: 15 minutes | Serves 4

1 tablespoon butter
2 cloves garlic, smashed
½ cup chopped yellow onion
1 pound (454 g) chicken breasts, cubed
10 ounces (283 g) button mushrooms, thinly sliced
1 cup chicken broth
½ teaspoon shallot powder
½ teaspoon turmeric powder
½ teaspoon dried basil
½ teaspoon dried sage
½ teaspoon cayenne pepper
⅓ teaspoon ground black pepper
Kosher salt, to taste
½ cup heavy cream
1 cup shredded Colby cheese

1. Set your Instant Pot to Sauté and melt the butter. 2. Add the garlic, onion, chicken, and mushrooms and sauté for about 4 minutes, or until the vegetables are softened. 3. Add the remaining ingredients except the heavy cream and cheese to the Instant Pot and stir to incorporate. 4. Lock the lid. Select the Meat/Stew mode and set the cooking time for 6 minutes at High Pressure. 5. When the timer beeps, perform a natural pressure release for 10 minutes, then release any remaining pressure. Carefully remove the lid. 6. Stir in the heavy cream until heated through. Pour the mixture into a baking dish and scatter the cheese on top. 7. Bake in the preheated oven at 400°F (205°C) until the cheese bubbles. 8. Allow to cool for 5 minutes and serve.

Per Serving:
calories: 439 | fat: 29g | protein: 34g | carbs: 10g | net carbs: 8g | fiber: 2g

Chicken Thighs with Cilantro

Prep time: 15 minutes | Cook time: 25 minutes | Serves 4

1 tablespoon olive oil
Juice of ½ lime
1 tablespoon coconut aminos
1½ teaspoons Montreal chicken seasoning
8 bone-in chicken thighs, skin on
2 tablespoons chopped fresh cilantro

1. In a gallon-size resealable bag, combine the olive oil, lime juice, coconut aminos, and chicken seasoning. Add the chicken thighs, seal the bag, and massage the bag to ensure the chicken is thoroughly coated. Refrigerate for at least 2 hours, preferably overnight. 2. Preheat the air fryer to 400°F (204°C). 3. Remove the chicken from the marinade (discard the marinade) and arrange in a single layer in the air fryer basket. Pausing halfway through the cooking time to flip the chicken, air fry for 20 to 25 minutes, until a thermometer inserted into the thickest part registers 165°F (74°C). 4. Transfer the chicken to a serving platter and top with the cilantro before serving.

Per Serving:
calories: 692 | fat: 53g | protein: 49g | carbs: 2g | fiber: 0g | sodium: 242mg

Buffalo Chicken Crust Pizza

Prep time: 10 minutes | Cook time: 30 minutes | Serves 2

Buffalo Sauce:
¼ cup Frank's RedHot sauce
¼ cup (½ stick) unsalted butter
2¼ teaspoons apple cider vinegar
Crust:
2 (5-ounce) cans chunk chicken breast in water, drained
¼ cup grated Parmesan cheese
1 large egg
Toppings:
4 ounces fresh mozzarella cheese, sliced
1 tablespoon sliced scallions (optional)

1. Preheat the oven to 350°F and line a pizza stone or metal pizza pan with parchment paper. 2. Make the sauce: Put the hot sauce, butter, and vinegar in a small saucepan over medium heat. Once the butter melts, stir to combine and remove from the heat. Set aside. 3. Prepare the crust: Spread the drained chicken on the lined pizza stone/pan and bake for 10 minutes to remove all the moisture. Remove from the oven and transfer the chicken to a medium-sized bowl. Increase the oven temperature to 500°F. 4. To the bowl with the chicken, add the Parmesan cheese and egg. Mix thoroughly with a fork. 5. Place a clean sheet of parchment paper on the counter and pour the chicken mixture onto it. Spread the chicken into a thin layer with a rubber spatula. Place another piece of parchment paper on top of the chicken mixture and flatten it into a ¼-inch-thick circle using a rolling pin. Remove the top piece of parchment, transfer the bottom piece of parchment with the crust on it to the pizza stone/pan, and bake the crust for 8 minutes, until slightly browned and hardened. 6. Remove the crust from the oven and top with the Buffalo sauce and mozzarella cheese. Bake for 6 to 8 more minutes, until the cheese is melted and starting to brown. Remove from the oven, top with the sliced scallions, if using, and cut into 6 slices. 7. Store leftovers in a sealed container in the refrigerator for up to 3 days. Reheat in a 250°F oven.

Per Serving:
calories: 600 | fat: 45g | protein: 48g | carbs: 2g | net carbs: 2g | fiber: 0g

Chicken Croquettes with Creole Sauce

Prep time: 30 minutes | Cook time: 10 minutes | Serves 4

2 cups shredded cooked chicken
½ cup shredded Cheddar cheese
2 eggs
¼ cup finely chopped onion
¼ cup almond meal
1 tablespoon poultry seasoning
Olive oil

Creole Sauce:
¼ cup mayonnaise
¼ cup sour cream
1½ teaspoons Dijon mustard
1½ teaspoons fresh lemon juice
½ teaspoon garlic powder
½ teaspoon Creole seasoning

1. In a large bowl, combine the chicken, Cheddar, eggs, onion, almond meal, and poultry seasoning. Stir gently until thoroughly combined. Cover and refrigerate for 30 minutes. 2. Meanwhile, to make the Creole sauce: In a small bowl, whisk together the mayonnaise, sour cream, Dijon mustard, lemon juice, garlic powder, and Creole seasoning until thoroughly combined. Cover and refrigerate until ready to serve. 3. Preheat the air fryer to 400°F (204°C). Divide the chicken mixture into 8 portions and shape into patties. 4. Working in batches if necessary, arrange the patties in a single layer in the air fryer basket and coat both sides lightly with olive oil. Pausing halfway through the cooking time to flip the patties, air fry for 10 minutes, or until lightly browned and the cheese is melted. Serve with the Creole sauce.

Per Serving:

calories: 460 | fat: 35g | protein: 28g | carbs: 7g | net carbs: 4g | fiber: 3g

Chicken with Parmesan Topping

Prep time: 15 minutes | Cook time: 40 minutes | Serves 4

4 chicken breast halves, skinless and boneless
Salt and black pepper, to taste
¼ cup green chilies, chopped
5 bacon slices, chopped
6 ounces cream cheese
¼ cup onion, chopped
½ cup mayonnaise
½ cup Grana Padano cheese, grated
1 cup cheddar cheese, grated
2 ounces pork rinds, crushed
2 tablespoons olive oil
½ cup Parmesan cheese, shredded

1. Season the chicken with salt and pepper. Heat the olive oil in a pan over medium heat and fry the chicken for approximately 4-6 minutes until cooked through with no pink showing. Remove to a baking dish. 2. In the same pan, fry bacon until crispy and remove to a plate. Sauté the onion for 3 minutes, until soft. Remove from heat, add in the fried bacon, cream cheese, 1 cup of water, Grana Padano cheese, mayonnaise, chilies, and cheddar cheese, and spread over the chicken. 3. Bake in the oven for 10-15 minutes at 370°F. Remove and sprinkle with mixed Parmesan cheese and pork rinds and return to the oven. Bake for another 10-15 minutes until the cheese melts. Serve immediately.

Per Serving:

calories: 773 | fat: 57g | protein: 58g | carbs: 7g | net carbs: 6g | fiber: 1g

Buttery Garlic Chicken

Prep time: 5 minutes | Cook time: 40 minutes | Serves 2

2 tablespoons ghee, melted
2 boneless skinless chicken breasts
Pink Himalayan salt
Freshly ground black pepper
1 tablespoon dried Italian seasoning
4 tablespoons butter
2 garlic cloves, minced
¼ cup grated Parmesan cheese

1. Preheat the oven to 375°F. Choose a baking dish that is large enough to hold both chicken breasts and coat it with the ghee. 2. Pat dry the chicken breasts and season with pink Himalayan salt, pepper, and Italian seasoning. Place the chicken in the baking dish. 3. In a medium skillet over medium heat, melt the butter. Add the minced garlic, and cook for about 5 minutes. You want the garlic very lightly browned but not burned. 4. Remove the butter-garlic mixture from the heat, and pour it over the chicken breasts. 5. Roast the chicken in the oven for 30 to 35 minutes, until cooked through. Sprinkle some of the Parmesan cheese on top of each chicken breast. Let the chicken rest in the baking dish for 5 minutes. 6. Divide the chicken between two plates, spoon the butter sauce over the chicken, and serve.

Per Serving:

calories: 642 | fat: 45g | protein: 57g | carbs: 2g | net carbs: 2g | fiber: 0g

Herb and Lemon Whole Chicken

Prep time: 5 minutes | Cook time: 30 to 32 minutes | Serves 4

3 teaspoons garlic powder
3 teaspoons salt
2 teaspoons dried parsley
2 teaspoons dried rosemary
1 teaspoon pepper
1 (4-pound / 1.8-kg) whole chicken
2 tablespoons coconut oil
1 cup chicken broth
1 lemon, zested and quartered

1. Combine the garlic powder, salt, parsley, rosemary, and pepper in a small bowl. Rub this herb mix over the whole chicken. 2. Set your Instant Pot to Sauté and heat the coconut oil. 3. Add the chicken and brown for 5 to 7 minutes. Using tongs, transfer the chicken to a plate. 4. Pour the broth into the Instant Pot and scrape the bottom with a rubber spatula or wooden spoon until no seasoning is stuck to pot, then insert the trivet. 5. Scatter the lemon zest over chicken. Put the lemon quarters inside the chicken. Place the chicken on the trivet. 6. Secure the lid. Select the Meat/Stew mode and set the cooking time for 25 minutes at High Pressure. 7. Once cooking is complete, do a natural pressure release for 10 minutes, then release any remaining pressure. Carefully open the lid. 8. Shred the chicken and serve warm.

Per Serving:

calories: 860 | fat: 63g | protein: 55g | carbs: 3g | net carbs: 2g | fiber: 1g

Crunchy Chicken Milanese

Prep time: 10 minutes | Cook time: 10 minutes | Serves 2

2 boneless skinless chicken breasts
½ cup coconut flour
1 teaspoon ground cayenne pepper
Pink Himalayan salt
Freshly ground black pepper
1 egg, lightly beaten
½ cup crushed pork rinds
2 tablespoons olive oil

1. Pound the chicken breasts with a heavy mallet until they are about ½ inch thick. (If you don't have a kitchen mallet, you can use the thick rim of a heavy plate.) 2. Prepare two separate prep plates and one small, shallow bowl: •On plate 1, put the coconut flour, cayenne pepper, pink Himalayan salt, and pepper. Mix together. •Crack the egg into the small bowl, and lightly beat it with a fork or whisk. •On plate 2, put the crushed pork rinds. 3. In a large skillet over medium-high heat, heat the olive oil. 4. Dredge 1 chicken breast on both sides in the coconut-flour mixture. Dip the chicken into the egg, and coat both sides. Dredge the chicken in the pork-rind mixture, pressing the pork rinds into the chicken so they stick. Place the coated chicken in the hot skillet and repeat with the other chicken breast. 5. Cook the chicken for 3 to 5 minutes on each side, until brown, crispy, and cooked through, and serve.

Per Serving:

calories: 604 | fat: 29g | protein: 65g | carbs: 17g | net carbs: 7g | fiber: 10g

"K.F.C." Keto Fried Chicken

Prep time: 15 minutes | Cook time: 10 minutes | Serves 4

1 cup vegetable oil, for frying
2 large eggs
2 tablespoons heavy whipping cream
⅔ cup blanched almond flour
⅔ cup grated Parmesan cheese
¼ teaspoon salt
½ teaspoon black pepper
½ teaspoon paprika
½ teaspoon ground cayenne
1 pound (approximately 4) boneless, skinless chicken thighs

1 In a medium pot over medium heat add vegetable oil. Make sure it is about 1" deep. Heat oil to 350°F, frequently monitoring to maintain the temperature by adjusting heat during frying. 2 In a medium bowl, add eggs and heavy whipping cream. Beat until well mixed. 3 In a separate medium bowl, add almond flour, Parmesan cheese, salt, pepper, paprika, and cayenne and mix. 4 Cut each thigh into two even pieces. If wet, pat dry. 5 Coat each piece first in the dry breading, then in the egg wash, and then the breading again. 6 Shake off any excess breading and lower the chicken into the hot oil. Fry until deep brown and cooked through, about 3–5 minutes on each side, and then drain on paper towels. 7 Repeat until all chicken is cooked. Serve right away while hot and crispy.

Per Serving:

calories: 753 | fat: 62g | protein: 36g | carbs: 8g | net carbs: 6g | fiber: 2g

Chicken with Lettuce

Prep time: 15 minutes | Cook time: 14 minutes | Serves 4

1 pound (454 g) chicken breast tenders, chopped into bite-size pieces
½ onion, thinly sliced
½ red bell pepper, seeded and thinly sliced
½ green bell pepper, seeded and thinly sliced
1 tablespoon olive oil
1 tablespoon fajita seasoning
1 teaspoon kosher salt
Juice of ½ lime
8 large lettuce leaves
1 cup prepared guacamole

1. Preheat the air fryer to 400°F (204°C). 2. In a large bowl, combine the chicken, onion, and peppers. Drizzle with the olive oil and toss until thoroughly coated. Add the fajita seasoning and salt and toss again. 3. Working in batches if necessary, arrange the chicken and vegetables in a single layer in the air fryer basket. Pausing halfway through the cooking time to shake the basket, air fry for 14 minutes, or until the vegetables are tender and a thermometer inserted into the thickest piece of chicken registers 165°F (74°C). 4. Transfer the mixture to a serving platter and drizzle with the fresh lime juice. Serve with the lettuce leaves and top with the guacamole.

Per Serving:

calories: 273 | fat: 15g | protein: 27g | carbs: 9g | fiber: 5g | sodium: 723mg

Chicken with Monterey Jack Cheese

Prep time: 15 minutes | Cook time: 35 minutes | Serves 3

2 tablespoons butter
1 teaspoon garlic, minced
1 pound chicken breasts
1 teaspoon creole seasoning
¼ cup scallions, chopped
½ cup tomatoes, chopped
½ cup chicken stock
¼ cup whipping cream
½ cup Monterey Jack cheese, grated
¼ cup fresh cilantro, chopped
Salt and black pepper, to taste
4 ounces cream cheese
8 eggs
A pinch of garlic powder

1. Set a pan over medium heat and warm 1 tablespoon butter. Add chicken, season with creole seasoning and cook each side for 2 minutes; remove to a plate. Melt the rest of the butter and stir in garlic and tomatoes; cook for 4 minutes. Return the chicken to the pan and pour in stock; cook for 15 minutes. Place in whipping cream, scallions, salt, Monterey Jack cheese, and pepper; cook for 2 minutes. 2. In a blender, combine the cream cheese with garlic powder, salt, eggs, and pepper, and pulse well. Place the mixture into a lined baking sheet, and then bake for 10 minutes in the oven at 325°F. Allow the cheese sheet to cool down, place on a cutting board, roll, and slice into medium slices. Split the slices among bowls and top with chicken mixture. Sprinkle with chopped cilantro to serve.

Per Serving:

calories: 571 | fat: 39g | protein: 43g | carbs: 8g | net carbs: 6g | fiber: 1g

Caprese Chicken Thighs

Prep time: 10 minutes | Cook time: 28 minutes | Serves 4

⅓ cup olive oil
3 tablespoons balsamic vinegar, divided into 2 tablespoons and 1 tablespoon
1 teaspoon Italian seasoning
½ teaspoon garlic powder
½ teaspoon sea salt
¼ teaspoon black pepper
8 boneless, skinless chicken thighs (2½ ounces / 71 g each)
4 ounces (113 g) fresh Mozzarella cheese, cut into 8 slices
2 medium Roma (plum) tomatoes, thinly sliced
2 tablespoons fresh basil, cut into ribbons

1. In a large bowl, whisk together the oil, 2 tablespoons of balsamic vinegar, the Italian seasoning, garlic powder, sea salt, and black pepper. 2. Add the chicken thighs and push down into the marinade. Set aside for 20 minutes, or refrigerate until ready to use. 3. Meanwhile, preheat the oven to 375ºF (190ºC). Line a sheet pan with foil or parchment paper. 4. Shake off any excess marinade from each piece of chicken and arrange on the baking sheet in a single layer without touching. 5. Top each chicken thigh with a slice of Mozzarella, covering most of it. You may need to cut a piece in half to cover the chicken better. Place 2 slices of tomato on top of the Mozzarella. 6. Roast for 23 to 28 minutes, until the chicken is cooked through. You may need to pour off extra liquid from the pan at the end. 7. Drizzle the chicken with the remaining 1 tablespoon balsamic vinegar (or with a reduction by simmering more balsamic vinegar in a small saucepan). Garnish with basil ribbons.

Per Serving:

calories: 564 | fat: 46g | protein: 31g | carbs: 4g | net carbs: 4g | fiber: 0g

Parmesan Baked Chicken

Prep time: 5 minutes | Cook time: 20 minutes | Serves 2

2 tablespoons ghee
2 boneless skinless chicken breasts
Pink Himalayan salt
Freshly ground black pepper
½ cup mayonnaise
¼ cup grated Parmesan cheese
1 tablespoon dried Italian seasoning
¼ cup crushed pork rinds

1. Preheat the oven to 425°F. Choose a baking dish that is large enough to hold both chicken breasts and coat it with the ghee. 2. Pat dry the chicken breasts with a paper towel, season with pink Himalayan salt and pepper, and place in the prepared baking dish. 3. In a small bowl, mix to combine the mayonnaise, Parmesan cheese, and Italian seasoning. 4. Slather the mayonnaise mixture evenly over the chicken breasts, and sprinkle the crushed pork rinds on top of the mayonnaise mixture. 5. Bake until the topping is browned, about 20 minutes, and serve.

Per Serving:

calories: 850 | fat: 67g | protein: 60g | carbs: 2g | net carbs: 2g | fiber: 0g

Chicken Gumbo

Prep time: 20 minutes | Cook time: 30 minutes | Serves 5

2 sausages, sliced
3 chicken breasts, cubed
1 cup celery, chopped
2 tablespoons dried oregano
2 bell peppers, seeded and chopped
1 onion, peeled and chopped
2 cups tomatoes, chopped
4 cups chicken broth
3 tablespoons dried thyme
2 tablespoons garlic powder
2 tablespoons dry mustard
1 teaspoon cayenne powder
1 tablespoon chili powder
Salt and black pepper, to taste
6 tablespoons cajun seasoning
3 tablespoons olive oil

1. In a pot over medium heat warm olive oil. Add the sausages, chicken, pepper, onion, dry mustard, chili, tomatoes, thyme, bell peppers, salt, oregano, garlic powder, cayenne, and cajun seasoning. 2. Cook for 10 minutes. Add the remaining ingredients and bring to a boil. Reduce the heat and simmer for 20 minutes covered. Serve hot divided between bowls.

Per Serving:

calories: 376 | fat: 17g | protein: 36g | carbs: 20g | net carbs: 16g | fiber: 6g

Pesto Chicken

Prep time: 5 minutes | Cook time: 25 minutes | Serves 2

2 (6-ounce / 170-g) boneless, skinless chicken breasts, butterflied
½ teaspoon salt
¼ teaspoon pepper
¼ teaspoon dried parsley
¼ teaspoon garlic powder
2 tablespoons coconut oil
1 cup water
¼ cup whole-milk ricotta cheese
¼ cup pesto
¼ cup shredded whole-milk Mozzarella cheese
Chopped parsley, for garnish (optional)

1. Sprinkle the chicken breasts with salt, pepper, parsley, and garlic powder. 2. Set your Instant Pot to Sauté and melt the coconut oil. 3. Add the chicken and brown for 3 to 5 minutes. Remove the chicken from the pot to a 7-cup glass bowl. 4. Pour the water into the Instant Pot and use a wooden spoon or rubber spatula to make sure no seasoning is stuck to bottom of pot. 5. Scatter the ricotta cheese on top of the chicken. Pour the pesto over chicken, and sprinkle the Mozzarella cheese over chicken. Cover with aluminum foil. Add the trivet to the Instant Pot and place the bowl on the trivet. 6. Secure the lid. Select the Manual mode and set the cooking time for 20 minutes at High Pressure. 7. Once cooking is complete, do a natural pressure release for 10 minutes, then release any remaining pressure. Carefully open the lid. 8. Serve the chicken garnished with the chopped parsley, if desired.

Per Serving:

calories: 519 | fat: 32g | protein: 46g | carbs: 4g | net carbs: 4g | fiber: 1g

Thanksgiving Turkey Breast

Prep time: 5 minutes | Cook time: 30 minutes | Serves 4

1½ teaspoons fine sea salt
1 teaspoon ground black pepper
1 teaspoon chopped fresh rosemary leaves
1 teaspoon chopped fresh sage
1 teaspoon chopped fresh tarragon
1 teaspoon chopped fresh thyme leaves
1 (2-pound / 907-g) turkey breast
3 tablespoons ghee or unsalted butter, melted
3 tablespoons Dijon mustard

1. Spray the air fryer with avocado oil. Preheat the air fryer to 390°F (199°C). 2. In a small bowl, stir together the salt, pepper, and herbs until well combined. Season the turkey breast generously on all sides with the seasoning. 3. In another small bowl, stir together the ghee and Dijon. Brush the ghee mixture on all sides of the turkey breast. 4. Place the turkey breast in the air fryer basket and air fry for 30 minutes, or until the internal temperature reaches 165°F (74°C). Transfer the breast to a cutting board and allow it to rest for 10 minutes before cutting it into ½-inch-thick slices. 5. Store leftovers in an airtight container in the refrigerator for up to 4 days or in the freezer for up to a month. Reheat in a preheated 350°F (177°C) air fryer for 4 minutes, or until warmed through.

Per Serving:

calories: 351 | fat: 18g | protein: 44g | carbs: 3g | net carbs: 2g | fiber: 1g

Bruschetta and Cheese Stuffed Chicken

Prep time: 10 minutes | Cook time: 10 minutes | Serves 4

6 ounces (170 g) diced Roma tomatoes
2 tablespoons avocado oil
1 tablespoon thinly sliced fresh basil, plus more for garnish
1½ teaspoons balsamic vinegar
Pinch of salt
Pinch of black pepper
4 boneless, skinless chicken breasts (about 2 pounds / 907 g)
12 ounces (340 g) goat cheese, divided
2 teaspoons Italian seasoning, divided
1 cup water

1. Prepare the bruschetta by mixing the tomatoes, avocado oil, basil, vinegar, salt, and pepper in a small bowl. Let it marinate until the chicken is done. 2. Pat the chicken dry with a paper towel. Butterfly the breast open but do not cut all the way through. Stuff each breast with 3 ounces (85 g) of the goat cheese. Use toothpicks to close the edges. 3. Sprinkle ½ teaspoon of the Italian seasoning on top of each breast. 4. Pour the water into the pot. Place the trivet inside. Lay a piece of aluminum foil on top of the trivet and place the chicken breasts on top. It is okay if they overlap. 5. Close the lid and seal the vent. Cook on High Pressure for 10 minutes. Quick release the steam. 6. Remove the toothpicks and top each breast with one-fourth of the bruschetta.

Per Serving:

calories: 581 | fat: 34g | protein: 64g | carbs: 5g | net carbs: 4g | fiber: 1g

Garlic & Ginger Chicken with Peanut Sauce

Prep time: 10 minutes | Cook time: 14 minutes | Serves 6

1 tablespoon wheat-free soy sauce
1 tablespoon sugar-free fish sauce
1 tablespoon lime juice
1 teaspoon cilantro
1 teaspoon minced garlic
1 teaspoon minced ginger
1 tablespoon olive oil
1 tablespoon rice wine vinegar
1 teaspoon cayenne pepper
1 teaspoon erythritol
6 chicken thighs
Peanut sauce:
½ cup peanut butter
1 teaspoon minced garlic
1 tablespoon lime juice
2 tablespoons water
1 teaspoon minced ginger
1 tablespoon chopped jalapeño
2 tablespoons rice wine vinegar
2 tablespoons erythritol
1 tablespoon fish sauce

1. Combine all chicken ingredients in a large Ziploc bag. Seal the bag and shake to combine. Refrigerate for 1 hour. Remove from fridge about 15 minutes before cooking. 2. Preheat the grill to medium heat and cook the chicken for 7 minutes per side. Whisk together all sauce ingredients in a mixing bowl. Serve the chicken drizzled with peanut sauce.

Per Serving:

calories: 526 | fat: 38g | protein: 39g | carbs: 11g | net carbs: 8g | fiber: 3g

Marjoram Chicken Wings with Cream Cheese

Prep time: 7 minutes | Cook time: 10 minutes | Serves 2

1 teaspoon marjoram
1 teaspoon cream cheese
½ green pepper
½ teaspoon salt
½ teaspoon ground black pepper
14 ounces (397 g) chicken wings
¾ cup water
1 teaspoon coconut oil

1. Rub the chicken wings with the marjoram, salt, and ground black pepper. 2. Blend the green pepper until you get a purée. 3. Rub the chicken wings in the green pepper purée. 4. Then toss the coconut oil in the instant pot bowl and preheat it on the Sauté mode. 5. Add the chicken wings and cook them for 3 minutes from each side or until light brown. 6. Then add cream cheese and water. 7. Cook the meal on Manual mode for 4 minutes at High Pressure. 8. When the time is over, make a quick pressure release. 9. Let the cooked chicken wings chill for 1 to 2 minutes and serve them!

Per Serving:

calories: 411 | fat: 18g | protein: 58g | carbs: 2g | net carbs: 1g | fiber: 1g

Chicken Patties

Prep time: 15 minutes | Cook time: 12 minutes | Serves 4

1 pound (454 g) ground chicken thigh meat
½ cup shredded Mozzarella cheese
1 teaspoon dried parsley
½ teaspoon garlic powder
¼ teaspoon onion powder
1 large egg
2 ounces (57 g) pork rinds, finely ground

1. In a large bowl, mix ground chicken, Mozzarella, parsley, garlic powder, and onion powder. Form into four patties. 2. Place patties in the freezer for 15 to 20 minutes until they begin to firm up. 3. Whisk egg in a medium bowl. Place the ground pork rinds into a large bowl. 4. Dip each chicken patty into the egg and then press into pork rinds to fully coat. Place patties into the air fryer basket. 5. Adjust the temperature to 360ºF (182ºC) and air fry for 12 minutes. 6. Patties will be firm and cooked to an internal temperature of 165ºF (74ºC) when done. Serve immediately.

Per Serving:
calories: 265 | fat: 15g | protein: 29g | carbs: 1g | fiber: 0g | sodium: 285mg

Fried Chicken Breasts

Prep time: 30 minutes | Cook time: 12 to 14 minutes | Serves 4

1 pound (454 g) boneless, skinless chicken breasts
¾ cup dill pickle juice
¾ cup finely ground blanched almond flour
¾ cup finely grated Parmesan cheese
½ teaspoon sea salt
½ teaspoon freshly ground black pepper
2 large eggs
Avocado oil spray

1. Place the chicken breasts in a zip-top bag or between two pieces of plastic wrap. Using a meat mallet or heavy skillet, pound the chicken to a uniform ½-inch thickness. 2. Place the chicken in a large bowl with the pickle juice. Cover and allow to brine in the refrigerator for up to 2 hours. 3. In a shallow dish, combine the almond flour, Parmesan cheese, salt, and pepper. In a separate, shallow bowl, beat the eggs. 4. Drain the chicken and pat it dry with paper towels. Dip in the eggs and then in the flour mixture, making sure to press the coating into the chicken. Spray both sides of the coated breasts with oil. 5. Spray the air fryer basket with oil and put the chicken inside. Set the temperature to 400ºF (204ºC) and air fry for 6 to 7 minutes. 6. Carefully flip the breasts with a spatula. Spray the breasts again with oil and continue cooking for 6 to 7 minutes more, until golden and crispy.

Per Serving:
calories: 450 | fat: 27g | protein: 44g | carbs: 6g | net carbs: 4g | fiber: 2g

Chipotle Dry-Rub Wings

Prep time: 10 minutes | Cook time: 45 minutes | Serves 4

Chipotle Rub:
1 tablespoon ground chipotle pepper
1 teaspoon paprika
1 teaspoon ground cumin
1 teaspoon ground mustard
1 teaspoon garlic powder
1 teaspoon onion powder
1 teaspoon pink Himalayan salt
2 pounds chicken wings
1 teaspoon baking powder

1. Preheat the oven to 250°F and place a wire baking rack inside a rimmed baking sheet. 2. Put the seasonings for the rub in a small bowl and stir with a fork. Divide the spice rub into 2 equal portions. 3. Cut the wings in half, if whole (see Tip), and place in a large zip-top plastic bag. Add the baking powder and half of the spice rub to the bag and shake thoroughly to coat the wings. 4. Lay the wings on the baking rack in a single layer. Bake for 25 minutes. 5. Turn the heat up to 450°F and bake the wings for an additional 20 minutes, until golden brown and crispy. 6. Once the wings are done, place them in a large plastic container with the remaining half of the spice rub and shake to coat. Serve immediately.

Per Serving:
calories: 507 | fat: 36g | protein: 42g | carbs: 3g | net carbs: 3g | fiber: 0g

Pancetta & Chicken Casserole

Prep time: 10 minutes | Cook time: 25 minutes | Serves 3

8 pancetta strips, chopped
⅓ cup Dijon mustard
Salt and black pepper, to taste
1 onion, chopped
1 tablespoon olive oil
1½ cups chicken stock
3 chicken breasts, skinless and boneless
¼ teaspoon sweet paprika

1. In a bowl, combine paprika, black pepper, salt, and mustard. Sprinkle this on chicken breasts and massage. Set a pan over medium heat, stir in the pancetta, cook until it browns, and remove to a plate. 2Place oil in the same pan and heat over medium heat, add in the chicken breasts, cook for each side for 2 minutes and set aside. Put in the stock, and bring to a simmer. Stir in black pepper, pancetta, salt, and onion. Return the chicken to the pan as well, stir gently, and simmer for 20 minutes over medium heat, turning the meat halfway through. Split the chicken on serving plates, sprinkle the sauce over it to serve.

Per Serving:
calories: 438 | fat: 23g | protein: 47g | carbs: 8g | net carbs: 7g | fiber: 2g

Turmeric Chicken Nuggets

Prep time: 10 minutes | Cook time: 9 minutes | Serves 5

8 ounces (227 g) chicken fillet
1 teaspoon ground turmeric
½ teaspoon ground coriander
½ cup almond flour
2 eggs, beaten
½ cup butter

1. Chop the chicken fillet roughly into the medium size pieces. 2. In the mixing bowl, mix up ground turmeric, ground coriander, and almond flour. 3. Then dip the chicken pieces in the beaten egg and coat in the almond flour mixture. 4. Toss the butter in the instant pot and melt it on Sauté mode for 4 minutes. 5. Then put the coated chicken in the hot butter and cook for 5 minutes or until the nuggets are golden brown.

Per Serving:

calories: 343 | fat: 29g | protein: 18g | carbs: 3g | net carbs: 2g | fiber: 1g

Zucchini Spaghetti with Turkey Bolognese Sauce

Prep time: 10 minutes | Cook time: 35 minutes | Serves 6

3 cups sliced mushrooms
2 teaspoons olive oil
1 pound ground turkey
3 tablespoons pesto sauce
1 cup diced onion
2 cups broccoli florets
6 cups zucchini, spiralized

1. Heat the oil in a skillet. Add zucchini and cook for 2-3 minutes, stirring continuously; set aside. 2. Add turkey to the skillet and cook until browned, about 7-8 minutes. Transfer to a plate. Add onion and cook until translucent, about 3 minutes. Add broccoli and mushrooms, and cook for 7 more minutes. Return the turkey to the skillet. Stir in the pesto sauce. Cover the pan, lower the heat, and simmer for 15 minutes. Stir in zucchini pasta and serve immediately.

Per Serving:

calories: 279 | fat: 19g | protein: 22g | carbs: 5g | net carbs: 3g | fiber: 2g

Pecorino Chicken

Prep time: 10 minutes | Cook time: 15 minutes | Serves 3

2 ounces (57 g) Pecorino cheese, grated
10 ounces (283 g) chicken breast, skinless, boneless
1 tablespoon butter
¾ cup heavy cream
½ teaspoon salt
½ teaspoon red hot pepper

1. Chop the chicken breast into the cubes. 2. Toss butter in the instant pot and preheat it on the Sauté mode. 3. Add the chicken cubes. 4. Sprinkle the poultry with the salt and red hot pepper. 5. Add cream and mix up together all the ingredients. 6. Close the lid of the instant pot and seal it. 7. Set Poultry mode and put a timer on 15 minutes. 8. When the time is over, let the chicken rest for 5 minutes more. 9. Transfer the meal on the plates and sprinkle with the grated cheese. The cheese shouldn't melt immediately.

Per Serving:

calories: 340 | fat: 25g | protein: 28g | carbs: 1g | net carbs: 1g | fiber: 0g

Poblano Chicken

Prep time: 10 minutes | Cook time: 29 minutes | Serves 4

2 Poblano peppers, sliced
16 ounces (454 g) chicken fillet
½ teaspoon salt
½ cup coconut cream
1 tablespoon butter
½ teaspoon chili powder

1. Heat up the butter on Sauté mode for 3 minutes. 2. Add Poblano and cook them for 3 minutes. 3. Meanwhile, cut the chicken fillet into the strips and sprinkle with salt and chili powder. 4. Add the chicken strips to the instant pot. 5. Then add coconut cream and close the lid. Cook the meal on Sauté mode for 20 minutes.

Per Serving:

calories: 320 | fat: 18g | protein: 34g | carbs: 4g | net carbs: 3g | fiber: 1g

Chicken Cordon Bleu

Prep time: 20 minutes | Cook time: 15 to 20 minutes | Serves 4

4 small boneless, skinless chicken breasts
Salt and pepper, to taste
4 slices deli ham
4 slices deli Swiss cheese (about 3 to 4 inches square)
2 tablespoons olive oil
2 teaspoons marjoram
¼ teaspoon paprika

1. Split each chicken breast horizontally almost in two, leaving one edge intact. 2. Lay breasts open flat and sprinkle with salt and pepper to taste. 3. Place a ham slice on top of each chicken breast. 4. Cut cheese slices in half and place one half atop each breast. Set aside remaining halves of cheese slices. 5. Roll up chicken breasts to enclose cheese and ham and secure with toothpicks. 6. Mix together the olive oil, marjoram, and paprika. Rub all over outsides of chicken breasts. 7. Place chicken in air fryer basket and air fry at 360ºF (182ºC) for 15 to 20 minutes, until well done and juices run clear. 8. Remove all toothpicks. To avoid burns, place chicken breasts on a plate to remove toothpicks, then immediately return them to the air fryer basket. 9. Place a half cheese slice on top of each chicken breast and cook for a minute or so just to melt cheese.

Per Serving:

calories: 309 | fat: 18g | protein: 33g | carbs: 1g | net carbs: 1g | fiber: 0g

Cheese Stuffed Chicken

Prep time: 15 minutes | Cook time: 20 minutes | Serves 4

12 ounces (340 g) chicken fillet
4 ounces (113 g) provolone cheese, sliced
1 tablespoon cream cheese
½ teaspoon dried cilantro
½ teaspoon smoked paprika
1 cup water, for cooking

1. Beat the chicken fillet well and rub it with dried cilantro and smoked paprika. 2. Then spread it with cream cheese and top with Provolone cheese. 3. Roll the chicken fillet into the roll and wrap in the foil. 4. Pour water and insert the rack in the instant pot. 5. Place the chicken roll on the rack. Close and seal the lid. 6. Cook it on Manual mode (High Pressure) for 20 minutes. 7. Make a quick pressure release and slice the chicken roll into the servings.

Per Serving:

calories: 271 | fat: 15g | protein: 32g | carbs: 1g | net carbs: 1g | fiber: 0g

Coconut Curry Chicken

Prep time: 15 minutes | Cook time: 3 to 4 hours | Serves 6

1 tablespoon coconut oil
1 teaspoon cumin seeds
2 medium onions, grated
7 to 8 ounces (198 to 227 g) canned plum tomatoes
1 teaspoon salt
1 teaspoon turmeric
½ to 1 teaspoon Kashmiri chili powder (optional)
2 to 3 fresh green chiles, chopped
1 cup coconut cream
12 chicken thighs, skinned, trimmed, and cut into bite-size chunks
1 teaspoon garam masala
Handful fresh coriander leaves, chopped

1. Heat the oil in a frying pan (or in the slow cooker if you have a sear setting). Add the cumin seeds. When sizzling and aromatic, add the onions and cook until they are browning, about 5 to 7 minutes. 2. In a blender, purée the tomatoes and add them to the pan with the salt, turmeric, chili powder (if using), and fresh green chiles. 3. Stir together and put everything in the slow cooker. Pour in the coconut cream. Add the meat and stir to coat with the sauce. 4. Cover and cook on low for 4 hours, or on high for 3 hours. 5. Taste the sauce and adjust the seasoning. If the sauce is very liquidy, turn the cooker to high and cook for 30 minutes more with the lid off. 6. Add the garam masala and throw in the fresh coriander leaves to serve.

Per Serving:

calories: 648 | fat: 32g | protein: 78g | carbs: 9g | net carbs: 7g | fiber: 2g

Chicken Fajitas with Bell Peppers

Prep time: 10 minutes | Cook time: 5 minutes | Serves 4

1½ pounds (680 g) boneless, skinless chicken breasts
¼ cup avocado oil
2 tablespoons water
1 tablespoon Mexican hot sauce
2 cloves garlic, minced
1 teaspoon lime juice
1 teaspoon ground cumin
1 teaspoon salt
1 teaspoon erythritol
¼ teaspoon chili powder
¼ teaspoon smoked paprika
5 ounces (142 g) sliced yellow bell pepper strips
5 ounces (142 g) sliced red bell pepper strips
5 ounces (142 g) sliced green bell pepper strips

1. Slice the chicken into very thin strips lengthwise. Cut each strip in half again. Imagine the thickness of restaurant fajitas when cutting. 2. In a measuring cup, whisk together the avocado oil, water, hot sauce, garlic, lime juice, cumin, salt, erythritol, chili powder, and paprika to form a marinade. Add to the pot, along with the chicken and peppers. 3. Close the lid and seal the vent. Cook on High Pressure for 5 minutes. Quick release the steam.

Per Serving:

calories: 319 | fat: 18g | protein: 34g | carbs: 6g | net carbs: 4g | fiber: 2g

Easy Chicken Chili

Prep time: 10 minutes | Cook time: 25 minutes | Serves 4

4 chicken breasts, skinless, boneless, cubed
1 tablespoon butter
½ onion, chopped
2 cups chicken broth
8 ounces diced tomatoes
2 ounces tomato puree
1 tablespoon chili powder
1 tablespoon cumin
½ tablespoon garlic powder
1 serrano pepper, minced
½ cup shredded cheddar cheese
Salt and black pepper to taste

1. Set a large pan over medium-high heat and add the chicken. Cover with water and bring to a boil. Cook until no longer pink, for 10 minutes. Transfer the chicken to a flat surface to shred with forks. 2. In a large pot, pour in the butter and set over medium heat. Sauté onion until transparent for 5 minutes. Stir in the chicken, tomatoes, cumin, serrano pepper, garlic powder, tomato puree, broth, and chili powder. Adjust the seasoning and let the mixture boil. Reduce heat to simmer for about 10 minutes. Divide chili among bowls and top with shredded cheese to serve.

Per Serving:

calories: 331 | fat: 12g | protein: 44g | carbs: 9g | net carbs: 7g | fiber: 2g

Buttered Duck Breast

Prep time: 10 minutes | Cook time: 12 minutes | Serves 1

1 medium duck breast, skin scored
1 tablespoon heavy cream
2 tablespoons butter
Salt and black pepper, to taste
1 cup kale
¼ teaspoon fresh sage

1. Set the pan over medium heat and warm half of the butter. Place in sage and heavy cream, and cook for 2 minutes. Set another pan over medium heat. Place in the remaining butter and duck breast as the skin side faces down, cook for 4 minutes, flip, and cook for 3 more minutes. 2. Place the kale to the pan containing the sauce, cook for 1 minute. Set the duck breast on a flat surface and slice. Arrange the duck slices on a platter and drizzle over the sauce.

Per Serving:
calories: 485 | fat: 37g | protein: 35g | carbs: 3g | net carbs: 2g | fiber: 1g

Creamy Stuffed Chicken with Parma Ham

Prep time: 10 minutes | Cook time: 25 minutes | Serves 4

4 chicken breasts
2 tablespoons olive oil
3 cloves garlic, minced
3 shallots, finely chopped
4 tablespoons dried mixed herbs
8 slices Parma ham
8 ounces cream cheese
2 lemons, zested Salt to taste

1. Preheat the oven to 350°F. 2. Heat the oil in a small skillet and sauté the garlic and shallots with a pinch of salt and lemon zest for 3 minutes; let it cool. After, stir the cream cheese and mixed herbs into the shallot mixture. 3. Score a pocket in each chicken breast, fill the holes with the cream cheese mixture and cover with the cut-out chicken. Wrap each breast with two Parma ham and secure the ends with a toothpick. Lay the chicken parcels on a greased baking sheet and cook in the oven for 20 minutes. Remove to rest for 4 minutes before serving with green salad and roasted tomatoes.

Per Serving:
calories: 557 | fat: 35g | protein: 50g | carbs: 9g | net carbs: 7g | fiber: 1g

Chicken Skewers with Celery Fries

Prep time: 5 minutes | Cook time: 40 minutes | Serves 4

2 chicken breasts
½ teaspoon salt
¼ teaspoon ground black pepper
2 tablespoons olive oil
¼ cup chicken broth
For the fries
1 pound celery root
2 tablespoons olive oil
½ teaspoon salt
¼ teaspoon ground black pepper

1. Set oven to 400°F. Grease and line a baking sheet. In a bowl, mix oil, spices and the chicken; set in the fridge for 10 minutes while covered. Peel and chop celery root to form fry shapes and place into a separate bowl. Apply oil to coat and add pepper and salt for seasoning. Arrange to the baking tray in an even layer and bake for 10 minutes. 2. Take the chicken from the refrigerator and thread onto the skewers. Place over the celery, pour in the chicken broth, then set in the oven for 30 minutes. Serve with lemon wedges.

Per Serving:
calories: 293 | fat: 15g | protein: 22g | carbs: 18g | net carbs: 14g | fiber: 4g

Chapter 4 Beef, Pork, and Lamb

Braised Short Ribs

Prep time: 15 minutes | Cook time: 2 hours 30 minutes | Serves 2

2 tablespoons butter
4 bone-in beef chuck short ribs (about 2 pounds / 907 g)
Pink Himalayan sea salt
Freshly ground black pepper
1 garlic clove
2 sprigs fresh thyme
1 sprig fresh rosemary
1½ cups beef broth
1½ cups red wine

1. Preheat the oven to 350°F (180°C). 2. In a large sauté pan or skillet, melt the butter over medium heat. 3. Season the ribs on all sides with salt and pepper. 4. Add the ribs to the skillet, sear on both sides for 4 to 6 minutes, until uniformly browned. 5. Transfer the ribs to an 8-inch baking pan; leave the drippings in the skillet. 6. Add the garlic, thyme, and rosemary to the skillet and stir for 2 to 3 minutes, until the garlic is browned. 7. Add the broth and wine, and stir to combine. Simmer over low heat until the liquid is reduced by about one-fourth. 8. Pour the sauce over the short ribs and cover the baking pan with aluminum foil. Bake for 2½ hours, until the ribs are very tender. 9. Using a slotted spoon or a fork, transfer the ribs to a serving dish. Pour the cooking liquid through a mesh strainer into a medium bowl. Discard the solids. Drizzle a small amount of the strained liquid over the ribs before serving.

Per Serving:
calories: 696 | fat: 55g | protein: 39g | carbs: 2g | net carbs: 2g | fiber: 0g

Cheesy Southwestern Meat Loaf

Prep time: 30 minutes | Cook time: 1 hour | Serves 8

½ cup avocado or extra-virgin olive oil, divided
2 cups shredded (not spiralized) zucchini, from 2 small or 1 large zucchini
1½ teaspoons salt, divided
1 pound (454 g) ground beef, preferably grass-fed
1 pound (454 g) ground pork chorizo
½ cup chopped cilantro
¼ cup chopped scallions, green and white parts
1 large egg, beaten
1 tablespoon chopped chipotle pepper with adobo sauce
1 teaspoon garlic powder
¼ cup almond flour
2 cups shredded Mexican cheese blend or Cheddar cheese, divided
1 tablespoon tomato paste (no sugar added)

1. Preheat the oven to 375°F (190°C). Coat a loaf pan with 2 tablespoons of avocado oil. 2. Line a colander with a layer of paper towels and add the shredded zucchini. Sprinkle with ½ teaspoon of salt, tossing to coat. Let sit for 10 minutes, then press down with another layer of paper towels to release some of the excess moisture. 3. While the zucchini drains, in a large bowl, combine the ground beef, chorizo, cilantro, scallions, ¼ cup of oil, egg, chipotle with adobo, garlic powder, and remaining 1 teaspoon of salt. Mix well with a fork. 4. Add the almond flour to the drained zucchini and toss to coat. Add the zucchini to the meat mixture and mix until well combined. Add half of the mixture to the prepared pan and spread evenly. Top with 1 cup of shredded cheese, spreading evenly. Top with the remaining half of the mixture and spread evenly. In a small bowl, whisk together the tomato paste and remaining 2 tablespoons of oil and spread evenly on top of the meat mixture. Sprinkle with the remaining 1 cup of cheese. Bake for 50 to 55 minutes, or until cooked through. Let sit for 10 minutes before cutting.

Per Serving:
calories: 623 | fat: 53g | protein: 33g | carbs: 4g | net carbs: 3g | fiber: 1g

Stuffed Pork with Red Cabbage Salad

Prep time: 10 minutes | Cook time: 30 minutes | Serves 4

Zest and juice from 2 limes
2 garlic cloves, minced
¾ cup olive oil
1 cup fresh cilantro, chopped
1 cup fresh mint, chopped
1 teaspoon dried oregano
Salt and black pepper, to taste
1 teaspoon cumin
4 pork loin steaks
2 pickles, chopped
4 ham slices
6 Swiss cheese slices
2 tablespoons mustard
For the Salad
1 head red cabbage, shredded
2 tablespoons vinegar
3 tablespoons olive oil
Salt to taste

1. In a food processor, blitz the lime zest, oil, oregano, black pepper, cumin, cilantro, lime juice, garlic, mint, and salt. Rub the steaks with the mixture and toss well to coat; set aside for some hours in the fridge. 2. Arrange the steaks on a working surface, split the pickles, mustard, cheese, and ham on them, roll, and secure with toothpicks. Heat a pan over medium heat, add in the pork rolls, cook each side for 2 minutes and remove to a baking sheet. Bake in the oven at 350°F for 25 minutes. Prepare the red cabbage salad by mixing all salad ingredients and serve with the meat.

Per Serving:
calories: 1023 | fat: 87g | protein: 44g | carbs: 13g | net carbs: 11g | fiber: 3g

Ground Beef Stroganoff

Prep time: 10 minutes | Cook time: 20 minutes | serves 6

- 1½ pounds ground beef
- ½ cup finely chopped onions
- 2 cloves garlic, minced
- 4 ounces white mushrooms, sliced
- 4 ounces cream cheese (½ cup), softened
- 1 cup beef broth
- ¼ cup heavy whipping cream
- ¼ cup water
- 1 tablespoon Worcestershire sauce
- Salt and ground black pepper
- ½ cup sour cream

1. In a large skillet over medium heat, cook the ground beef with the onions, garlic, and mushrooms, crumbling the meat with a large spoon it as cooks, until the meat is browned and the onions are softened and translucent, about 10 minutes. Drain the fat, if necessary. 2. Stir in the cream cheese and cook until melted. Add the broth, cream, water, and Worcestershire sauce and stir to combine. Continue to simmer for 5 minutes. 3. Season to taste with salt and pepper. Stir in the sour cream and serve. Leftovers can be stored in an airtight container in the refrigerator for up to 5 days.

Per Serving:

calories: 396 | fat: 32g | protein: 22g | carbs: 23g | net carbs: 2g | fiber: 0g

Jamaican Pork Oven Roast

Prep time: 5 minutes | Cook time: 4 hours | Serves 12

- 4 pounds pork roast
- 1 tablespoon olive oil
- ¼ cup jerk spice blend
- ½ cup vegetable stock
- Salt and black pepper, to taste

1. Rub the pork with olive oil and the spice blend. Heat a dutch oven over medium heat and sear the meat well on all sides; add in the stock. Cover the pot, reduce the heat, and let cook for 4 hours.

Per Serving:

calories: 265 | fat: 11g | protein: 36g | carbs: 0g | net carbs: 0g | fiber: 0g

Beef Sausage Casserole

Prep time: 10 minutes | Cook time: 25 minutes | Serves 8

- ⅓ cup almond flour
- 2 eggs
- 2 pounds beef sausage, chopped
- Salt and black pepper, to taste
- 1 tablespoon dried parsley
- ¼ teaspoon red pepper flakes
- ¼ cup Parmesan cheese, grated
- ¼ teaspoon onion powder
- ½ teaspoon garlic powder
- ¼ teaspoon dried oregano
- 1 cup ricotta cheese
- 1 cup sugar-free marinara sauce
- 1½ cups cheddar cheese, shredded

1. In a bowl, combine the sausage, black pepper, pepper flakes, oregano, eggs, Parmesan cheese, onion powder, almond flour, salt, parsley, and garlic powder. Form balls, lay them on a greased baking sheet, place in the oven at 370ºF, and bake for 15 minutes. 2. Remove the balls from the oven and cover with half of the marinara sauce. Pour ricotta cheese all over followed by the rest of the marinara sauce. Scatter the cheddar cheese and bake in the oven for 10 minutes. Allow the meatballs casserole to cool before serving.

Per Serving:

calories: 519 | fat: 39g | protein: 36g | carbs: 6g | net carbs: 4g | fiber: 2g

Beef Meatballs

Prep time: 5 minutes | Cook time: 32 minutes | Serves 5

- ½ cup pork rinds, crushed
- 1 egg
- Salt and black pepper, to taste
- 1½ pounds ground beef
- 10 ounces canned onion soup
- 1 tablespoon almond flour
- ¼ cup free-sugar ketchup
- 3 teaspoons Worcestershire sauce
- ½ teaspoon dry mustard
- ¼ cup water

1. In a bowl, combine ⅓ cup of the onion soup with the beef, pepper, pork rinds, egg, and salt. Heat a pan over medium heat, shape the mixture into 12 meatballs. Brown in the pan for 12 minutes on both sides. 2. In a separate bowl, combine the rest of the soup with the almond flour, dry mustard, ketchup, Worcestershire sauce, and water. Pour this over the beef meatballs, cover the pan, and cook for 20 minutes as you stir occasionally. Split among serving bowls and serve.

Per Serving:

calories: 417 | fat: 30g | protein: 31g | carbs: 6g | net carbs: 5g | fiber: 1g

Veal Stew

Prep time: 10 minutes | Cook time: 2 hours | Serves 6

- 2 tablespoons olive oil
- 3 pounds veal shoulder, cubed
- 1 onion, chopped
- 1 garlic clove, minced
- Salt and black pepper, to taste
- 1 cup water
- 1½ cups red wine
- 12 ounces canned tomato sauce
- 1 carrot, chopped
- 1 cup mushrooms, chopped
- ½ cup green beans
- 2 teaspoons dried oregano

1. Set a pot over medium heat and warm the oil. Brown the veal for 5-6 minutes. Stir in the onion, and garlic, and cook for 3 minutes. Place in the wine, oregano, carrot, black pepper, salt, tomato sauce, water, and mushrooms, bring to a boil, reduce the heat to low. Cook for 1 hour and 45 minutes, then add in the green beans and cook for 5 minutes. Adjust the seasoning and split among serving bowls to serve.

Per Serving:

calories: 415 | fat: 21g | protein: 44g | carbs: 7g | net carbs: 5g | fiber: 2g

Chili Cheese Pot Pie

Prep time: 15 minutes | Cook time: 45 minutes | serves 6

Filling:
2 pounds ground beef
½ cup diced onions, or 2 tablespoons dried minced onions
2 cloves garlic, minced
1 (14½-ounce) can petite diced tomatoes
1½ tablespoons chili powder
2 teaspoons ground cumin
1 teaspoon smoked paprika

Biscuit Topping:
1½ cups finely ground blanched almond flour
2 teaspoons baking powder
½ teaspoon garlic powder
¼ teaspoon salt
½ cup shredded cheddar cheese
¼ cup sour cream
2 large eggs
2 tablespoons salted butter, melted but not hot

1. Make the filling: In a 12-inch cast-iron skillet or other ovenproof skillet, cook the ground beef with the onions and garlic over medium heat, crumbling the meat with a large spoon as it cooks, until the meat is browned and the onions and garlic are translucent, about 10 minutes. Drain the fat, if necessary. 2. Stir in the tomatoes and seasonings. Simmer over low heat for 15 minutes, then remove from the heat. 3. Preheat the oven to 375°F. 4. Make the biscuit topping: In a bowl, whisk together the almond flour, baking powder, garlic powder, and salt until well combined. In a separate bowl, stir together the cheese, sour cream, eggs, and melted butter. Add the wet ingredients to the dry ingredients and gently stir until well combined. 5. Drop the biscuit topping mixture by the large spoonful onto the chili beef mixture in the skillet. 6. Bake for 20 minutes or until the biscuits are cooked through and browned on top. Leftovers can be stored in an airtight container in the refrigerator for up to 5 days.

Per Serving:
calories: 477 | fat: 37g | protein: 24g | carbs: 10g | net carbs: 7g | fiber: 4g

Beef Flank Steak with Sage

Prep time: 13 minutes | Cook time: 7 minutes | Serves 2

⅓ cup sour cream
½ cup green onion, chopped
1 tablespoon mayonnaise
3 cloves garlic, smashed
1 pound (454 g) beef flank steak, trimmed and cubed
2 tablespoons fresh sage, minced
½ teaspoon salt
⅓ teaspoon black pepper, or to taste

1. Season your meat with salt and pepper; arrange beef cubes on the bottom of a baking dish that fits in your air fryer. 2. Stir in green onions and garlic; air fry for about 7 minutes at 385°F (196°C). 3. Once your beef starts to tender, add the cream, mayonnaise, and sage; air fry an additional 8 minutes. Bon appétit!

Per Serving:
calories: 542 | fat: 29g | protein: 49g | carbs: 14g | net carbs: 10g | fiber: 1g

Garlicky Pork with Bell Peppers

Prep time: 15 minutes | Cook time: 25 minutes | Serves 4

3 tablespoons butter
4 pork steaks, bone-in
1 cup chicken stock
Salt and black pepper, to taste
A pinch of lemon pepper
3 tablespoons olive oil
6 garlic cloves, minced
2 tablespoons fresh parsley, chopped
4 bell peppers, sliced
1 lemon, sliced

1. Heat a pan with 2 tablespoons oil and 2 tablespoons butter over medium heat. Add in the pork steaks, season with black pepper and salt, and cook until browned; remove to a plate. In the same pan, warm the rest of the oil and butter, add garlic and bell peppers and cook for 4 minutes. 2Pour the chicken stock, lemon slices, salt, lemon pepper, and black pepper, and cook everything for 5 minutes. Return the pork steaks to the pan and cook for 10 minutes. Split the sauce and steaks among plates and sprinkle with parsley to serve.

Per Serving:
calories: 528 | fat: 39g | protein: 30g | carbs: 19g | net carbs: 14g | fiber: 5g

Mojito Lamb Chops

Prep time: 30 minutes | Cook time: 5 minutes | Serves 2

Marinade:
2 teaspoons grated lime zest
½ cup lime juice
¼ cup avocado oil
¼ cup chopped fresh mint leaves
4 cloves garlic, roughly chopped
2 teaspoons fine sea salt
½ teaspoon ground black pepper
4 (1-inch-thick) lamb chops
Sprigs of fresh mint, for garnish (optional)
Lime slices, for serving (optional)

1. Make the marinade: Place all the ingredients for the marinade in a food processor or blender and purée until mostly smooth with a few small chunks. Transfer half of the marinade to a shallow dish and set the other half aside for serving. Add the lamb to the shallow dish, cover, and place in the refrigerator to marinate for at least 2 hours or overnight. 2. Spray the air fryer basket with avocado oil. Preheat the air fryer to 390ºF (199ºC). 3. Remove the chops from the marinade and place them in the air fryer basket. Air fry for 5 minutes, or until the internal temperature reaches 145ºF (63ºC) for medium doneness. 4. Allow the chops to rest for 10 minutes before serving with the rest of the marinade as a sauce. Garnish with fresh mint leaves and serve with lime slices, if desired. Best served fresh.

Per Serving:
calories: 597 | fat: 43g | protein: 47g | carbs: 8g | net carbs: 7g | fiber: 1g

Sloppy Joe Chili

Prep time: 20 minutes | Cook time: 40 minutes | Serves 6

Spice Blend:
1 tablespoon smoked paprika
1 teaspoon granulated garlic
1 teaspoon granulated onion
½ teaspoon sea salt
½ teaspoon ground black pepper
Sloppy Joe Mixture:
2 slices thick-cut bacon, chopped
1 large yellow onion, finely diced
1 medium green bell pepper, finely diced
1 medium red bell pepper, finely diced
Sea salt and ground black pepper, to taste
Pinch of ground cinnamon
1 clove garlic, minced or grated
4 portobello mushrooms, cut into ½-inch pieces
2 pounds (907 g) ground beef, 85% lean
1 (28-ounce / 794-g) can diced tomatoes
3 tablespoons coconut aminos
2 tablespoons ketchup, homemade or store-bought
1 tablespoon apple cider vinegar
2 teaspoons Dijon mustard
For Garnish:
1 small red onion, diced
⅓ cup full-fat sour cream (optional)

Make This on the Stovetop: 1. In a small bowl, mix together all the ingredients for the spice blend. Set aside. 2. Place the bacon in a large stockpot over medium-high heat. Cook, stirring occasionally, until the fat has rendered, about 4 minutes. 3. Add the onion and bell peppers, lightly season with salt and pepper, add the cinnamon, and sauté until the onions are translucent and beginning to brown, about 5 minutes. Add the garlic and cook for 1 minute more, until fragrant. 4. Turn the heat down to medium, add the mushrooms, and lightly season with salt and pepper. Cook for 5 minutes, then stir in the spice blend and add the beef. Let the meat cook for a few minutes to begin to brown, then add the diced tomatoes, coconut aminos, ketchup, vinegar, mustard, and cinnamon. Stir to combine, then turn the heat down to medium-low and simmer for 15 to 20 minutes, until the meat is cooked through. 5. To serve, spoon the sloppy joe mixture onto serving plates and garnish with the red onion and sour cream, if desired. Make This in a Slow Cooker: 1. In a small bowl, mix together all the ingredients for the spice blend. Set aside. 2. Place the bacon in a skillet or sauté pan over medium-high heat and cook, stirring occasionally, until the fat has rendered, about 4 minutes. 3. Transfer the bacon and the rendered fat to a slow cooker with all of the remaining ingredients and the spice blend. Cook on low for 3 to 4 hours. Make This in an Instant Pot or Other Multicooker: Use 1 (6-ounce / 170-g) can tomato paste instead of 1 (28-ounce / 794-g) can diced tomatoes. 1. In a small bowl, mix together all the ingredients for the spice blend. Set aside. 2. Set the Instant Pot to the sauté function (normal). Once hot, place the bacon in the pot and cook, stirring occasionally, until rendered, 3 to 4 minutes. Add the onion, bell peppers, and garlic, lightly season with salt and pepper, and sauté until translucent and beginning to brown, about 5 minutes. 3. Add the remaining ingredients and the spice blend to the pot, reset the cooker to manual, and cook on high pressure for 20 minutes. When cooking is finished, allow the cooker to depressurize on its own; don't flip the valve to release it.

Per Serving:

calories: 421 | fat: 24g | protein: 34g | carbs: 20g | net carbs: 15g | fiber: 5g

Blue Cheese Steak Salad

Prep time: 30 minutes | Cook time: 22 minutes | Serves 4

2 tablespoons balsamic vinegar
2 tablespoons red wine vinegar
1 tablespoon Dijon mustard
1 tablespoon Swerve
1 teaspoon minced garlic
Sea salt and freshly ground black pepper, to taste
¾ cup extra-virgin olive oil
1 pound (454 g) boneless sirloin steak
Avocado oil spray
1 small red onion, cut into ¼-inch-thick rounds
6 ounces (170 g) baby spinach
½ cup cherry tomatoes, halved
3 ounces (85 g) blue cheese, crumbled

1. In a blender, combine the balsamic vinegar, red wine vinegar, Dijon mustard, Swerve, and garlic. Season with salt and pepper and process until smooth. With the blender running, drizzle in the olive oil. Process until well combined. Transfer to a jar with a tight-fitting lid, and refrigerate until ready to serve (it will keep for up to 2 weeks). 2. Season the steak with salt and pepper and let sit at room temperature for at least 45 minutes, time permitting. 3. Set the air fryer to 400ºF (204ºC). Spray the steak with oil and place it in the air fryer basket. Air fry for 6 minutes. Flip the steak and spray it with more oil. Air fry for 6 minutes more for medium-rare or until the steak is done to your liking. 4. Transfer the steak to a plate, tent with a piece of aluminum foil, and allow it to rest. 5. Spray the onion slices with oil and place them in the air fryer basket. Cook at 400ºF (204ºC) for 5 minutes. Flip the onion slices and spray them with more oil. Air fry for 5 minutes more. 6. Slice the steak diagonally into thin strips. Place the spinach, cherry tomatoes, onion slices, and steak in a large bowl. Toss with the desired amount of dressing. Sprinkle with crumbled blue cheese and serve.

Per Serving:

calories: 625 | fat: 51g | protein: 29g | carbs: 15g | net carbs: 11g | fiber: 4g

Peppercorn Pork with Salsa Verde

Prep time: 10 minutes | Cook time: 40 minutes | Serves 3

12 ounces (340 g) pork shoulder, sliced
½ cup salsa verde
½ cup water
¾ teaspoon peppercorns
½ teaspoon salt

1. Toss the butter in the instant pot and sauté it for 1 minute or until it is melted. 2. After this, add pork shoulder, salt, and peppercorns; sauté the ingredients for 10 minutes. 3. After this, add water and salsa verde. 4. Set the Bean/Chili mode and set the timer on 30 minutes (High Pressure). 5. When the time is over, make a natural pressure release.

Per Serving:

calories: 342 | fat: 24g | protein: 27g | carbs: 2g | net carbs: 2g | fiber: 0g

Sausage Bagels

**Prep time: 5 minutes | Cook time: 45 minutes |
Makes 2 bagels**

1 pound (454 g) ground pork
1 teaspoon onion powder
1 teaspoon garlic powder
Salt, to taste
Freshly ground black pepper, to taste
1 egg

1. Preheat the oven to 400ºF (205ºC). 2. In a large bowl, combine the pork, onion powder, and garlic powder. Season with salt and pepper. Stir to combine. 3. In a small bowl, whisk the egg. Add it to the bowl and stir until everything is well incorporated. 4. Divide the pork mixture in half and form two large balls. Use your thumbs to make an indentation in the middle, resembling a bagel. Flatten the balls slightly. Transfer to a small baking dish and bake for 40 to 45 minutes or until the pork is cooked through and meat has browned. Let them cool before slicing and serving.

Per Serving:

calories: 640 | fat: 51g | protein: 42g | carbs: 2g | net carbs: 2g | fiber: 0g

Paprika Pork Chops

**Prep time: 5 minutes | Cook time: 10 minutes |
Serves 4**

4 pork chops
Salt and black pepper, to taste
3 tablespoons paprika
¾ cup cumin powder
1 teaspoon chili powder

1. In a bowl, combine the paprika with black pepper, cumin, salt, and chili. Place in the pork chops and rub them well. Heat a grill over medium temperature, add in the pork chops, cook for 5 minutes, flip, and cook for 5 minutes. Serve with steamed veggies.

Per Serving:

calories: 355 | fat: 19g | protein: 42g | carbs: 3g | net carbs: 1g | fiber: 2g

Simple Liver and Onions

**Prep time: 10 minutes | Cook time: 25 minutes |
Serves 4**

½ cup grass-fed butter
¼ cup extra-virgin olive oil
2 onions, thinly sliced
½ cup white wine
1 pound calf's liver, trimmed and cut into strips
1 tablespoon balsamic vinegar
2 tablespoons chopped fresh parsley
Sea salt, for seasoning
Freshly ground black pepper, for seasoning

1. Sauté the onions. In a large skillet over medium heat, warm the butter and olive oil. Add the onions to the skillet and sauté them until they've softened, about 5 minutes. Stir in the white wine and reduce the heat to medium-low. Cover the skillet and cook, stirring frequently, until the onions are very soft and lightly browned, about 15 minutes. Transfer the onions with a slotted spoon to a plate. 2. Cook the liver. Increase the heat to high and stir in the liver strips and the vinegar. Sauté the liver until it's done the way you like it, about 4 minutes for medium rare. 3. Finish the dish. Return the onions to the skillet along with the parsley, stirring to combine them. Season the liver and onions with salt and pepper. 4. Serve. Divide the liver and onions between four plates and serve immediately.

Per Serving:

calories: 497 | fat: 40g | protein: 23g | carbs: 8g | net carbs: 5g | fiber: 3g

Chorizo and Beef Burger

**Prep time: 10 minutes | Cook time: 15 minutes |
Serves 4**

¾ pound (340 g) 80/20 ground beef
¼ pound (113 g) Mexican-style ground chorizo
¼ cup chopped onion
5 slices pickled jalapeños, chopped
2 teaspoons chili powder
1 teaspoon minced garlic
¼ teaspoon cumin

1. In a large bowl, mix all ingredients. Divide the mixture into four sections and form them into burger patties. 2. Place burger patties into the air fryer basket, working in batches if necessary. 3. Adjust the temperature to 375ºF (191ºC) and air fry for 15 minutes. 4. Flip the patties halfway through the cooking time. Serve warm.

Per Serving:

calories: 270 | fat: 20g | protein: 21g | carbs: 2g | net carbs: 1g | fiber: 1g

Pepperoni Low-Carb Tortilla Pizza

Prep time: 5 minutes | Cook time: 5 minutes | Serves 2

2 tablespoons olive oil
2 large low-carb tortillas (I use Mission brand)
4 tablespoons low-sugar tomato sauce (I use Rao's)
1 cup shredded mozzarella cheese
2 teaspoons dried Italian seasoning
½ cup pepperoni

1. In a medium skillet over medium-high heat, heat the olive oil. Add the tortilla. 2. Spoon the tomato sauce onto the tortilla, spreading it out. Sprinkle on the cheese, Italian seasoning, and pepperoni. Work quickly so the tortilla doesn't burn. 3. Cook until the tortilla is crispy on the bottom, about 3 minutes. Transfer to a cutting board, and cut into slices. Put the slices on a serving plate and serve hot.

Per Serving:

calories: 547 | fat: 44g | protein: 27g | carbs: 17g | net carbs: 8g | fiber: 9g

Cajun Bacon Pork Loin Fillet

Prep time: 30 minutes | Cook time: 20 minutes | Serves 6

1½ pounds (680 g) pork loin fillet or pork tenderloin
3 tablespoons olive oil
2 tablespoons Cajun spice mix
Salt, to taste
6 slices bacon
Olive oil spray

1. Cut the pork in half so that it will fit in the air fryer basket. 2. Place both pieces of meat in a resealable plastic bag. Add the oil, Cajun seasoning, and salt to taste, if using. Seal the bag and massage to coat all of the meat with the oil and seasonings. Marinate in the refrigerator for at least 1 hour or up to 24 hours. 3. Remove the pork from the bag and wrap 3 bacon slices around each piece. Spray the air fryer basket with olive oil spray. Place the meat in the air fryer. Set the air fryer to 350°F (177°C) for 15 minutes. Increase the temperature to 400°F (204°C) for 5 minutes. Use a meat thermometer to ensure the meat has reached an internal temperature of 145°F (63°C). 4. Let the meat rest for 10 minutes. Slice into 6 medallions and serve.

Per Serving:

calories: 289 | fat: 19g | protein: 27g | carbs: 0g | net carbs: 0g | fiber: 0g

Parmesan Pork Chops and Roasted Asparagus

Prep time: 10 minutes | Cook time: 25 minutes | Serves 2

¼ cup grated Parmesan cheese
¼ cup crushed pork rinds
1 teaspoon garlic powder
2 boneless pork chops
Pink Himalayan salt
Freshly ground black pepper
Olive oil, for drizzling
½ pound asparagus spears, tough ends snapped off

1. Preheat the oven to 350°F. Line a baking sheet with aluminum foil or a silicone baking mat. 2. In a medium bowl, mix to combine the Parmesan cheese, pork rinds, and garlic powder. 3. Pat the pork chops dry with a paper towel, and season with pink Himalayan salt and pepper. 4. Place a pork chop in the bowl with the Parmesan–pork rind mixture, and press the "breading" to the pork chop so it sticks. Place the coated pork chop on the prepared baking sheet. Repeat for the second pork chop. 5. Drizzle a small amount of olive oil over each pork chop. 6. Place the asparagus on the baking sheet around the pork chops. Drizzle with olive oil, and season with pink Himalayan salt and pepper. Sprinkle any leftover Parmesan cheese–pork rind mixture over the asparagus. 7. Bake for 20 to 25 minutes. Thinner pork chops will cook faster than thicker ones. 8. Serve hot.

Per Serving:

calories: 370 | fat: 21g | protein: 40g | carbs: 6g | net carbs: 4g | fiber: 3g

Beef Shoulder Roast

Prep time: 15 minutes | Cook time: 46 minutes | Serves 6

2 tablespoons peanut oil
2 pounds (907 g) shoulder roast
¼ cup coconut aminos
1 teaspoon porcini powder
1 teaspoon garlic powder
1 cup beef broth
2 cloves garlic, minced
2 tablespoons champagne vinegar
½ teaspoon hot sauce
1 teaspoon celery seeds
1 cup purple onions, cut into wedges
1 tablespoon flaxseed meal, plus 2 tablespoons water

1. Press the Sauté button to heat up the Instant Pot. Then, heat the peanut oil and cook the beef shoulder roast for 3 minutes on each side. 2. In a mixing dish, combine coconut aminos, porcini powder, garlic powder, broth, garlic, vinegar, hot sauce, and celery seeds. 3. Pour the broth mixture into the Instant Pot. Add the onions to the top. 4. Secure the lid. Choose Meat/Stew mode and set cooking time for 40 minutes on High Pressure. 5. Once cooking is complete, use a natural pressure release for 15 mintues, then release any remaining pressure. Carefully remove the lid. 6. Make the slurry by mixing flaxseed meal with 2 tablespoons of water. Add the slurry to the Instant Pot. 7. Press the Sauté button and allow it to cook until the cooking liquid is reduced and thickened slightly. Serve warm.

Per Serving:

calories: 313 | fat: 16g | protein: 34g | carbs: 7g | net carbs: 3g | fiber: 3g

Swiss-Style Italian Sausage

Prep time: 20 minutes | Cook time: 22 minutes | Serves 6

¼ cup olive oil
2 pounds Italian pork sausage, chopped
1 onion, sliced
4 sun-dried tomatoes, sliced thin
Salt and black pepper, to taste
½ pound Gruyere cheese, grated
3 yellow bell peppers, seeded and chopped
3 orange bell peppers, seeded and chopped
A pinch of red pepper flakes
½ cup fresh parsley, chopped

1. Set a pan over medium heat and warm oil, place in the sausage slices, cook each side for 3 minutes, remove to a bowl, and set aside. Stir in tomatoes, bell peppers, and onion, and cook for 5 minutes. Season with black pepper, pepper flakes, and salt and mix well. Cook for 1 minute, and remove from heat. 2. Lay sausage slices onto a baking dish, place the bell pepper mixture on top, scatter with the Gruyere cheese, set in the oven at 340° F. Bake for 10 minutes, until the cheese melts. Serve topped with parsley.

Per Serving:

calories: 919 | fat: 75g | protein: 40g | carbs: 15g | net carbs: 12g | fiber: 3g

Beef Back Ribs with Barbecue Glaze

Prep time: 10 minutes | Cook time: 35 minutes | Serves 4

½ cup water
1 (3-pound / 1.4-kg) rack beef back ribs, prepared with rub of choice
¼ cup unsweetened tomato purée
¼ teaspoon Worcestershire sauce
¼ teaspoon garlic powder
2 teaspoons apple cider vinegar
¼ teaspoon liquid smoke
¼ teaspoon smoked paprika
3 tablespoons Swerve
Dash of cayenne pepper

1. Pour the water in the pot and place the trivet inside. 2. Arrange the ribs on top of the trivet. 3. Close the lid. Select Manual mode and set cooking time for 25 minutes on High Pressure. 4. Meanwhile, prepare the glaze by whisking together the tomato purée, Worcestershire sauce, garlic powder, vinegar, liquid smoke, paprika, Swerve, and cayenne in a medium bowl. Heat the broiler. 5. When timer beeps, quick release the pressure. Open the lid. Remove the ribs and place on a baking sheet. 6. Brush a layer of glaze on the ribs. Put under the broiler for 5 minutes. 7. Remove from the broiler and brush with glaze again. Put back under the broiler for 5 more minutes, or until the tops are sticky. 8. Serve immediately.

Per Serving:

calories: 758 | fat: 27g | protein: 34g | carbs: 1g | net carbs: 1g | fiber: 0g

Shoulder Chops with Lemon-Thyme Gravy

Prep time: 30 minutes | Cook time: 40 minutes | Serves 6

¼ cup (60 ml) refined avocado oil or melted coconut oil, for frying
2½ pounds (1.2 kg) bone-in pork shoulder blade chops (aka shoulder chops, blade steaks, or pork shoulder steaks), about ½ inch (1.25 cm) thick
1½ teaspoons finely ground gray sea salt, divided
1 teaspoon ground black pepper
⅓ cup (80 ml) white wine, such as Pinot Grigio, Sauvignon Blanc, or unoaked Chardonnay
2 tablespoons unflavored gelatin
Grated zest of 1 lemon
Juice of 1 lemon
1 teaspoon dried thyme leaves
⅔ cup (160 ml) full-fat coconut milk

1. Place the oil in a large frying pan over high heat. While the oil is heating, sprinkle 1 teaspoon of the salt and the pepper on both sides of the chops. Place the chops in the hot oil and sear for 4 minutes per side. Transfer the seared chops to a clean plate. 2. Remove the pan from the heat. Leaving the fat in the pan, add the wine, gelatin, lemon zest, lemon juice, thyme, and remaining ½ teaspoon of salt. Whisk to combine. 3. Return the chops to the frying pan. Cover and cook over medium-low heat for 30 minutes, flipping them halfway through cooking. 4. Place an oven rack in the top position and turn on the broiler to low, if that is an option (if not, simply "broil" is fine). Place the chops in an oven-safe pan (I like to use cast iron) and set the pan on the top rack of the oven. Broil the chops for 3 minutes per side, or until just browned. Allow to rest for 5 minutes. 5. Meanwhile, add the coconut milk to the liquid in the frying pan. Cook over medium heat for 15 minutes, whisking occasionally, until slightly thickened. 6. If serving individually instead of family style, remove the bones from each chop and divide the steaks into 6 servings. Serve the chops drizzled with the gravy.

Per Serving:

calories: 511 | fat: 40g | protein: 33g | carbs: 2g | net carbs: 2g | fiber: 0g

Pork Goulash with Cauliflower

Prep time: 10 minutes | Cook time: 15 minutes | Serves 4

1 red bell pepper, seeded and chopped
2 tablespoons olive oil
1½ pounds ground pork
Salt and black pepper, to taste
2 cups cauliflower florets
1 onion, chopped
14 ounces canned diced tomatoes
¼ teaspoon garlic powder
1 tablespoon tomato puree
1½ cups water

1. Heat olive oil in a pan over medium heat, stir in the pork, and brown for 5 minutes. Place in the bell pepper and onion, and cook for 4 minutes. Stir in the water, tomatoes, and cauliflower, bring to a simmer and cook for 5 minutes while covered. Place in the black pepper, tomato paste, salt, and garlic powder. Stir well, remove from the heat, split into bowls, and enjoy.

Per Serving:

calories: 559 | fat: 43g | protein: 31g | carbs:11 g | net carbs: 6g | fiber: 5g

Beef Provençal

Prep time: 10 minutes | Cook time: 35 minutes | Serves 4

12 ounces beef steak racks
2 fennel bulbs, sliced
Salt and black pepper, to taste
3 tablespoons olive oil
½ cup apple cider vinegar
1 teaspoon herbs de Provence
1 tablespoon swerve

1. In a bowl, mix the fennel with 2 tablespoons of oil, swerve, and vinegar, toss to coat well, and set to a baking dish. Season with herbs de Provence, pepper and salt, and cook in the oven at 400ºF for 15 minutes. 2. Sprinkle black pepper and salt to the beef, place into an oiled pan over medium heat, and cook for a couple of minutes. Place the beef to the baking dish with the fennel, and bake for 20 minutes. Split everything among plates and enjoy.

Per Serving:

calories: 251 | fat: 15g | protein: 19g | carbs: 8g | net carbs: 4g | fiber: 4g

Chapter 4 Beef, Pork, and Lamb | 43

Sausage and Peppers

Prep time: 7 minutes | Cook time: 35 minutes | Serves 4

Oil, for spraying
2 pounds (907 g) hot or sweet Italian sausage links, cut into thick slices
4 large bell peppers of any color, seeded and cut into slices
1 onion, thinly sliced
1 tablespoon olive oil
1 tablespoon chopped fresh parsley
1 teaspoon dried oregano
1 teaspoon dried basil
1 teaspoon balsamic vinegar

1. Line the air fryer basket with parchment and spray lightly with oil. 2. In a large bowl, combine the sausage, bell peppers, and onion. 3. In a small bowl, whisk together the olive oil, parsley, oregano, basil, and balsamic vinegar. Pour the mixture over the sausage and peppers and toss until evenly coated. 4. Using a slotted spoon, transfer the mixture to the prepared basket, taking care to drain out as much excess liquid as possible. 5. Air fry at 350°F (177°C) for 20 minutes, stir, and cook for another 15 minutes, or until the sausage is browned and the juices run clear.

Per Serving:

calories: 378 | fat: 23g | protein: 39g | carbs: 6g | net carbs: 4g | fiber: 2g

Italian Beef Meatloaf

Prep time: 10 minutes | Cook time: 25 minutes | Serves 6

1 pound (454 g) ground beef
1 cup crushed pork rinds
1 egg
¼ cup grated Parmesan cheese
¼ cup Italian dressing
2 teaspoons Italian seasoning
½ cup water
½ cup sugar-free tomato sauce
1 tablespoon chopped fresh herbs (such as parsley or basil)
1 clove garlic, minced

1. In large bowl, combine the beef, pork rinds, egg, cheese, dressing, and Italian seasoning. Use a wooden spoon to incorporate everything into the meat, but do not overwork the meat or it will turn out tough. 2. Turn the meat mixture out onto a piece of aluminum foil. Use your hands to shape into a loaf. Wrap the foil up around the meat like a packet, but do not cover the top. Place the trivet in the pot and add the water. Place the meatloaf on top of the trivet. 3. Close the lid and seal the vent. Cook on High Pressure 20 minutes. Quick release the steam. 4. While the meat is cooking, whisk together the tomato sauce, herbs, and garlic in a small bowl. Heat the broiler. 5. Remove the meat and foil packet from the pot. Place on a baking sheet and spread the tomato sauce mixture on top. Broil until the glaze becomes sticky, about 5 minutes. Slice into six equal pieces.

Per Serving:

calories: 358 | fat: 25g | protein: 29g | carbs: 2g | net carbs: 2g | fiber: 0g

Spaghetti Squash and Ground Pork Stir-Fry with Kale

Prep time: 10 minutes | Cook time: 1 hour 25 minutes | Serves 3 to 4

1 medium spaghetti squash, halved lengthwise and seeded
2 tablespoons avocado or macadamia nut oil, divided
1 pound (454 g) ground free-range pork
Salt and freshly ground black pepper, to taste
1 bunch kale, stems removed, leaves chopped (2 to 3 cups)
1 teaspoon garlic powder
1 teaspoon onion powder
1 teaspoon dried parsley
½ teaspoon dry mustard powder
½ teaspoon dried rosemary
½ teaspoon dried oregano

1. Preheat the oven to 400°F (205°C). Line a baking sheet with aluminum foil. 2. Brush the cut side of the spaghetti squash with 1 tablespoon of the oil. Place it cut side down on the baking sheet and roast for 45 minutes to 1 hour, or until tender when pierced with a fork. Remove from the oven and let sit until cool enough to handle. 3. In a large skillet or a wok, heat the oil over medium-high heat. Add the ground pork and season with salt and pepper. Cook for about 5 minutes, stirring and breaking the meat up into pieces. 4. Scoop the squash flesh (the spaghetti strands) into the skillet or wok and stir to combine with the meat. Reserve the spaghetti squash shells for serving, if you'd like. 5. Add the kale, garlic and onion powders, parsley, dry mustard powder, rosemary, oregano, and salt and pepper to taste. Mix everything together until well combined and cook for 10 minutes, or until the meat is no longer pink and the kale is wilted. 6. To serve, scoop the pork mixture into the reserved spaghetti squash shells or simply serve up in bowls or on plates!

Per Serving:

calories: 355 | fat: 23g | protein: 23g | carbs: 14g | net carbs: 8g | fiber: 6g

Paprika Pork Ribs

Prep time: 10 minutes | Cook time: 30 minutes | Serves 4

1 pound (454 g) pork ribs
1 tablespoon ground paprika
1 teaspoon ground turmeric
3 tablespoons avocado oil
1 teaspoon salt
½ cup beef broth

1. Rub the pork ribs with ground paprika, turmeric, salt, and avocado oil. 2. Then pour the beef broth in the instant pot. 3. Arrange the pork ribs in the instant pot. Close and seal the lid. 4. Cook the pork ribs for 30 minutes on Manual mode (High Pressure). 5. When the time is finished, make a quick pressure release and chop the ribs into servings.

Per Serving:

calories: 335 | fat: 22g | protein: 31g | carbs: 2g | net carbs: 1g | fiber: 1g

Cilantro Pork

Prep time: 10 minutes | Cook time: 85 minutes | Serves 4

1 pound (454 g) boneless pork shoulder
¼ cup chopped fresh cilantro
1 cup water
1 teaspoon salt
1 teaspoon coconut oil
½ teaspoon mustard seeds

1. Pour water in the instant pot. 2. Add pork shoulder, fresh cilantro, salt, coconut oil, and mustard seeds. 3. Close and seal the lid. Cook the meat on High Pressure (Manual mode) for 85 minutes. 4. Then make a quick pressure release and open the lid. 5. The cooked meat has to be served with the remaining liquid from the instant pot.

Per Serving:

calories: 343 | fat: 25g | protein: 26g | carbs: 0g | net carbs: 0g | fiber: 0g

Rosemary Pork Belly

Prep time: 10 minutes | Cook time: 75 minutes | Serves 4

10 ounces (283 g) pork belly
1 teaspoon dried rosemary
½ teaspoon dried thyme
¼ teaspoon ground cinnamon
1 teaspoon salt
1 cup water

1. Rub the pork belly with dried rosemary, thyme, ground cinnamon, and salt and transfer in the instant pot bowl. 2. Add water, close and seal the lid. 3. Cook the pork belly on Manual mode (High Pressure) for 75 minutes. 4. Remove the cooked pork belly from the instant pot and slice it into servings.

Per Serving:

calories: 329 | fat: 19g | protein: 33g | carbs: 0g | net carbs: 0g | fiber: 0g

Easy Zucchini Beef Lasagna

Prep time: 10 minutes | Cook time: 45 minutes | Serves 4

1 pound ground beef
2 large zucchinis, sliced lengthwise
3 cloves garlic
1 medium white onion, finely chopped
3 tomatoes, chopped
Salt and black pepper to taste
2 teaspoons sweet paprika
1 teaspoon dried thyme
1 teaspoon dried basil
1 cup shredded mozzarella cheese
1 tablespoon olive oil
Cooking spray

1. Preheat the oven to 370ºF and lightly grease a baking dish with cooking spray. 2. Heat the olive oil in a skillet and cook the beef for 4 minutes while breaking any lumps as you stir. Top with onion, garlic, tomatoes, salt, paprika, and pepper. Stir and continue cooking for 5 minutes. 3. Then, lay ⅓ of the zucchini slices in the baking dish. Top with ⅓ of the beef mixture and repeat the layering process two more times with the same quantities. Season with basil and thyme. 4. Finally, sprinkle the mozzarella cheese on top and tuck the baking dish in the oven. Bake for 35 minutes. Remove the lasagna and let it rest for 10 minutes before serving.

Per Serving:

calories: 396 | fat: 27g | protein: 27g | carbs: 12g | net carbs: 9g | fiber: 3g

Lamb Koobideh

Prep time: 15 minutes | Cook time: 30 minutes | Serves 4

1 pound (454 g) ground lamb
1 egg, beaten
1 tablespoon lemon juice
1 teaspoon ground turmeric
½ teaspoon garlic powder
1 teaspoon chives, chopped
½ teaspoon ground black pepper
1 cup water

1. In a mixing bowl, combine all the ingredients except for water. 2. Shape the mixture into meatballs and press into ellipse shape. 3. Pour the water and insert the trivet in the Instant Pot. 4. Put the prepared ellipse meatballs in a baking pan and transfer on the trivet. 5. Close the lid and select Manual mode. Set cooking time for 30 minutes on High Pressure. 6. When timer beeps, make a quick pressure release. Open the lid. 7. Serve immediately

Per Serving:

calories: 231 | fat: 10g | protein: 33g | carbs: 1g | net carbs: 1g | fiber: 0g

Grilled Herbed Pork Kebabs

Prep time: 10 minutes | Cook time: 15 minutes | Serves 4

¼ cup good-quality olive oil
1 tablespoon minced garlic
2 teaspoons dried oregano
1 teaspoon dried basil
1 teaspoon dried parsley
½ teaspoon sea salt
¼ teaspoon freshly ground black pepper
1 (1-pound) pork tenderloin, cut into 1½-inch pieces

1. Marinate the pork. In a medium bowl, stir together the olive oil, garlic, oregano, basil, parsley, salt, and pepper. Add the pork pieces and toss to coat them in the marinade. Cover the bowl and place it in the refrigerator for 2 to 4 hours. 2. Make the kebabs. Divide the pork pieces between four skewers, making sure to not crowd the meat. 3. Grill the kebabs. Preheat your grill to medium-high heat. Grill the skewers for about 12 minutes, turning to cook all sides of the pork, until the pork is cooked through. 4. Serve. Rest the skewers for 5 minutes. Divide the skewers between four plates and serve them immediately.

Per Serving:

calories: 261 | fat: 18g | protein: 24g | carbs: 1g | net carbs: 1g | fiber: 0g

Baked Pork Meatballs in Pasta Sauce

Prep time: 10 minutes | Cook time: 35 minutes | Serves 6

2 pounds (907 g) ground pork
1 tablespoon olive oil
1 cup pork rinds, crushed
3 cloves garlic, minced
½ cup coconut milk
2 eggs, beaten
½ cup grated Parmesan cheese
½ cup grated asiago cheese
Salt and black pepper to taste
¼ cup chopped parsley
2 jars sugar-free marinara sauce
½ teaspoon Italian seasoning
1 cup Italian blend kinds of cheeses
Chopped basil to garnish

1. Preheat the oven to 400ºF, line a cast iron pan with foil and oil it with cooking spray. Set aside. 2. Combine the coconut milk and pork rinds in a bowl. Mix in the ground pork, garlic, Asiago cheese, Parmesan cheese, eggs, salt, and pepper, just until combined. Form balls of the mixture and place them in the prepared pan. Bake in the oven for 20 minutes at a reduced temperature of 370ºF. 3. Transfer the meatballs to a plate. Pour half of the marinara sauce in the baking pan. Place the meatballs back in the pan and pour the remaining marinara sauce all over them. Sprinkle with the Italian blend cheeses, drizzle with the olive oil, and then sprinkle with Italian seasoning. 4. Cover the pan with foil and put it back in the oven to bake for 10 minutes. After, remove the foil, and cook for 5 minutes. Once ready, take out the pan and garnish with basil. Serve on a bed of squash spaghetti.

Per Serving:

calories: 575 | fat: 43g | protein: 39g | carbs: 8g | net carbs: 5g | fiber: 3g

Cottage Pie

Prep time: 20 minutes | Cook time: 30 minutes | Serves 4

Pie:
2 tablespoons extra-virgin olive oil
2 celery stalks, chopped
½ medium onion, chopped
2 garlic cloves, minced
1 pound (454 g) ground beef
¼ cup chicken broth
1 tablespoon tomato paste
1 teaspoon pink Himalayan sea salt
1 teaspoon freshly ground black pepper
½ teaspoon ground white pepper
Topping:
2 (12-ounce / 340-g) packages cauliflower rice, cooked and drained
1 cup shredded low-moisture mozzarella cheese
2 tablespoons heavy (whipping) cream
2 tablespoons butter
½ teaspoon pink Himalayan sea salt
½ teaspoon freshly ground black pepper
¼ teaspoon ground white pepper
¼ teaspoon garlic powder

1. Preheat the oven to 400ºF (205ºC). 2. To make the pie: In a large sauté pan or skillet, heat the olive oil over medium heat. Add the celery and onion and cook for 8 to 10 minutes, until the onion is tender. 3. Add the garlic and cook for an additional minute, until fragrant. 4. Add the ground beef, breaking it up with a wooden spoon or spatula. Continue to cook the beef for 7 to 10 minutes, until fully browned. 5. Stir in the broth and tomato paste and stir to coat the meat. Sprinkle in the salt, black pepper, and white pepper. 6. Transfer the meat mixture to a 9-by-13-inch baking dish. 7. To make the topping: In a food processor, combine the cauliflower rice, mozzarella, cream, butter, salt, black pepper, white pepper, and garlic powder. Purée on high speed until the mixture is smooth, scraping down the sides of the bowl as necessary. 8. Spread the cauliflower mash over the top of the meat and smooth the top. 9. Bake for 10 minutes, until the topping is just lightly browned. Let cool for 5 minutes, then serve.

Per Serving:

calories: 564 | fat: 44g | protein: 30g | carbs: 13g | net carbs: 7g | fiber: 6g

Buttery Beef and Spinach

Prep time: 2 minutes | Cook time: 10 minutes | Serves 4

1 pound (454 g) 85% lean ground beef
1 cup water
4 cups fresh spinach
¾ teaspoon salt
¼ cup butter
¼ teaspoon pepper
¼ teaspoon garlic powder

1. Press the Sauté button and add ground beef to Instant Pot. Brown beef until fully cooked and spoon into 7-cup glass bowl. Drain grease and replace pot. 2. Pour water into pot and place steam rack in bottom. Place baking dish on steam rack and add fresh spinach, salt, butter, pepper, and garlic powder to ground beef. Cover with aluminum foil. Click lid closed. 3. Press the Manual button and adjust time for 2 minutes. When timer beeps, quick-release the pressure. Remove aluminum foil and stir.

Per Serving:

calories: 272 | fat: 19g | protein: 18g | carbs: 1g | net carbs: 0g | fiber: 1g

Chapter 5 Fish and Seafood

Cheesy Garlic Salmon

Prep time: 10 minutes | Cook time: 12 minutes | Serves 4

½ cup Asiago cheese
2 tablespoons freshly squeezed lemon juice
2 tablespoons butter, at room temperature
2 teaspoons minced garlic
1 teaspoon chopped fresh basil
1 teaspoon chopped fresh oregano
4 (5-ounce) salmon fillets
1 tablespoon olive oil

1. Preheat the oven to 350°F. Line a baking sheet with parchment paper and set aside. 2. In a small bowl, stir together the Asiago cheese, lemon juice, butter, garlic, basil, and oregano. 3. Pat the salmon dry with paper towels and place the fillets on the baking sheet skin-side down. Divide the topping evenly between the fillets and spread it across the fish using a knife or the back of a spoon. 4. Drizzle the fish with the olive oil and bake until the topping is golden and the fish is just cooked through, about 12 minutes. 5. Serve.

Per Serving:
calories: 357 | fat: 28g | protein: 24g | carbs: 2g | net carbs: 2g | fiber: 0g

Tilapia Fillets with Arugula

Prep time: 5 minutes | Cook time: 4 minutes | Serves 4

1 lemon, juiced
1 cup water
1 pound (454 g) tilapia fillets
½ teaspoon cayenne pepper, or more to taste
2 teaspoons butter, melted
Sea salt and ground black pepper, to taste
½ teaspoon dried basil
2 cups arugula

1. Pour the fresh lemon juice and water into your Instant Pot and insert a steamer basket. 2. Brush the fish fillets with the melted butter. 3. Sprinkle with the cayenne pepper, salt, and black pepper. Place the tilapia fillets in the basket. Sprinkle the dried basil on top. 4. Lock the lid. Select the Manual mode and set the cooking time for 4 minutes at Low Pressure. 5. When the timer beeps, perform a quick pressure release. Carefully remove the lid. 6. Serve with the fresh arugula.

Per Serving:
calories: 134 | fat: 4g | protein: 23g | carbs: 1g | net carbs: 1g | fiber: 0g

Snapper Scampi

Prep time: 5 minutes | Cook time: 8 to 10 minutes | Serves 4

4 (6 ounces / 170 g) skinless snapper or arctic char fillets
1 tablespoon olive oil
3 tablespoons lemon juice, divided
½ teaspoon dried basil
Pinch salt
Freshly ground black pepper, to taste
2 tablespoons butter
2 cloves garlic, minced

1. Rub the fish fillets with olive oil and 1 tablespoon of the lemon juice. Sprinkle with the basil, salt, and pepper, and place in the air fryer basket. 2. Air fry the fish at 380ºF (193ºC) for 7 to 8 minutes or until the fish just flakes when tested with a fork. Remove the fish from the basket and put on a serving plate. Cover to keep warm. 3. In a baking pan, combine the butter, remaining 2 tablespoons lemon juice, and garlic. Bake in the air fryer for 1 to 2 minutes or until the garlic is sizzling. Pour this mixture over the fish and serve

Per Serving:
calories: 256 | fat: 11g | protein: 35g | carbs: 1g | net carbs: 1g | fiber: 0g

Seared Scallops with Chorizo and Asiago Cheese

Prep time: 10 minutes | Cook time: 15 minutes | Serves 4

2 tablespoons ghee
16 fresh scallops
8 ounces chorizo, chopped
1 red bell pepper, seeds removed, sliced
1 cup red onions, finely chopped
1 cup asiago cheese, grated
Salt and black pepper to taste

1. Melt half of the ghee in a skillet over medium heat, and cook the onion and bell pepper for 5 minutes until tender. Add the chorizo and stir-fry for another 3 minutes. Remove and set aside. 2. Pat dry the scallops with paper towels, and season with salt and pepper. Add the remaining ghee to the skillet and sear the scallops for 2 minutes on each side to have a golden brown color. Add the chorizo mixture back and warm through. Transfer to serving platter and top with asiago cheese.

Per Serving:
calories: 573 | fat: 44g | protein: 34g | carbs: 7g | net carbs: 6g | fiber: 1g

Cod Fillets with Cherry Tomatoes

Prep time: 2 minutes | Cook time: 15 minutes | Serves 4

2 tablespoons butter
¼ cup diced onion
1 clove garlic, minced
1 cup cherry tomatoes, halved
¼ cup chicken broth
¼ teaspoon dried thyme
¼ teaspoon salt
⅛ teaspoon pepper
4 (4-ounce / 113-g) cod fillets
1 cup water
¼ cup fresh chopped Italian parsley

1. Set your Instant Pot to Sauté. Add and melt the butter. Once hot, add the onions and cook until softened. Add the garlic and cook for another 30 seconds. 2. Add the tomatoes, chicken broth, thyme, salt, and pepper. Continue to cook for 5 to 7 minutes, or until the tomatoes start to soften. 3. Pour the sauce into a glass bowl. Add the fish fillets. Cover with foil. 4. Pour the water into the Instant Pot and insert a trivet. Place the bowl on top. 5. Lock the lid. Select the Manual mode and set the cooking time for 3 minutes at Low Pressure. 6. Once cooking is complete, do a quick pressure release. Carefully open the lid. 7. Sprinkle with the fresh parsley and serve.

Per Serving:
calories: 159 | fat: 8g | protein: 22g | carbs: 3g | net carbs: 2g| fiber: 1g

Basil Alfredo Sea Bass

Prep time: 15 minutes | Cook time: 30 minutes | Serves 4

Sea Bass:
4 (6-ounce / 170-g) sea bass pieces
2 tablespoons olive oil
Pesto:
1 cup tightly packed fresh basil leaves
¼ cup grated Parmesan cheese
3 tablespoons pine nuts, or walnuts
1 tablespoon water
½ teaspoon salt
Freshly ground black pepper, to taste
3 tablespoons olive oil
Alfredo Sauce:
2 tablespoons butter
1 tablespoon olive oil
1 garlic clove, minced
1 cup heavy (whipping) cream
¾ cup Parmesan cheese
Salt, to taste
Freshly ground black pepper, to taste

Make the Sea Bass 1. Preheat the oven to 375ºF (190ºC). 2. Rub the sea bass with the olive oil and place it in a baking dish or on a rimmed baking sheet. Bake for 20 to 25 minutes or until the fish is completely opaque and the flesh flakes easily with a fork. Make the Pesto 1. In a blender or food processor (I prefer a blender because I like this very finely chopped/blended), combine the basil, Parmesan, pine nuts, water, and salt. Season with pepper. 2. With the blender running, stream the olive oil in. Set aside. Make the Alfredo Sauce 1. In a small saucepan over medium heat, melt the butter and olive oil together. 2. Stir in the garlic and cream. Bring to a low simmer and cook for 5 to 7 minutes until thickened. 3. Slowly add the Parmesan, stirring well to mix as it melts. Continue to stir until smooth. Season with salt and pepper. Set aside. 4. In a small bowl, stir together ½ cup of pesto and ½ cup of Alfredo sauce. Spoon over the fish before serving. Refrigerate leftovers in an airtight container for up to 4 days.

Per Serving:
calories: 768 | fat: 64g | protein: 45g | carbs: 4g | net carbs: 4g | fiber: 0g

Zoodles in Clam Sauce

Prep time: 5 minutes | Cook time: 7 minutes | Serves 2

¼ cup MCT oil, duck fat, or bacon fat
2 tablespoons minced onions
2 cloves garlic, minced
1 (6½-ounce / 184-g) can whole clams, drained and chopped
¼ teaspoon fine sea salt
⅛ teaspoon freshly ground black pepper
2 cups zoodles
Fresh basil leaves, for garnish (optional)

1. Heat the oil in a cast-iron skillet over medium heat. Add the onions and garlic and cook until the onions are translucent, about 4 minutes. Add the chopped clams and heat for 3 minutes. Season with the salt and pepper. 2. Serve over zoodles, garnished with basil, if desired. 3. Store extra sauce and zoodles separately in airtight containers in the fridge for up to 3 days. Reheat in a skillet over medium heat until warmed.

Per Serving:
calories: 355 | fat: 29g | protein: 16g | carbs: 8g | net carbs: 7g | fiber: 1g

Pork Rind Salmon Cakes

Prep time: 10 minutes | Cook time: 10 minutes | Serves 2

6 ounces canned Alaska wild salmon, drained
2 tablespoons crushed pork rinds
1 egg, lightly beaten
3 tablespoons mayonnaise, divided
Pink Himalayan salt
Freshly ground black pepper
1 tablespoon ghee
½ tablespoon Dijon mustard

1. In a medium bowl, mix to combine the salmon, pork rinds, egg, and 1½ tablespoons of mayonnaise, and season with pink Himalayan salt and pepper. 2. With the salmon mixture, form patties the size of hockey pucks or smaller. Keep patting the patties until they keep together. 3. In a medium skillet over medium-high heat, melt the ghee. When the ghee sizzles, place the salmon patties in the pan. Cook for about 3 minutes per side, until browned. Transfer the patties to a paper towel–lined plate. 4. In a small bowl, mix together the remaining 1½ tablespoons of mayonnaise and the mustard. 5. Serve the salmon cakes with the mayo-mustard dipping sauce.

Per Serving:
calories: 362 | fat: 31g | protein: 24g | carbs: 1g | net carbs: 1g | fiber: 0g

Coconut Shrimp with Spicy Dipping Sauce

Prep time: 15 minutes | Cook time: 8 minutes | Serves 4

1 (2½-ounce / 71-g) bag pork rinds
¾ cup unsweetened shredded coconut flakes
¾ cup coconut flour
1 teaspoon onion powder
1 teaspoon garlic powder
2 eggs
1½ pounds (680 g) large shrimp, peeled and deveined
½ teaspoon salt
¼ teaspoon freshly ground black pepper
Spicy Dipping Sauce:
½ cup mayonnaise
2 tablespoons Sriracha
Zest and juice of ½ lime
1 clove garlic, minced

1. Preheat the air fryer to 390°F (199°C). 2. In a food processor fitted with a metal blade, combine the pork rinds and coconut flakes. Pulse until the mixture resembles coarse crumbs. Transfer to a shallow bowl. 3. In another shallow bowl, combine the coconut flour, onion powder, and garlic powder; mix until thoroughly combined. 4. In a third shallow bowl, whisk the eggs until slightly frothy. 5. In a large bowl, season the shrimp with the salt and pepper, tossing gently to coat. 6. Working a few pieces at a time, dredge the shrimp in the flour mixture, followed by the eggs, and finishing with the pork rind crumb mixture. Arrange the shrimp on a baking sheet until ready to air fry. 7. Working in batches if necessary, arrange the shrimp in a single layer in the air fryer basket. Pausing halfway through the cooking time to turn the shrimp, air fry for 8 minutes until cooked through. 8. To make the sauce: In a small bowl, combine the mayonnaise, Sriracha, lime zest and juice, and garlic. Whisk until thoroughly combined. Serve alongside the shrimp.

Per Serving:

calories: 473 | fat: 33g | protein: 30g | carbs: 13g | net carbs: 7g | fiber: 6g

Oven-Baked Dijon Salmon

Prep time: 5 minutes | Cook time: 10 minutes | Serves 4

4 (6-ounce / 170-g) salmon fillets
2 tablespoons olive oil
Salt, to taste
Freshly ground black pepper, to taste
¼ cup grainy Dijon mustard

1. Preheat the oven to 450°F (235°C). 2. Drizzle the fillets with the olive oil and season with salt and pepper. Brush the mustard over each piece of fish and place on a baking sheet. Bake for 10 to 12 minutes or until the salmon is opaque and flakes easily with a fork. (Cook a few minutes longer if you prefer it cooked more than medium.)

Per Serving:

calories: 370 | fat: 25g | protein: 34g | carbs: 1g | net carbs: 0g | fiber: 1g

Salmon Poke

Prep time: 5 minutes | Cook time: 0 minutes | Serves 2

½ pound (227 g) sushi-grade salmon, chopped into ½-inch cubes
¼ small red onion, finely chopped
1 tablespoon dried chives
½ tablespoon capers
1 tablespoon dried basil
1 teaspoon Dijon mustard
½ teaspoon olive oil
Juice of ½ small lemon
Salt and freshly ground black pepper, to taste
1 cucumber, sliced into rounds, for serving (optional)

1. Put the salmon, red onion, and chives in a mixing bowl. Add the capers, basil, mustard, olive oil, and lemon juice and season with salt and pepper. Mix the contents of the bowl together until everything is evenly coated. 2. If desired, spoon the poke onto cucumber rounds (enough to cover the cucumber slice, but not so much that it's falling off). You can certainly eat this poke by itself, too, though.

Per Serving:

calories: 177 | fat: 9g | protein: 23g | carbs: 1g | net carbs: 1g | fiber: 0g

Halibut in a Butter and Garlic Blanket

Prep time: 10 minutes | Cook time: 20 minutes | Serves 4

Coconut oil, for greasing
4 (4-ounce / 113-g) halibut fillets, about 1-inch thick
½ cup (1 stick) butter, cut into squares
2 tablespoons finely chopped scallion
1 tablespoon minced garlic
½ lemon
Sea salt and freshly ground black pepper, to taste

1. Preheat the oven to 400°F (205°C). 2. Cut out four 12-inch squares of aluminum foil, and grease them with coconut oil. Place one halibut fillet on each foil square. Place two pats of butter on each fillet. Sprinkle the scallion and garlic over the fillets, dividing equally, and then squeeze the lemon half over the fillets, finally topping with a healthy sprinkle of salt and pepper. 3. Pull the sides of each foil square up to create a pouch around the halibut, and then roll the top like a paper lunch bag. The fish should be completely enclosed, but there should be room in the foil pouches to allow steam to circulate and cook the fish. Place the foil pouches on a large baking sheet. 4. Bake for about 20 minutes until the fish is opaque throughout. 5. Remove the fish from the foil pouches before serving but save the "juice" to serve over any veggies that you choose to serve with the dish.

Per Serving:

1 fillet: calories: 313 | fat: 25g | protein: 21g | carbs: 1g | net carbs: 1g | fiber: 0g

Cajun Cod Fillet

Prep time: 10 minutes | Cook time: 4 minutes | Serves 2

10 ounces (283 g) cod fillet
1 tablespoon olive oil
1 teaspoon Cajun seasoning
2 tablespoons coconut aminos

1. Sprinkle the cod fillet with coconut aminos and Cajun seasoning. 2. Then heat up olive oil in the instant pot on Sauté mode. 3. Add the spiced cod fillet and cook it for 4 minutes from each side. 4. Then cut it into halves and sprinkle with the oily liquid from the instant pot.

Per Serving:
calories: 189 | fat: 8g | protein: 25g | carbs: 3g | net carbs: 3g | fiber: 0g

Sole Asiago

Prep time: 10 minutes | Cook time: 8 minutes | Serves 4

4 (4 ounces) sole fillets
¾ cup ground almonds
¼ cup Asiago cheese
2 eggs, beaten
2½ tablespoons melted coconut oil

1. Preheat the oven to 350°F. Line a baking sheet with parchment paper and set aside. 2. Pat the fish dry with paper towels. 3. Stir together the ground almonds and cheese in a small bowl. 4. Place the bowl with the beaten eggs in it next to the almond mixture. 5. Dredge a sole fillet in the beaten egg and then press the fish into the almond mixture so it is completely coated. Place on the baking sheet and repeat until all the fillets are breaded. 6. Brush both sides of each piece of fish with the coconut oil. 7. Bake the sole until it is cooked through, about 8 minutes in total. 8. Serve immediately.

Per Serving:
calories: 406 | fat: 31g | protein: 29g | carbs: 6g | net carbs: 3g | fiber: 3g

Lemony Salmon

Prep time: 30 minutes | Cook time: 10 minutes | Serves 4

1½ pounds (680 g) salmon steak
½ teaspoon grated lemon zest
Freshly cracked mixed peppercorns, to taste
⅓ cup lemon juice
Fresh chopped chives, for garnish
½ cup dry white wine
½ teaspoon fresh cilantro, chopped
Fine sea salt, to taste

1. To prepare the marinade, place all ingredients, except for salmon steak and chives, in a deep pan. Bring to a boil over medium-high flame until it has reduced by half. Allow it to cool down. 2. After that, allow salmon steak to marinate in the refrigerator approximately 40 minutes. Discard the marinade and transfer the fish steak to the preheated air fryer. 3. Air fry at 400ºF (204ºC) for 9 to 10 minutes. To finish, brush hot fish steaks with the reserved marinade, garnish with fresh chopped chives, and serve right away!

Per Serving:
calories: 319 | fat: 17g | protein: 37g | carbs: 3g | net carbs: 2g | fiber: 1g

Shrimp Zoodle Alfredo

Prep time: 10 minutes | Cook time: 10 minutes | Serves 4

10 ounces (283 g) salmon fillet (2 fillets)
4 ounces (113 g) Mozzarella, sliced
4 cherry tomatoes, sliced
1 teaspoon erythritol
1 teaspoon dried basil
½ teaspoon ground black pepper
1 tablespoon apple cider vinegar
1 tablespoon butter
1 cup water, for cooking

1. Melt the butter on Sauté mode and add shrimp. 2. Sprinkle them with seafood seasoning and sauté then for 2 minutes. 3. After this, spiralizer the zucchini with the help of the spiralizer and add in the shrimp. 4. Add coconut cream and close the lid. Cook the meal on Sauté mode for 8 minutes.

Per Serving:
calories: 213 | fat: 16g | protein: 12g | carbs: 7g | net carbs: 5g | fiber: 2g

Pan-Seared Scallops with Lemon Butter

Prep time: 10 minutes | Cook time: 20 minutes | Serves 4

1 pound (454 g) scallops, rinsed under cold water and patted dry with a paper towel
Salt, to taste
Freshly ground black pepper, to taste
4 tablespoons butter, divided
1 lemon, halved
Zest of ½ lemon

1. Season the scallops on both sides with salt and pepper. 2. In a large nonstick skillet over medium-high heat, melt 2 tablespoons of butter. 3. Add the scallops. Cook for 5 to 7 minutes per side or until the scallops begin to get crispy. 4. Squeeze 1 lemon half over the scallops. Transfer the scallops to a serving platter. 5. Return the skillet to low heat. Add the remaining 2 tablespoons of butter. 6. Stir in the lemon zest and squeeze the remaining lemon half into the skillet. Stir continuously until the butter reduces slightly, 4 to 5 minutes. Pour the sauce over the scallops and serve immediately. Refrigerate leftovers in an airtight container for up to 2 days.

Per Serving:
calories: 200 | fat: 12g | protein: 19g | carbs: 3g | net carbs: 3g | fiber: 0g

Sushi

Prep time: 15 minutes | Cook time: 3 to 5 minutes | Serves 2 to 4

4 cups cauliflower rice
2 tablespoons grass-fed gelatin
1 tablespoon apple cider vinegar
1 teaspoon salt
2 to 4 nori sheets
½ pound (227 g) sushi-grade fish, thinly sliced
1 small avocado, halved, pitted, peeled, and thinly sliced
1 small cucumber (or any other vegetable you'd like), thinly sliced
Sesame seeds, for topping (optional)
Coconut aminos or tamari, wasabi, sugar-free pickled ginger, sliced avocado, and/or avocado oil mayonnaise mixed with sugar-free hot sauce, for serving (optional)

1. In a shallow pot with a lid, combine the cauliflower with 3 tablespoons of water. Turn the heat to medium, cover the pot, and steam for 3 to 5 minutes. 2. Drain the cauliflower and transfer to a mixing bowl. Stir in the gelatin, vinegar, and salt. Stir together until the mixture is smooth and sticky. Set aside. 3. Fold a dish towel in half lengthwise and place it on your counter. Cover the towel in plastic wrap. 4. Place a nori sheet on top of the plastic wrap, then spread with a layer of the cauliflower rice. 5. Layer slices of fish, avocado, and cucumber over the cauliflower on the end of the nori sheet closest to you. 6. Starting at the end closest to you, gently roll the nori sheet over all the ingredients, using the towel as your rolling aid. (Emphasis on the word "gently" because you don't want to tear the nori sheet.) When you're done rolling, remove the towel and plastic wrap as you slide the roll onto a plate or cutting board. Using a sharp knife, cut the roll into equal pieces. Repeat steps 4 through 7 with the remaining nori and filling ingredients. 7. Sprinkle sesame seeds on top of your sushi, if desired, and serve with any of the other optional ingredients you'd like.

Per Serving:
calories: 295 | fat: 15g | protein: 30g | carbs: 10g | net carbs: 2g | fiber: 8g

Simply Broiled or Air-Fried Salmon

Prep time: 5 minutes | Cook time: 30 minutes | Serves 2 to 4

1 tablespoon olive, avocado, or macadamia nut oil
1 pound (454 g) salmon fillet or steak (with or without skin), cut into 2 to 4 equal pieces
Salt and freshly ground black pepper, to taste
Dried herbs and spices of your choice (optional)
Steamed or roasted asparagus or spaghetti squash, for serving

1. Preheat the broiler. Line a broiling pan with aluminum foil and grease with the oil. If air-frying, line the air fryer basket with foil and grease with the oil. 2. Season the salmon with salt, pepper, and any other herbs and spices you'd like. Then lay it in the broiling pan (skin-side down, if applicable) or place it in the air-fryer basket. 3. Broil the salmon in the oven for about 30 minutes, checking for doneness (it should form a crisp crust) after about 20 minutes, or cook in the air fryer at 400ºF (205ºC) for 25 to 30 minutes. To crisp up skin in the broiler, flip the salmon when there are about 5 minutes left of cooking. 4. Serve the salmon with steamed or roasted vegetables.

Per Serving:
calories: 258 | fat: 18g | protein: 24g | carbs: 0g | net carbs: 0g | fiber: 0g

Pan-Seared Lemon-Garlic Salmon

Prep time: 5 minutes | Cook time: 10 minutes | Serves 2

1 tablespoon extra-virgin olive oil
2 (8-ounce / 227-g) salmon fillets
1 lemon, halved
Pink Himalayan sea salt
Freshly ground black pepper
2 tablespoons butter
1 tablespoon chopped fresh parsley
2 garlic cloves, minced

1. In a medium sauté pan or skillet, heat the olive oil over medium-high heat. 2. Squeeze the juice from a lemon half over the fillets. Season the salmon with salt and pepper. 3. Place the salmon skin-side up in the skillet. Cook for 4 to 5 minutes, then flip the fish and cook for an additional 2 to 3 minutes on the other side. 4. Add the butter, the juice from the other lemon half, the parsley, and garlic to the pan. Toss to combine. Allow the fish to cook for 2 to 3 more minutes, until the flesh flakes easily with a fork. 5. Transfer the fish to a serving plate, then top with the butter sauce and serve.

Per Serving:
calories: 489 | fat: 33g | protein: 45g | carbs: 0g | net carbs: 0g | fiber: 0g

Garlic Lemon Scallops

Prep time: 5 minutes | Cook time: 10 minutes | Serves 4

4 tablespoons salted butter, melted
4 teaspoons peeled and finely minced garlic
½ small lemon, zested and juiced
8 (1-ounce / 28-g) sea scallops, cleaned and patted dry
¼ teaspoon salt
¼ teaspoon ground black pepper

1. In a small bowl, mix butter, garlic, lemon zest, and lemon juice. Place scallops in an ungreased round nonstick baking dish. Pour butter mixture over scallops, then sprinkle with salt and pepper. 2. Place dish into air fryer basket. Adjust the temperature to 360ºF (182ºC) and bake for 10 minutes. Scallops will be opaque and firm, and have an internal temperature of 135ºF (57ºC) when done. Serve warm.

Per Serving:
calories: 113 | fat: 9g | protein: 4g | carbs: 3g | net carbs: 2g | fiber: 0g

Tuna Stuffed Poblano Peppers

Prep time: 15 minutes | Cook time: 12 minutes | Serves 4

7 ounces (198 g) canned tuna, shredded
1 teaspoon cream cheese
¼ teaspoon minced garlic
2 ounces (57 g) Provolone cheese, grated
4 poblano pepper
1 cup water, for cooking

1. Remove the seeds from poblano peppers. 2. In the mixing bowl, mix up shredded tuna, cream cheese, minced garlic, and grated cheese. 3. Then fill the peppers with tuna mixture and put it in the baking pan. 4. Pour water and insert the baking pan in the instant pot. 5. Cook the meal on Manual mode (High Pressure) for 12 minutes. Then make a quick pressure release.

Per Serving:
calories: 153 | fat: 8g | protein: 17g | carbs: 2g | net carbs: 1g | fiber: 1g

Dill Lemon Salmon

Prep time: 10 minutes | Cook time: 4 minutes | Serves 4

1 pound (454 g) salmon fillet
1 tablespoon butter, melted
2 tablespoons lemon juice
1 teaspoon dried dill
1 cup water

1. Cut the salmon fillet on 4 servings. 2. Line the instant pot baking pan with foil and put the salmon fillets inside in one layer. 3. Then sprinkle the fish with dried dill, lemon juice, and butter. 4. Pour water in the instant pot and insert the rack. 5. Place the baking pan with salmon on the rack and close the lid. 6. Cook the meal on Manual mode (High Pressure) for 4 minutes. Allow the natural pressure release for 5 minutes and remove the fish from the instant pot.

Per Serving:
calories: 178 | fat: 10g | protein: 22g | carbs: 0g | net carbs: 0g | fiber: 0g

Pistachio-Crusted Salmon

Prep time: 5 minutes | Cook time: 20 minutes | Serves 4

4 salmon fillets
½ teaspoon pepper
1 teaspoon salt
¼ cup mayonnaise
½ cup chopped pistachios
Sauce
1 chopped shallot
2 teaspoons lemon zest
1 tablespoon olive oil
A pinch of black pepper
1 cup heavy cream

1. Preheat the oven to 370°F. 2. Brush the salmon with mayonnaise and season with salt and pepper. Coat with pistachios, place in a lined baking dish and bake for 15 minutes. 3. Heat olive oil in a saucepan and sauté the shallot for 3 minutes. Stir in the rest of the sauce ingredients. Bring the mixture to a boil and cook until thickened. Serve the fish with the sauce.

Per Serving:
calories: 473 | fat: 33g | protein: 36g | carbs: 8g | net carbs: 6g | fiber: 2g

Muffin Top Tuna Pops

Prep time: 10 minutes | Cook time: 25 minutes | Serves 6

1 (5-ounce) can tuna in water, drained
2 large eggs
¾ cup shredded Cheddar cheese
¾ cup shredded pepper jack cheese
¼ cup full-fat sour cream
¼ cup full-fat mayonnaise
¼ cup chopped yellow onion
1 tablespoon dried parsley
¼ teaspoon salt
18 pieces sliced jalapeño from jar
2 tablespoons unsalted butter

1 Preheat oven to 350°F. Grease six cups of a muffin tin. 2 Combine all ingredients except the jalapeño slices and butter in a medium mixing bowl. 3 Evenly fill six muffin cups with the mixture, topping each with three jalapeño slices. 4 Bake 25 minutes. Serve warm with butter.

Per Serving:
calories: 275 | fat: 22g | protein: 14g | carbs: 1g | net carbs: 1g | fiber: 0g

Parmesan Lobster Tails

Prep time: 5 minutes | Cook time: 7 minutes | Serves 4

4 (4 ounces / 113 g) lobster tails
2 tablespoons salted butter, melted
1½ teaspoons Cajun seasoning, divided
¼ teaspoon salt
¼ teaspoon ground black pepper
¼ cup grated Parmesan cheese
½ ounce (14 g) plain pork rinds, finely crushed

1. Cut lobster tails open carefully with a pair of scissors and gently pull meat away from shells, resting meat on top of shells. 2. Brush lobster meat with butter and sprinkle with 1 teaspoon Cajun seasoning, ¼ teaspoon per tail. 3. In a small bowl, mix remaining Cajun seasoning, salt, pepper, Parmesan, and pork rinds. Gently press ¼ mixture onto meat on each lobster tail. 4. Carefully place tails into ungreased air fryer basket. Adjust the temperature to 400°F (204°C) and air fry for 7 minutes. Lobster tails will be crispy and golden on top and have an internal temperature of at least 145°F (63°C) when done. Serve warm.

Per Serving:
calories: 218 | fat: 11g | protein: 25g | carbs: 3g | net carbs: 2g | fiber: 0g

Cod with Jalapeño

Prep time: 5 minutes | Cook time: 14 minutes | Serves 4

4 cod fillets, boneless
1 jalapeño, minced
1 tablespoon avocado oil
½ teaspoon minced garlic

1. In the shallow bowl, mix minced jalapeño, avocado oil, and minced garlic. 2. Put the cod fillets in the air fryer basket in one layer and top with minced jalapeño mixture. 3. Cook the fish at 365°F (185°C) for 7 minutes per side.

Per Serving:
calories: 130 | fat: 3g | protein: 23g | carbs: 0g | net carbs: 0g | fiber: 0g

Coconut Shrimp Curry

Prep time: 10 minutes | Cook time: 4 minutes | Serves 5

15 ounces (425 g) shrimp, peeled
1 teaspoon chili powder
1 teaspoon garam masala
1 cup coconut milk
1 teaspoon olive oil
½ teaspoon minced garlic

1. Heat up the instant pot on Sauté mode for 2 minutes. 2. Then add olive oil. Cook the ingredients for 1 minute. 3. Add shrimp and sprinkle them with chili powder, garam masala, minced garlic, and coconut milk. 4. Carefully stir the ingredients and close the lid. 5. Cook the shrimp curry on Manual mode for 1 minute. Make a quick pressure release.

Per Serving:
calories: 222 | fat: 14g | protein: 21g | carbs: 4g | net carbs: 3g | fiber: 1g

Fried Red Snapper

Prep time: 10 minutes | Cook time: 20 minutes | Serves 4

1 cup coconut flour
1 whole red snapper (about 1½ pounds)
1 cup coconut oil
½ teaspoon pink Himalayan salt
Sauce:
2 tablespoons soy sauce
1 tablespoon toasted sesame oil
Juice of 1 lime
¼ teaspoon garlic powder
¼ teaspoon ginger powder
¼ teaspoon onion powder
¼ teaspoon paprika
¼ teaspoon ground black pepper
Lime wedges, for serving

1. Place the coconut flour in a zip-top plastic bag. Pat the snapper dry with paper towels, score the skin, and place it in the bag with the flour. Seal the bag and shake thoroughly to coat the fish. Set aside. 2. Put the coconut oil in a 12-inch or larger heavy skillet (preferably cast-iron) over medium-high heat. (Make sure the skillet is large enough to fit the fish.) Place a deep-fry thermometer in the oil and heat until it reaches 350°F. 3. Place the snapper in the hot oil and shallow-fry for 10 minutes on each side, until brown and crispy on the outside. Set aside on a large plate and season with the salt. 4. In a small bowl, whisk together the ingredients for the sauce. 5. Pour the sauce evenly over the fried snapper and serve immediately with lime wedges. 6. Store leftovers in a sealed container in the refrigerator for up to 4 days. Reheat in the microwave for a couple minutes.

Per Serving:
calories: 183 | fat: 6g | protein: 26g | carbs: 6g | net carbs: 3g | fiber: 3g

Mackerel and Broccoli Casserole

Prep time: 15 minutes | Cook time: 15 minutes | Serves 5

1 cup shredded broccoli
10 ounces (283 g) mackerel, chopped
½ cup shredded Cheddar cheese
1 cup coconut milk
1 teaspoon ground cumin
1 teaspoon salt

1. Sprinkle the chopped mackerel with ground cumin and salt and transfer in the instant pot. 2. Top the fish with shredded broccoli and Cheddar cheese, 3. Then add coconut milk. Close and seal the lid. 4. Cook the casserole on Manual mode (High Pressure) for 15 minutes. 5. Allow the natural pressure release for 10 minutes and open the lid.

Per Serving:
calories: 312 | fat: 25g | protein: 18g | carbs: 4g | net carbs: 2g | fiber: 2g

White Fish with Cauliflower

Prep time: 30 minutes | Cook time: 13 minutes | Serves 4

½ pound (227 g) cauliflower florets
½ teaspoon English mustard
2 tablespoons butter, room temperature
½ tablespoon cilantro, minced
2 tablespoons sour cream
2½ cups cooked white fish
Salt and freshly cracked black pepper, to taste

1. Boil the cauliflower until tender. Then, purée the cauliflower in your blender. Transfer to a mixing dish. 2. Now, stir in the fish, cilantro, salt, and black pepper. 3. Add the sour cream, English mustard, and butter; mix until everything's well incorporated. Using your hands, shape into patties. 4. Place in the refrigerator for about 2 hours. Cook for 13 minutes at 395°F (202°C). Serve with some extra English mustard.

Per Serving:
calories: 297 | fat: 16g | protein: 33g | carbs: 5g | net carbs: 4g | fiber: 1g

Sardine Fritter Wraps

Prep time: 5 minutes | Cook time: 8 minutes | Serves 4

⅓ cup (80 ml) refined avocado oil, for frying
Fritters:
2 (4.375-ounce/125-g) cans sardines, drained
½ cup (55 g) blanched almond flour
2 large eggs
2 tablespoons finely chopped fresh parsley
2 tablespoons finely diced red bell pepper
2 cloves garlic, minced
½ teaspoon finely ground gray sea salt
¼ teaspoon ground black pepper
For Serving:
8 romaine lettuce leaves
1 small English cucumber, sliced thin
8 tablespoons (105 g) mayonnaise
Thinly sliced green onions

1. Pour the avocado oil into a large frying pan. Heat on medium for a couple of minutes. 2. Meanwhile, prepare the fritters: Place the fritter ingredients in a medium-sized bowl and stir to combine, being careful not to mash the heck out of the sardines. Spoon about 1 tablespoon of the mixture into the palm of your hand and roll it into a ball, then flatten it like a burger patty. Repeat with the remaining fritter mixture, making a total of 16 small patties. 3. Fry the fritters in the hot oil for 2 minutes per side, then transfer to a cooling rack. You may have to fry the fritters in batches if your pan isn't large enough to fit them all without overcrowding. 4. Meanwhile, divide the lettuce leaves among 4 dinner plates. Top with the sliced cucumber. When the fritters are done, place 2 fritters on each leaf. Top with a dollop of mayonnaise, sprinkle with sliced green onions, and serve!

Per Serving:
calories: 612 | fat: 56g | protein: 23g | carbs: 6g | net carbs: 4g | fiber: 2g

Lemon Shrimp Skewers

Prep time: 10 minutes | Cook time: 2 minutes | Serves 4

1 tablespoon lemon juice
1 teaspoon coconut aminos
12 ounces (340 g) shrimp, peeled
1 teaspoon olive oil
1 cup water

1. Put the shrimp in the mixing bowl. 2. Add lemon juice, coconut aminos, and olive oil. 3. Then string the shrimp on the skewers. 4. Pour water in the instant pot. 5. Then insert the trivet. 6. Put the shrimp skewers on the trivet. 7. Close the lid and cook the seafood on Manual mode (High Pressure) for 2 minutes. 8. When the time is finished, make a quick pressure release.

Per Serving:
calories: 113 | fat: 3g | protein: 19g | carbs: 2g | net carbs: 2g | fiber: 0g

Shrimp Alfredo

Prep time: 10 minutes | Cook time: 10 minutes | Serves 2

2 tablespoons butter
2 tablespoons olive oil, divided
1 garlic clove, minced
1 cup heavy (whipping) cream
¾ cup grated Parmesan cheese
Salt, to taste
Freshly ground black pepper, to taste
1 pound (454 g) shrimp, shells and tails removed, deveined

1. In a small saucepan over medium-low heat, melt together the butter and 1 tablespoon of olive oil. 2. Stir in the garlic and cream. Bring to a low simmer and cook for 5 to 7 minutes until thickened. 3. Slowly add the Parmesan, stirring well to mix as it melts. Continue to stir until smooth. Season with salt and pepper. Set aside. 4. In a skillet over medium heat, heat the remaining 1 tablespoon of olive oil. 5. Add the shrimp and sauté for about 3 minutes per side or until they turn pink. Remove from the heat and toss with the Alfredo sauce. Serve immediately. Refrigerate leftovers in an airtight container for up to 5 days.

Per Serving:
calories: 1034 | fat: 84g | protein: 63g | carbs: 7g | net carbs: 7g | fiber: 0g

Tuna with Herbs

Prep time: 20 minutes | Cook time: 17 minutes | Serves 4

1 tablespoon butter, melted
1 medium-sized leek, thinly sliced
1 tablespoon chicken stock
1 tablespoon dry white wine
1 pound (454 g) tuna
½ teaspoon red pepper flakes, crushed
Sea salt and ground black pepper, to taste
½ teaspoon dried rosemary
½ teaspoon dried basil
½ teaspoon dried thyme
2 small ripe tomatoes, puréed
1 cup Parmesan cheese, grated

1. Melt ½ tablespoon of butter in a sauté pan over medium-high heat. Now, cook the leek and garlic until tender and aromatic. Add the stock and wine to deglaze the pan. 2. Preheat the air fryer to 370°F (188°C). 3. Grease a casserole dish with the remaining ½ tablespoon of melted butter. Place the fish in the casserole dish. Add the seasonings. Top with the sautéed leek mixture. Add the tomato purée. Cook for 10 minutes in the preheated air fryer. Top with grated Parmesan cheese; cook an additional 7 minutes until the crumbs are golden. Bon appétit!

Per Serving:
calories: 441 | fat: 23g | protein: 54g | carbs: 7g | net carbs: 5g | fiber: 1g

Caprese Salmon

Prep time: 10 minutes | Cook time: 15 minutes | Serves 2

10 ounces (283 g) salmon fillet (2 fillets)	½ teaspoon ground black pepper
4 ounces (113 g) Mozzarella, sliced	1 tablespoon apple cider vinegar
4 cherry tomatoes, sliced	1 tablespoon butter
1 teaspoon erythritol	1 cup water, for cooking
1 teaspoon dried basil	

1. Grease the mold with butter and put the salmon inside. 2. Sprinkle the fish with erythritol, dried basil, ground black pepper, and apple cider vinegar. 3. Then top the salmon with tomatoes and Mozzarella. 4. Pour water and insert the steamer rack in the instant pot. 5. Put the fish on the rack. 6. Close and seal the lid. 7. Cook the meal on Manual mode at High Pressure for 15 minutes. Make a quick pressure release.

Per Serving:

calories: 447 | fat: 25g | protein: 46g | carbs: 15g | net carbs: 12g | fiber: 3g

Baked Tilapia and Parmesan

Prep time: 10 minutes | Cook time: 15 minutes | Serves 4

4 tablespoons (½ stick) butter, melted	fillets, patted dry
2 teaspoons garlic salt	4 ounces (113 g) grated Parmesan cheese
1 teaspoon freshly ground black pepper	4 ounces (113 g) crushed pork rinds
4 (4-ounce / 113-g) tilapia	

1. Preheat the oven to 400°F (205°C). Line a baking sheet with parchment paper and set aside. 2. In a small bowl, mix the melted butter, garlic salt, and pepper. Place the tilapia fillets on the prepared baking sheet, then drizzle or brush the butter mixture across each fillet. 3. Sprinkle each fillet with Parmesan cheese and crushed pork rinds. 4. Bake for about 13 minutes, and then turn the oven up to broil and broil for 2 more minutes.

Per Serving:

1 fillet: calories: 372 | fat: 24g | protein: 38g | carbs: 1g | net carbs: 1g | fiber: 0g

Tuna Salad Wrap

Prep time: 5 minutes | Cook time: 0 minutes | Serves 2

2 (5 ounce / 142 g) cans tuna packed in olive oil, drained	¼ teaspoon freshly ground black pepper
3 tablespoons mayonnaise	Pinch of dried or fresh dill
1 tablespoon chopped red onion	2 low-carb tortillas
2 teaspoons dill relish	2 romaine lettuce leaves
¼ teaspoon pink Himalayan sea salt	¼ cup grated Cheddar cheese

1. In a medium bowl, combine the tuna, mayonnaise, onion, relish, salt, pepper, and dill. 2. Place a lettuce leaf on each tortilla, then split the tuna mixture evenly between the wraps, spreading it evenly over the lettuce. 3. Sprinkle the Cheddar on top of each, then fold the tortillas and serve.

Per Serving:

calories: 549 | fat: 33g | protein: 42g | carbs: 21g | net carbs: 5g | fiber: 16g

Shrimp Bake

Prep time: 15 minutes | Cook time: 5 minutes | Serves 4

14 ounces (397 g) shrimp, peeled	1 cup Cheddar cheese, shredded
1 egg, beaten	½ teaspoon coconut oil
½ cup coconut milk	1 teaspoon ground coriander

1. In the mixing bowl, mix shrimps with egg, coconut milk, Cheddar cheese, coconut oil, and ground coriander. 2. Then put the mixture in the baking ramekins and put in the air fryer. 3. Cook the shrimps at 400°F (204°C) for 5 minutes.

Per Serving:

calories: 289 | fat: 19g | protein: 29g | carbs: 2g | net carbs: 1g | fiber: 1g

Chapter 6 Snacks and Appetizers

Creole Pancetta and Cheese Balls

Prep time: 5 minutes | Cook time: 5 minutes | Serves 6

1 cup water
6 eggs
4 slices pancetta, chopped
⅓ cup grated Cheddar cheese
¼ cup cream cheese
¼ cup mayonnaise
1 teaspoon Creole seasonings
Sea salt and ground black pepper, to taste

1. Pour the water into the Instant Pot and insert a steamer basket. Place the eggs in the basket. 2. Lock the lid. Select the Manual mode and set the cooking time for 5 minutes at Low Pressure. 3. When the timer beeps, perform a quick pressure release. Carefully remove the lid. 4. Allow the eggs to cool for 10 to 15 minutes. Peel the eggs and chop them, then transfer to a bowl. Add the remaining ingredients and stir to combine well. 5. Shape the mixture into balls with your hands. Serve chilled.

Per Serving:

calories: 239 | fat: 19g | protein: 14g | carbs: 3g | net carbs: 3g | fiber: 0g

Chinese Spare Ribs

Prep time: 3 minutes | Cook time: 24 minutes | Serves 6

1½ pounds (680 g) spare ribs
Salt and ground black pepper, to taste
2 tablespoons sesame oil
½ cup chopped green onions
½ cup chicken stock
2 tomatoes, crushed
2 tablespoons sherry
1 tablespoon coconut aminos
1 teaspoon ginger-garlic paste
½ teaspoon crushed red pepper flakes
½ teaspoon dried parsley
2 tablespoons sesame seeds, for serving

1. Season the spare ribs with salt and black pepper to taste. 2. Set your Instant Pot to Sauté and heat the sesame oil. 3. Add the seasoned spare ribs and sear each side for about 3 minutes. 4. Add the remaining ingredients except the sesame seeds to the Instant Pot and stir well. 5. Secure the lid. Select the Meat/Stew mode and set the cooking time for 18 minutes at High Pressure. 6. When the timer beeps, perform a natural pressure release for 10 minutes, then release any remaining pressure. Carefully remove the lid. 7. Serve topped with the sesame seeds.

Per Serving:

calories: 336 | fat: 16g | protein: 43g | carbs: 3g | net carbs: 2g | fiber: 1g

Baked Brie with Pecans

Prep time: 5 minutes | Cook time: 10 minutes | Serves 6

1 (¾ pound / 340 g) wheel Brie cheese
3 ounces (85 g) pecans, chopped
2 garlic cloves, minced
2 tablespoons minced fresh rosemary leaves
1½ tablespoons olive oil
Salt and freshly ground black pepper, to taste

1. Preheat the oven to 400ºF (205ºC). 2. Line a baking sheet with parchment paper and place the Brie on it. 3. In a small bowl, stir together the pecans, garlic, rosemary, and olive oil. Season with salt and pepper. Spoon the mixture in an even layer over the Brie. Bake for about 10 minutes until the cheese is warm and the nuts are lightly browned. 4. Remove and let it cool for 1 to 2 minutes before serving.

Per Serving:

calories: 318 | fat: 29g | protein: 13g | carbs: 3g | net carbs: 2g | fiber: 1g

Granola Clusters

Prep time: 5 minutes | Cook time: 15 minutes | Serves 2

¼ cup almonds
¼ cup pecans
¼ cup macadamia nuts
1 large egg white
2 tablespoons ground flaxseed
1 tablespoon coconut oil, melted
1 tablespoon pumpkin seeds
1 tablespoon chia seeds
1 tablespoon unsweetened coconut flakes
1 tablespoon granulated erythritol
¼ teaspoon vanilla extract
⅛ teaspoon pink Himalayan sea salt

1. Preheat the oven to 325ºF (163ºC). Line a baking sheet with parchment paper. 2. In a food processor, combine the almonds, pecans, macadamia nuts, egg white, flaxseed, coconut oil, pumpkin seeds, chia seeds, coconut flakes, erythritol, vanilla, and salt. Pulse until the largest chunks of nuts are about the size of a pea. 3. Spread the mixture evenly on the baking sheet. Bake for 15 to 18 minutes, until the granola is lightly browned. 4. Let cool for about 20 minutes, then break into clusters.

Per Serving:

calories: 482 | fat: 45g | protein: 12g | carbs: 15g | net carbs: 5g | fiber: 10g

Cucumber Salmon Coins

Prep time: 5 minutes | Cook time: 0 minutes | Serves 2

¼ cup (52 g) mayonnaise
Grated zest of ½ lemon
1 tablespoon plus 1 teaspoon lemon juice
1 teaspoon Dijon mustard
1 clove garlic, minced
¼ teaspoon finely ground sea salt
⅛ teaspoon ground black pepper
1 English cucumber (about 12 in/30.5 cm long), sliced crosswise into coins
8 ounces (225 g) smoked salmon, separated into small pieces
2 fresh chives, sliced

1. Place the mayonnaise, lemon zest, lemon juice, mustard, garlic, salt, and pepper in a small bowl and whisk to combine. 2. Divide the cucumber coins between 2 plates. Top each coin with a piece of smoked salmon, then drizzle with the mayonnaise mixture and sprinkle with sliced chives. 3. Serve right away or store in the fridge for up to 1 day.

Per Serving:
calories: 337 | fat: 25g | protein: 22g | carbs: 5g | net carbs: 4g | fiber: 2g

Warm Herbed Olives

Prep time: 5 minutes | Cook time: 4 minutes | Serves 4

¼ cup good-quality olive oil
4 ounces green olives
4 ounces Kalamata olives
½ teaspoon dried thyme
¼ teaspoon fennel seeds
Pinch red pepper flakes

1. Sauté the olives. In a large skillet over medium heat, warm the olive oil. Sauté the olives, thyme, fennel seeds, and red pepper flakes until the olives start to brown, 3 to 4 minutes. 2. Serve. Put the olives into a bowl and serve them warm.

Per Serving:
calories: 165 | fat: 17g | protein: 1g | carbs: 3g | net carbs: 2g | fiber: 1g

Easy Baked Zucchini Chips

Prep time: 5 minutes | Cook time: 2½ hours | Serves 4

2 medium zucchini (10 ounces / 283 g total)
1 tablespoon olive oil or avocado oil
½ teaspoon sea salt

1. Preheat the oven to 200ºF (93ºC). 2. Use a mandoline or a sharp knife to slice the zucchini into ⅛-inch-thick slices. 3. Place the zucchini in a large bowl. Add the olive oil and toss to thoroughly coat. Sprinkle lightly with sea salt. Toss to coat again. 4. Place ovenproof wire cooling racks on top of two baking sheets, then top those with parchment paper. (The cooling rack method allows for better air circulation.) Arrange the zucchini slices in a single layer. It's fine if they touch, but make sure they don't overlap. 5. Bake side by side for about 2½ hours, rotating the pans front to back halfway through, until the chips are golden and just starting to get crispy. 6. Allow the chips to cool in the oven with the heat off and the door propped slightly open. This is a crucial step, as they will be soft initially and crisp up when they cool using this method.

Per Serving:
calories: 46 | fat: 4g | protein: 2g | carbs: 4g | net carbs: 2g | fiber: 2g

Keto Taco Shells

Prep time: 5 minutes | Cook time: 20 minutes | Serves 4

6 ounces (170 g) shredded cheese

1. Preheat the oven to 350ºF (180ºC). 2. Line a baking sheet with a silicone baking mat or parchment paper. 3. Separate the cheese into 4 (1½-ounce / 43-g) portions and make small circular piles a few inches apart (they will spread a bit in the oven). Pat the cheese down so all the piles are equally thick. Bake for 10 to 12 minutes or until the edges begin to brown. Cool for just a couple of minutes. 4. Lay a wooden spoon or spatula across two overturned glasses. Repeat to make a second setup, and carefully transfer a baked cheese circle to drape over the length of each spoon or spatula. Let them cool into the shape of a taco shell. 5. Fill with your choice of protein and top with chopped lettuce, avocado, salsa, sour cream, or whatever else you like on your tacos. These taco shells will keep refrigerated in an airtight container for a few days, but they are best freshly made and still a little warm.

Per Serving:
1 taco shell: calories: 168 | fat: 14g | protein: 11g | carbs: 1g | net carbs: 1g | fiber: 0g

Lemon-Cheese Cauliflower Bites

Prep time: 5 minutes | Cook time: 8 minutes | Serves 6

1 cup water
1 pound (454 g) cauliflower, broken into florets
Sea salt and ground black pepper, to taste
2 tablespoons extra-virgin olive oil
2 tablespoons lemon juice
1 cup grated Cheddar cheese

1. Pour the water into the Instant Pot and insert a steamer basket. Place the cauliflower florets in the basket. 2. Lock the lid. Select the Manual mode and set the cooking time for 3 minutes at Low Pressure. 3. When the timer beeps, perform a quick pressure release. Carefully remove the lid. 4. Season the cauliflower with salt and pepper. Drizzle with olive oil and lemon juice. Sprinkle the grated cheese all over the cauliflower. 5. Press the Sauté button to heat the Instant Pot. Allow to cook for about 5 minutes, or until the cheese melts. Serve warm.

Per Serving:
calories: 136 | fat: 10g | protein: 7g | carbs: 5g | net carbs: 3g | fiber: 2g

Easy Peasy Peanut Butter Cookies

Prep time: 15 minutes | Cook time: 7 to 12 minutes | Makes 15 cookies

½ cup coconut flour
¼ cup sugar-free sweetener
½ teaspoon baking soda
4 tablespoons (low-carb or handmade) peanut butter
2 tablespoons butter, at room temperature
2 large eggs
1 teaspoon vanilla extract

1. Preheat the oven to 350ºF (180ºC). Line a baking sheet with parchment paper and set aside. 2. In a bowl, combine the flour, sweetener, and baking soda, mixing to blend. 3. Add the peanut butter, butter, eggs, and vanilla, and mix well to incorporate. 4. Drop by even spoonfuls onto the prepared baking sheet to make 15 cookies. 5. Using the back of a fork, press the cookies down a little and make decorative criss-cross marks. 6. Cook for 7 to 8 minutes for soft cookies or 10 to 12 minutes for crispy cookies.

Per Serving:
1 cookie: calories: 70 | fat: 5g | protein: 3g | carbs: 3g | net carbs: 2g | fiber: 1g

Sweet and Spicy Beef Jerky

Prep time: 15 minutes | Cook time: 4 to 6 hours | Serves 16

3 pounds flat-iron steak
Marinade:
½ cup soy sauce
½ cup apple cider vinegar
¼ cup Frank's RedHot sauce
½ teaspoon liquid stevia
2 teaspoons liquid smoke
2 teaspoons ground black pepper
1½ teaspoons garlic powder
1 teaspoon onion powder
Special equipment:
10 (12-inch) bamboo skewers

1. Marinate the steak: Slice the steak into thin jerky-sized strips, about ¼ inch thick, and put them in a gallon-sized ziptop plastic bag. Add the marinade ingredients, seal the bag, and shake to fully coat the meat. 2. Seal the bag tightly (removing any excess air) and place it in a bowl to catch any leakage. Place the bowl in the refrigerator for at least 4 hours or up to 24 hours. 3. Make the jerky: Adjust the racks in your oven so that one is in the highest position and one is in the lowest position. Preheat the oven to 190°F. 4. Remove the steak strips from the marinade and pat them as dry as possible using paper towels; discard the remaining marinade. 5. Using bamboo skewers, pierce the tip of each meat strip so that there are anywhere from 5 to 7 strips hanging on each skewer. Be sure to leave space between the strips so that air can circulate around them. Hang the skewers from the top oven rack and place a rimmed baking sheet on the lowest rack to catch any drippings. 6. Bake for 4 to 6 hours, until the jerky is dry to the touch. 7. Store in a zip-top plastic bag in the refrigerator for up to 10 days.

Per Serving:
calories: 150 | fat: 10g | protein: 16g | carbs: 1g | net carbs: 1g | fiber: 0g

Cinnamon Sugar Muffins

Prep time: 15 minutes | Cook time: 18 minutes | Makes 12 muffins

2 cups (220 g) blanched almond flour
⅔ cup (130 g) erythritol
1 tablespoon plus 1 teaspoon baking powder
1 tablespoon plus 1 teaspoon ground cinnamon
½ teaspoon finely ground sea salt
4 large eggs
½ cup (120 ml) milk (nondairy or regular)
½ cup (120 ml) melted coconut oil or ghee
2 teaspoons vanilla extract
⅔ cup (100 g) hulled hemp seeds
Cinnamon Sugar Topping:
2 tablespoons melted coconut oil or ghee
¼ cup (45 g) granulated erythritol
2 teaspoons ground cinnamon

1. Preheat the oven to 350°F (177°C). Line a standard-size 12-well muffin pan with muffin liners, or use a silicone muffin pan, which won't require liners. 2. Place the almond flour, erythritol, baking powder, cinnamon, and salt in a large bowl. Mix until combined. 3. In a small bowl, whisk the eggs, milk, melted oil, and vanilla. Add the egg mixture to the flour mixture and stir until fully combined. Fold in the hemp seeds. 4. Divide the batter evenly among the muffin wells, filling each about three-quarters full. Bake for 15 to 18 minutes, until the tops are golden. Remove from the oven and let cool in the pan. 5. Meanwhile, prepare the cinnamon sugar topping: Place the melted oil in a small dish, then place the erythritol and cinnamon in another small bowl and stir to combine. 6. Once the muffins are cool enough to handle, brush the top of a muffin with melted oil and then, holding it above the cinnamon sugar bowl, sprinkle with the cinnamon sugar. Gently shake off the excess and repeat with the remaining muffins.

Per Serving:
calories: 281 | fat: 26g | protein: 5g | carbs: 7g | net carbs: 4g | fiber: 3g

90-Second Bread

Prep time: 5 minutes | Cook time: 90 seconds | Serves 1

1 heaping tablespoon coconut flour
½ teaspoon baking powder
1 large egg
1½ tablespoons butter, melted
Pinch salt

1. In a small, 3- to 4-inch diameter, microwave-safe bowl, combine the coconut flour, baking powder, egg, butter, and salt, and mix until well combined. 2. Place the bowl in the microwave and cook on high for 90 seconds. 3. Dump the bread from the bowl and allow to cool for a couple of minutes. 4. With a serrated knife, cut the bread in half horizontally to make two halves, if desired.

Per Serving:
calories: 204 | fat: 17g | protein: 8g | carbs: 5g | net carbs: 2g | fiber: 3g

Smoky "Hummus" and Veggies

Prep time: 15 minutes | Cook time: 20 minutes | serves 6

Nonstick coconut oil cooking spray
1 cauliflower head, cut into florets
¼ cup tahini
¼ cup cold-pressed olive oil, plus extra for drizzling
Juice of 1 lemon
1 tablespoon ground paprika
1 teaspoon sea salt
¼ cup chopped fresh parsley, for garnish
2 tablespoons pine nuts (optional)
Flax crackers, for serving
Sliced cucumbers, for serving
Celery pieces, for serving

1. Preheat the oven to 400°F and grease a baking sheet with cooking spray. 2. Spread the cauliflower florets out on the prepared baking sheet and bake for 20 minutes. 3. Remove the cauliflower from the oven and allow it to cool for 10 minutes. 4. In a food processor or high-powered blender, combine the cauliflower with the tahini, olive oil, lemon juice, paprika, and salt. Blend on high until a fluffy, creamy texture is achieved. If the mixture seems too thick, slowly add a few tablespoons of water until smooth. 5. Scoop the "hummus" into an airtight container and chill in the refrigerator for about 20 minutes. 6. Transfer the "hummus" to a serving bowl and drizzle with olive oil. Garnish with the parsley and pine nuts (if using). 7. Serve with your favorite flax crackers and sliced cucumbers and celery.

Per Serving:
calories: 169 | fat: 15g | protein: 4g | carbs: 9g | net carbs: 5g | fiber: 4g

Antipasto Skewers

Prep time: 10 minutes | Cook time: 0 minutes | Makes 8 skewers

8 ounces (227 g) fresh whole Mozzarella
16 fresh basil leaves
16 slices salami (4 ounces / 113 g)
16 slices coppa or other cured meat like prosciutto (4 ounces / 113 g)
8 artichoke hearts, packed in water (8 ounces / 227 g)
¼ cup vinaigrette made with olive oil or avocado oil and apple cider vinegar
Flaky salt and freshly ground black pepper, to taste

1. Cut the Mozzarella into 16 small chunks. 2. Skewer 2 pieces each of the Mozzarella, basil leaves, salami slices, and coppa slices, along with one artichoke heart, on each skewer. You'll probably want to fold the basil leaves in half and the salami and coppa in fourths (or more depending on size) before skewering. 3. Place the skewers in a small shallow dish and drizzle with the dressing, turning to coat. If possible, let them marinate for 30 minutes or more. Sprinkle lightly with flaky salt and the pepper before serving.

Per Serving:
calories: 200 | fat: 15g | protein: 11g | carbs: 4g | net carbs: 4g | fiber: 0g

Loaded Bacon and Cheddar Cheese Balls

Prep time: 10 minutes | Cook time: 0 minutes | Makes 16 balls

7 bacon slices, cooked until crisp, cooled, and crumbled
1 tablespoon chopped chives
8 ounces (227 g) cream cheese
1½ cups finely shredded Cheddar cheese
½ teaspoon smoked paprika
1 teaspoon onion powder
½ teaspoon sea salt
Olive oil or butter, for greasing

1. Line a plate or storage container with parchment paper. 2. In a small bowl, toss together the crumbled bacon and chives and set aside. 3. In a food processor or blender, mix together the cream cheese, Cheddar, paprika, onion powder, and salt. 4. Grease your hands with olive oil or butter to avoid sticking, and form 16 balls of cheese. Roll each ball in the bacon and chive "batter" as you go, and set them on the prepared plate or storage container. 5. Serve right away, or store in an airtight container in the refrigerator for up to 5 days.

Per Serving:
2 cheese balls: calories: 228 | fat: 20g | protein: 10g | carbs: 2g | net carbs: 2g | fiber: 0g

Fresh Rosemary Keto Bread

Prep time: 15 minutes | Cook time: 55 minutes | serves 6

1½ cups warm water, divided, plus up to ¼ cup more if needed
1 (¼-ounce) packet active dry yeast
1 teaspoon cane sugar
1 cup coconut flour
3 tablespoons ground psyllium husk
1 rosemary sprig
¾ cup tahini
Sea salt

1. In a small bowl, whisk together ½ cup of warm water with the yeast and sugar. Set aside for 10 minutes to allow the yeast to activate and foam. 2. In a separate small mixing bowl, whisk together the coconut flour, psyllium, and rosemary. 3. In a large mixing bowl, stir together the yeast mixture, tahini, and the remaining 1 cup of warm water. 4. Stir the dry ingredients into the wet ingredients, making sure there are no clumps or dry crumbles. If the dough is crumbly or not well combined, add up to ¼ cup of warm water, 1 tablespoon at a time, until the dough comes together. 5. Line a bread pan with parchment paper and press the dough into the pan. If you don't have parchment paper, use a greased pan. Set the dough to rise in a cool, dark place for 90 minutes. It should rise and expand to double its original size. 6. Preheat the oven to 350°F. 7. Bake the bread for 50 to 55 minutes, or until the crust is firm to the touch. 8. While the bread is still warm, remove it from the pan. Let it cool completely before slicing and serving.

Per Serving:
calories: 278 | fat: 18g | protein: 8g | carbs: 24g | net carbs: 10g | fiber: 14g

Crispy Grilled Kale Leaves

Prep time: 10 minutes | Cook time: 5 minutes | Serves 4

½ cup good-quality olive oil
2 teaspoons freshly squeezed lemon juice
½ teaspoon garlic powder
7 cups large kale leaves, thoroughly washed and patted dry
Sea salt, for seasoning
Freshly ground black pepper, for seasoning

1. Preheat the grill. Set the grill to medium-high heat. 2. Mix the dressing. In a large bowl, whisk together the olive oil, lemon juice, and garlic powder until it thickens. 3. Prepare the kale. Add the kale leaves to the bowl and use your fingers to massage the dressing thoroughly all over the leaves. Season the leaves lightly with salt and pepper. 4. Grill and serve. Place the kale leaves in a single layer on the preheated grill. Grill for 1 to 2 minutes, turn the leaves over, and grill the other side for 1 minute, until they're crispy. Put the leaves on a platter and serve.

Per Serving:
calories: 282 | fat: 28g | protein: 3g | carbs: 9g | net carbs: 6g | fiber: 3g

N'Oatmeal Bars

Prep time: 25 minutes | Cook time: 0 minutes | Makes 16 bars

1 cup (180 g) coconut oil
½ cup (95 g) erythritol, divided
2 cups (300 g) hulled hemp seeds
½ cup (50 g) unsweetened shredded coconut
⅓ cup (33 g) coconut flour
½ teaspoon vanilla extract
10 ounces (285 g) unsweetened baking chocolate, roughly chopped
½ cup (120 ml) full-fat coconut milk

1. Line a 9-inch (23 cm) square baking pan with parchment paper, draping it over all sides of the pan for easy lifting. 2. Place the coconut oil and half of the erythritol in a medium-sized saucepan and melt over medium heat, about 2 minutes. Continue to Step 3 if using confectioners'-style erythritol; if using granulated erythritol, continue to cook until the granules can no longer be felt on the back of the spoon. 3. Add the hulled hemp seeds, shredded coconut, coconut flour, and vanilla, stirring until coated. Set aside half of the mixture for the topping. Press the remaining half of the mixture into the prepared pan. 4. Transfer the pan with the base layer to the refrigerator for at least 10 minutes, until set. 5. Meanwhile, prepare the chocolate layer: Place the remaining erythritol, the baking chocolate, and coconut milk in a small saucepan over low heat. Stir frequently until melted and smooth. 6. Take the base out of the fridge and spoon the chocolate mixture over the base layer, spreading it evenly with a knife or the back of a spoon. If the base hasn't totally set, a couple of hulled hemp seeds will lift up and mix in with the chocolate, so don't rush it. 7. Crumble the reserved hemp seed mixture over the chocolate layer, pressing in gently. Cover and refrigerate for 2 to 3 hours or overnight. 8. Cut into 16 bars and enjoy!

Per Serving:
calories: 311 | fat: 30g | protein: 8g | carbs: 10g | net carbs: 4g | fiber: 5g

Hushpuppies

Prep time: 10 minutes | Cook time: 15 minutes | Makes 10 hushpuppies

High-quality oil, for frying
1 cup finely ground blanched almond flour
1 tablespoon coconut flour
1 teaspoon baking powder
½ teaspoon salt
¼ cup finely chopped onions
¼ cup heavy whipping cream
1 large egg, beaten

1. Attach a candy thermometer to a Dutch oven or other large heavy pot, then pour in 3 inches of oil and set over medium-high heat. Heat the oil to 375°F. 2. In a medium-sized bowl, stir together the almond flour, coconut flour, baking powder, and salt. Stir in the rest of the ingredients and mix until blended. Do not overmix. 3. Use a tablespoon-sized cookie scoop to gently drop the batter into the hot oil. Don't overcrowd the hushpuppies; cook them in two batches. Fry for 3 minutes, then use a mesh skimmer or slotted spoon to turn and fry them for 3 more minutes or until golden brown on all sides. 4. Use the skimmer or slotted spoon to remove the hushpuppies from the oil and place on a paper towel–lined plate to drain. They are best served immediately.

Per Serving:
calories: 172 | fat: 14g | protein: 6g | carbs: 5g | net carbs: 3g | fiber: 3g

Pesto-Stuffed Mushrooms

Prep time: 20 minutes | Cook time: 20 minutes | Makes 1 dozen mushrooms

1 dozen baby bella mushroom caps, cleaned
8 ounces (227 g) fresh Mozzarella
½ cup pesto
Sea salt and ground black pepper, to taste

1. Preheat the oven to 350ºF (180ºC). 2. Place the mushrooms on a rimmed baking sheet cup side down and bake for 10 minutes, or until some of the moisture is released. 3. While the mushrooms are baking, slice the Mozzarella into small pieces, approximately the size of the mushrooms. 4. Turn the mushrooms cup side up and fill each one with a spoonful of pesto and 1 or 2 pieces of Mozzarella. Return the mushrooms to the oven and bake for about 10 minutes, until golden brown on top. 5. Sprinkle with salt and pepper before serving.

Per Serving:
calories: 132 | fat: 11g | protein: 4g | carbs: 5g | net carbs: 4g | fiber: 1g

Cauliflower Fritters with Cheese

Prep time: 10 minutes | Cook time: 8 minutes | Serves 4

1 cup cauliflower, boiled
2 eggs, beaten
2 tablespoons almond flour
2 ounces (57 g) Cheddar
cheese, shredded
½ teaspoon garlic powder
1 tablespoon avocado oil

1. In a medium bowl, mash the cauliflower. Add the beaten eggs, flour, cheese, and garlic powder and stir until well incorporated. Make the fritters from the cauliflower mixture. 2. Set your Instant Pot to Sauté and heat the avocado oil. 3. Add the fritters to the hot oil and cook each side for 3 minutes until golden brown. 4. Serve hot.

Per Serving:

calories: 125 | fat: 10g | protein: 8g | carbs: 3g | net carbs: 1g | fiber: 1g

Herbed Zucchini Slices

Prep time: 5 minutes | Cook time: 5 minutes | Serves 4

2 tablespoons olive oil
2 garlic cloves, chopped
1 pound (454 g) zucchini, sliced
½ cup water
½ cup sugar-free tomato purée
1 teaspoon dried thyme
½ teaspoon dried rosemary
½ teaspoon dried oregano

1. Set your Instant Pot to Sauté and heat the olive oil. 2. Add the garlic and sauté for 2 minutes until fragrant. 3. Add the remaining ingredients to the Instant Pot and stir well. 4. Lock the lid. Select the Manual mode and set the cooking time for 3 minutes at Low Pressure. 5. When the timer beeps, perform a quick pressure release. Carefully remove the lid. 6. Serve warm.

Per Serving:

calories: 87 | fat: 8g | protein: 2g | carbs: 5g | net carbs: 3g | fiber: 2g

Zucchini Chips

Prep time: 10 minutes | Cook time: 2 hours | serves 6

1 large zucchini, cut into thin disks
1 teaspoon sea salt
2 tablespoons coconut oil
1 teaspoon dried dill
1 tablespoon freshly ground black pepper

1. Preheat the oven to 225°F. 2. Line a baking sheet with parchment paper. If you don't have parchment paper, use aluminum foil or a greased pan. 3. Sprinkle the zucchini slices with the salt and spread them out on paper towels. 4. With a separate paper towel, firmly press the zucchini slices and pat them dry (the dryer the better). 5. Toss the zucchini slices in the coconut oil, dill, and pepper, then spread them out on the prepared baking sheet. 6. Bake for 2 hours, or until they are golden and crisp. Check every 30 minutes or so for burn marks. If you begin to see them burn, remove the chips immediately. 7. Remove the chips from the oven and cool. 8. Once the chips have cooled, transfer them to a serving bowl or store in an airtight container for up to 3 days.

Per Serving:

calories: 52 | fat: 5g | protein: 1g | carbs: 3g | net carbs: 1g | fiber: 1g

Almond Sesame Crackers

Prep time: 15 minutes | Cook time: 15 minutes | Makes about 36 (1-inch-square) crackers

1½ cups almond flour
1 egg
3 tablespoons sesame seeds,
divided
Salt and freshly ground black pepper, to taste

1. Preheat the oven to 350ºF (180ºC). 2. Line a baking sheet with parchment paper. 3. In a large bowl, mix together the almond flour, egg, and 1½ tablespoons of sesame seeds. Transfer the dough to a sheet of parchment and pat it out flat with your clean hands. Cover with another piece of parchment paper and roll it into a large square, at least 10 inches wide. 4. Remove the top piece of parchment and use a pizza cutter or sharp knife to cut the dough into small squares, about 1 inch wide. Season with salt and pepper and sprinkle with the remaining 1½ tablespoons of sesame seeds. 5. Remove the crackers from the parchment and place them on the prepared baking sheet. Bake for about 15 minutes or until the crackers begin to brown. Cool before serving, and store any leftovers in an airtight bag or container on your counter for up to 2 weeks.

Per Serving:

10 crackers: calories: 108 | fat: 9g | protein: 5g | carbs: 3g | net carbs: 1g | fiber: 2g

Garlic Meatballs

Prep time: 20 minutes | Cook time: 15 minutes | Serves 6

7 ounces (198 g) ground beef
7 ounces (198 g) ground pork
1 teaspoon minced garlic
3 tablespoons water
1 teaspoon chili flakes
1 teaspoon dried parsley
1 tablespoon coconut oil
¼ cup beef broth

1. In the mixing bowl, mix up ground beef, ground pork, minced garlic, water, chili flakes, and dried parsley. 2. Make the medium size meatballs from the mixture. 3. After this, heat up coconut oil in the instant pot on Sauté mode. 4. Put the meatballs in the hot coconut oil in one layer and cook them for 2 minutes from each side. 5. Then add beef broth and close the lid. 6. Cook the meatballs for 10 minutes on Manual mode (High Pressure). 7. Then make a quick pressure release and transfer the meatballs on the plate.

Per Serving:

calories: 131 | fat: 6g | protein: 19g | carbs: 0g | net carbs: 0g | fiber: 0g

Keto Asian Dumplings

Prep time: 20 minutes | Cook time: 20 minutes | Serves 4

Dipping Sauce:
¼ cup gluten-free soy sauce
2 tablespoons sesame oil
1 tablespoon rice vinegar
1 teaspoon chili garlic sauce
Filling:
1 tablespoon sesame oil
2 garlic cloves
1 teaspoon grated fresh ginger
1 celery stalk, minced
½ onion, minced
1 carrot, minced
8 ounces (227 g) ground pork
8 ounces (227 g) shrimp, peeled, deveined, and finely chopped
2 tablespoons gluten-free soy sauce
½ teaspoon fish sauce
Salt and freshly ground black pepper, to taste
3 scallions, green parts only, chopped
1 head napa cabbage, rinsed, leaves separated (about 12 leaves)

Make the Dipping Sauce 1. In a small bowl, whisk together the soy sauce, sesame oil, vinegar, and chili garlic sauce. Set aside. Make the Filling 2. In a large skillet over medium heat, heat the sesame oil. 3. Add the garlic, ginger, celery, onion, and carrot. Sauté for 5 to 7 minutes until softened. 4. Add the pork. Cook for 5 to 6 minutes, breaking it up with a spoon, until it starts to brown. 5. Add the shrimp and stir everything together well. 6. Stir in the soy sauce and fish sauce. Season with a little salt and pepper. Give it a stir and add the scallions. Keep it warm over low heat until ready to fill the dumplings. 7. Steam the cabbage leaves: Place the leaves in a large saucepan with just 1 to 2 inches of boiling water. Cook for about 5 minutes or until the leaves become tender. Remove from the water and set aside to drain. 8. Lay each leaf out flat. Put about 2 tablespoons of filling in the center of one leaf. Wrap the leaf over itself, tucking the sides in so the whole thing is tightly wrapped. Secure with a toothpick. Continue with the remaining leaves and filling. Serve with the dipping sauce. Refrigerate leftovers in an airtight container for up to 3 days.

Per Serving:
3 dumplings: calories: 305 | fat: 17g | protein: 27g | carbs: 11g | net carbs: 8g | fiber: 3g

Fried Cabbage Wedges

Prep time: 5 minutes | Cook time: 15 minutes | Serves 6

1 large head green or red cabbage (about 2½ lbs/1.2 kg)
2 tablespoons coconut oil or avocado oil
2 teaspoons garlic powder
½ teaspoon finely ground sea salt
¾ cup (180 ml) green goddess dressing
Special Equipment:
12 (4-in/10-cm) bamboo skewers

1. Cut the cabbage in half through the core, from top to bottom. Working with each half separately, remove the core by cutting a triangle around it and pulling it out. Then lay the half cut side down and cut into 6 wedges. Press a bamboo skewer into each wedge to secure the leaves. Repeat with the other half. 2. Heat the oil in a large frying pan over medium-low heat. 3. Place the cabbage wedges in the frying pan and sprinkle with the garlic powder and salt. Cook for 10 minutes on one side, or until lightly browned, then cook for 5 minutes on the other side. Serve with the dressing on the side.

Per Serving:
calories: 252 | fat: 20g | protein: 3g | carbs: 12g | net carbs: 7g | fiber: 5g

Finger Tacos

Prep time: 15 minutes | Cook time: 0 minutes | serves 4

2 avocados, peeled and pitted
1 lime
1 tablespoon tamari
1 teaspoon sesame oil
1 teaspoon ginger powder
1 teaspoon togarashi (optional)
½ cup kale chiffonade
½ cup cabbage chiffonade
10 fresh mint leaves chiffonade
⅓ cup cauliflower rice
1 (0.18-ounce) package nori squares or seaweed snack sheets

1. Put the avocados into a large mixing bowl, and squeeze the lime over them. 2. Roughly mash the avocados with a fork, leaving the mixture fairly chunky. 3. Gently stir in the tamari, sesame oil, ginger powder, and togarashi (if using). 4. Gently fold in the kale, cabbage, mint, and cauliflower rice. 5. Arrange some nori squares on a plate. 6. Use a nori or seaweed sheet to pick up a portion of the avocado mixture and pop it into your mouth.

Per Serving:
calories: 180 | fat: 15g | protein: 4g | carbs: 13g | net carbs: 5g | fiber: 8g

Parmesan Chicken Balls with Chives

Prep time: 10 minutes | Cook time: 15 minutes | Serves 4

1 teaspoon coconut oil, softened
1 cup ground chicken
¼ cup chicken broth
1 tablespoon chopped chives
1 teaspoon cayenne pepper
3 ounces (85 g) Parmesan cheese, grated

1. Set your Instant Pot to Sauté and heat the coconut oil. 2. Add the remaining ingredients except the cheese to the Instant Pot and stir to mix well. 3. Secure the lid. Select the Manual mode and set the cooking time for 15 minutes at High Pressure. 4. Once cooking is complete, do a quick pressure release. Carefully open the lid. 5. Add the grated cheese and stir until combined. Form the balls from the cooked chicken mixture and allow to cool for 10 minutes, then serve.

Per Serving:
calories: 154 | fat: 9g | protein: 18g | carbs: 1g | net carbs: 1g | fiber: 0g

Sweet Pepper Nacho Bites

Prep time: 5 minutes | Cook time: 5 minutes | Makes 24 bites

12 mini sweet peppers (approximately 8 ounces / 227 g)
½ cup shredded Monterey Jack cheese
½ cup guacamole
Juice of 1 lime

1. Preheat the oven to 400°F (205°C). 2. Carefully cut each pepper in half lengthwise and remove the seeds. Place them cut side up on a rimmed baking sheet so they aren't touching. Place 1 teaspoon of shredded cheese inside each. Bake 3 to 5 minutes, until the cheese starts to melt. 3. Remove from the oven and top each with 1 teaspoon of guacamole. Squeeze the lime juice over top. Serve immediately.

Per Serving:
calories: 137 | fat: 12g | protein: 4g | carbs: 5g | net carbs: 3g | fiber: 2g

Lime Brussels Chips

Prep time: 15 minutes | Cook time: 10 minutes | Serves 2

3 cups Brussels sprouts leaves (from 1½ to 2 pounds fresh Brussels sprouts) Juice of ½ lime
2½ tablespoons avocado oil or melted coconut oil
Pink Himalayan salt

1 Preheat the oven to 400°F. Line a rimmed baking sheet with parchment paper. 2 Trim off the flat stem ends of the Brussels sprouts and separate the leaves. You should end up with 2 to 3 cups of leaves. 3 Place the separated leaves in a large bowl and add the lime juice. 4 Add the oil and season with salt to taste. Toss until the leaves are evenly coated. 5 Spread the leaves evenly on the prepared baking sheet and bake for 7 to 10 minutes, until lightly golden brown. tip: Trimming a little higher up than usual on the stem end of the Brussels sprouts helps the leaves come off easier.

Per Serving:
calories: 173 | fat: 18g | protein: 2g | carbs: 4g | net carbs: 2g | fiber: 2g

3-Ingredient Almond Flour Crackers

Prep time: 5 minutes | Cook time: 12 minutes | Serves 6

2 cups (8 ounces / 227 g) blanched almond flour
½ teaspoon sea salt
1 large egg, beaten

1. Preheat the oven to 350°F (180°C). Line a large baking sheet with parchment paper. 2. In a large bowl, mix together the almond flour and sea salt. Add the egg and mix well, until a dense, crumbly dough forms. (You can also mix in a food processor if you prefer.) 3. Place the dough between two large pieces of parchment paper. Use a rolling pin to roll out to a very thin rectangle, about 1/16 inch thick. (It will tend to roll into an oval shape, so just rip off pieces of dough and re-attach to form a more rectangular shape.) 4. Cut the cracker dough into rectangles. Place on the lined baking sheet. Prick with a fork a few times. Bake for 8 to 12 minutes, until golden.

Per Serving:
calories: 226 | fat: 19g | protein: 9g | carbs: 8g | net carbs: 4g | fiber: 4g

Ketone Gummies

Prep time: 10 minutes | Cook time: 5 minutes | Makes 8 gummies

½ cup (120 ml) lemon juice
8 hulled strawberries (fresh or frozen and defrosted)
2 tablespoons unflavored gelatin
2 teaspoons exogenous ketones
Special Equipment (optional):
Silicone mold with eight 2-tablespoon or larger cavities

1. Have on hand your favorite silicone mold. I like to use a large silicone ice cube tray and spoon 2 tablespoons of the mixture into each cavity, If you do not have a silicone mold, you can use an 8-inch (20-cm) square silicone or metal baking pan; if using a metal pan, line it with parchment paper, draping some over the sides for easy removal. 2. Place the lemon juice, strawberries, and gelatin in a blender or food processor and pulse until smooth. Transfer the mixture to a small saucepan and set over low heat for 5 minutes, or until it becomes very liquid-y and begins to simmer. 3. Remove from the heat and stir in the exogenous ketones. 4. Divide the mixture evenly among 8 cavities of the mold or pour into the baking pan. Transfer to the fridge and allow to set for 30 minutes. If using a baking pan, cut into 8 squares.

Per Serving:
calories: 19 | fat: 0g | protein: 3g | carbs: 1g | net carbs: 1g | fiber: 0g

Olive Pâté

Prep time: 10 minutes | Cook time: 0 minutes | serves 6

1 cup pitted green olives
1 cup pitted black olives
¼ cup cold-pressed olive oil
1 teaspoon freshly ground black pepper
2 thyme sprigs

1. In a food processor, combine all the ingredients and pulse until the mixture is thick and chunky. 2. Transfer the pâté to a small serving bowl and serve with crackers.

Per Serving:
calories: 171 | fat: 17g | protein: 0g | carbs: 4g | net carbs: 4g | fiber: 1g

Cayenne Beef Bites

Prep time: 5 minutes | Cook time: 23 minutes | Serves 6

2 tablespoons olive oil
1 pound (454 g) beef steak, cut into cubes
1 cup beef bone broth
¼ cup dry white wine
1 teaspoon cayenne pepper
½ teaspoon dried marjoram
Sea salt and ground black pepper, to taste

1. Set your Instant Pot to Sauté and heat the olive oil. 2. Add the beef and sauté for 2 to 3 minutes, stirring occasionally. 3. Add the remaining ingredients to the Instant Pot and combine well. 4. Lock the lid. Select the Manual mode and set the cooking time for 20 minutes at High Pressure. 5. When the timer beeps, perform a natural pressure release for 10 minutes, then release any remaining pressure. Carefully remove the lid. 6. Remove the beef from the Instant Pot to a platter and serve warm.

Per Serving:

calories: 173 | fat: 10g | protein: 19g | carbs: 1g | net carbs: 1g | fiber: 0g

Mac Fatties

Prep time: 10 minutes | Cook time: 0 minutes | Makes 20 fat cups

1¾ cups (280 g) roasted and salted macadamia nuts
⅓ cup (70 g) coconut oil
Rosemary Lemon Flavor:
1 teaspoon finely chopped fresh rosemary
¼ teaspoon lemon juice
Spicy Cumin Flavor:
½ teaspoon ground cumin
¼ teaspoon cayenne pepper
Turmeric Flavor:
½ teaspoon turmeric powder
¼ teaspoon ginger powder
Garlic Herb Flavor:
1¼ teaspoons dried oregano leaves
½ teaspoon paprika
½ teaspoon garlic powder

1. Place the macadamia nuts and oil in a blender or food processor. Blend until smooth, or as close to smooth as you can get it with the equipment you're using. 2. Divide the mixture among 4 small bowls, placing ¼ cup (87 g) in each bowl. 3. To the first bowl, add the rosemary and lemon juice and stir to combine. 4. To the second bowl, add the cumin and cayenne and stir to combine. 5. To the third bowl, add the turmeric and ginger and stir to combine. 6. To the fourth bowl, add the oregano, paprika, and garlic powder and stir to combine. 7. Set a 24-well silicone or metal mini muffin pan on the counter. If using a metal pan, line 20 of the wells with mini foil liners. (Do not use paper; it would soak up all the fat.) Spoon the mixtures into the wells, using about 1 tablespoon per well. 8. Place in the freezer for 1 hour, or until firm. Enjoy directly from the freezer.

Per Serving:

calories: 139 | fat: 14g | protein: 1g | carbs: 2g | net carbs: 1g | fiber: 1g

Broccoli with Garlic-Herb Cheese Sauce

Prep time: 5 minutes | Cook time: 3 minutes | Serves 4

½ cup water
1 pound (454 g) broccoli (frozen or fresh)
½ cup heavy cream
1 tablespoon butter
½ cup shredded Cheddar cheese
3 tablespoons garlic and herb cheese spread
Pinch of salt
Pinch of black pepper

1. Add the water to the pot and place the trivet inside. 2. Put the steamer basket on top of the trivet. Place the broccoli in the basket. 3. Close the lid and seal the vent. Cook on Low Pressure for 1 minute. Quick release the steam. Press Cancel. 4. Carefully remove the steamer basket from the pot and drain the water. If you steamed a full bunch of broccoli, pull the florets off the stem. (Chop the stem into bite-size pieces, it's surprisingly creamy.) 5. Turn the pot to Sauté mode. Add the cream and butter. Stir continuously while the butter melts and the cream warms up. 6. When the cream begins to bubble on the edges, add the Cheddar cheese, cheese spread, salt, and pepper. Whisk continuously until the cheeses are melted and a sauce consistency is reached, 1 to 2 minutes. 7. Top one-fourth of the broccoli with 2 tablespoons cheese sauce.

Per Serving:

calories: 134 | fat: 12g | protein:4 g | carbs: 5g | net carbs: 3g | fiber: 2g

Herbed Cashew Cheese

Prep time: 10 minutes | Cook time: 0 minutes | Makes 1½ cups

1 cup raw cashews
1 cup warm water
¼ cup extra-virgin olive oil
¼ cup water
2 tablespoons fresh lemon juice
1 clove garlic, minced or grated
2 tablespoons minced fresh chives
Sea salt and ground black pepper, to taste

1. Place the cashews in a small container and add the warm water. (If it doesn't cover the cashews completely, just add more warm water.) Soak for 1 to 4 hours unrefrigerated or up to overnight in the refrigerator. 2. Drain and rinse the cashews, then place them in a blender or food processor. Add the olive oil, the ¼ cup water, the lemon juice, and the garlic. Process until smooth and creamy, stopping occasionally to scrape down the sides of the processor, about 5 minutes total. Mix in the chives and add salt and pepper to taste. 3. If you'd like a lighter texture, add warm water, 1 tablespoon at a time, until you achieve the desired consistency.

Per Serving:

calories: 288 | fat: 25g | protein: 7g | carbs: 13g | net carbs: 12g | fiber: 1g

Cream Cheese and Berries

Prep time: 5 minutes | Cook time: 0 minutes | Serves 1

2 ounces (57 g) cream cheese
2 large strawberries, cut into thin slices or chunks
5 blueberries
⅛ cup chopped pecans

1. Place the cream cheese on a small plate or in a bowl. 2. Pour the berries and chopped pecans on top. Enjoy!

Per Serving:
calories: 330 | fat: 31g | protein: 6g | carbs: 7g | net carbs: 5g | fiber: 2g

Parmesan Crisps

Prep time: 5 minutes | Cook time: 5 minutes | Makes about 25 crisps

2 cups grated Parmesan cheese

1. Heat the oven to 400°F (205°C). Line a baking sheet with a silicone mat or parchment paper. Scoop a generous tablespoon of the cheese onto the sheet and flatten it slightly. Repeat with the rest of the cheese, leaving about 1 inch (2.5 cm) space in between them. 2. Bake for 3 to 5 minutes, until crisp.

Per Serving:
calories: 169 | fat: 11g | protein: 11g | carbs: 6g | net carbs: 6g | fiber: 0g

Haystack Cookies

Prep time: 10 minutes | Cook time: 5 minutes | Makes 20 cookies

½ cup (95 g) erythritol
¼ cup (60 ml) full-fat coconut milk
3 tablespoons coconut oil, ghee, or cacao butter
¼ cup (20 g) cocoa powder
⅓ cup (30 g) unflavored MCT oil powder (optional)
2 cups (200 g) unsweetened shredded coconut

1. Line a rimmed baking sheet or large plate with parchment paper or a silicone baking mat. 2. Place the erythritol, coconut milk, and oil in a large frying pan. Slowly bring to a simmer over medium-low heat, whisking periodically to prevent burning; this should take about 5 minutes. 3. When the mixture reaches a simmer, remove from the heat and stir in the cocoa powder. Once fully combined, stir in the MCT oil powder, if using, and then the shredded coconut. 4. Using a 1-tablespoon measuring spoon, carefully scoop out a portion of the mixture and press it into the spoon. Place the haystack on the lined baking sheet and repeat, making a total of 20 cookies. 5. Refrigerate for 30 to 45 minutes before enjoying.

Per Serving:
calories: 122 | fat: 11g | protein: 1g | carbs: 4g | net carbs: 2g | fiber: 2g

Curried Broccoli Skewers

Prep time: 15 minutes | Cook time: 1 minute | Serves 2

1 cup broccoli florets
½ teaspoon curry paste
2 tablespoons coconut cream
1 cup water, for cooking

1. In the shallow bowl mix up curry paste and coconut cream. 2. Then sprinkle the broccoli florets with curry paste mixture and string on the skewers. 3. Pour water and insert the steamer rack in the instant pot. 4. Place the broccoli skewers on the rack. Close and seal the lid. 5. Cook the meal on Manual mode (High Pressure) for 1 minute. 6. Make a quick pressure release.

Per Serving:
calories: 58 | fat: 4g | protein: 2g | carbs: 4g | net carbs: 2g | fiber: 2g

Red Wine Mushrooms

Prep time: 5 minutes | Cook time: 15 minutes | Serves 2

8 ounces (227 g) sliced mushrooms
¼ cup dry red wine
2 tablespoons beef broth
½ teaspoon garlic powder
¼ teaspoon Worcestershire sauce
Pinch of salt
Pinch of black pepper
¼ teaspoon xanthan gum

1. Add the mushrooms, wine, broth, garlic powder, Worcestershire sauce, salt, and pepper to the pot. 2. Close the lid and seal the vent. Cook on High Pressure for 13 minutes. Quick release the steam. Press Cancel. 3. Turn the pot to Sauté mode. Add the xanthan gum and whisk until the juices have thickened, 1 to 2 minutes.

Per Serving:
calories: 94 | fat: 1g | protein: 4g | carbs: 8g | net carbs: 6g | fiber: 2g

Lemon-Butter Mushrooms

Prep time: 10 minutes | Cook time: 4 minutes | Serves 2

1 cup cremini mushrooms, sliced
½ cup water
1 tablespoon lemon juice
1 teaspoon almond butter
1 teaspoon grated lemon zest
½ teaspoon salt
½ teaspoon dried thyme

1. Combine all the ingredients in the Instant Pot. 2. Secure the lid. Select the Manual mode and set the cooking time for 4 minutes at High Pressure. 3. Once cooking is complete, do a natural pressure release for 5 minutes, then release any remaining pressure. Carefully open the lid. 4. Serve warm.

Per Serving:
calories: 63 | fat: 5g | protein: 3g | carbs: 3g | net carbs: 2g | fiber: 1g

Garlic Herb Butter

Prep time: 10 minutes | Cook time: 8 minutes | Serves 4

⅓ cup butter
1 teaspoon dried parsley
1 tablespoon dried dill
½ teaspoon minced garlic
¼ teaspoon dried thyme

1. Preheat the instant pot on Sauté mode. 2. Then add butter and melt it. 3. Add dried parsley, dill, minced garlic, and thyme. Stir the butter mixture well. 4. Transfer it in the butter mold and refrigerate until it is solid.

Per Serving:
calories: 138 | fat: 15g | protein: 0g | carbs: 1g | net carbs: 1g | fiber: 0g

Chicken and Cabbage Salad

Prep time: 15 minutes | Cook time: 10 minutes | Serves 4

12 ounces (340 g) chicken fillet, chopped
1 teaspoon Cajun seasoning
1 tablespoon coconut oil
1 cup chopped Chinese cabbage
1 tablespoon avocado oil
1 teaspoon sesame seeds

1. Sprinkle the chopped chicken with the Cajun seasoning. 2. Set your Instant Pot to Sauté and heat the coconut oil. Add the chicken and cook for 10 minutes, stirring occasionally. 3. When the chicken is cooked, transfer to a salad bowl. Add the cabbage, avocado oil, and sesame seeds and gently toss to combine. Serve immediately.

Per Serving:
calories: 207 | fat: 11g | protein: 25g | carbs: 1g | net carbs: 0g | fiber: 0g

Baked Crab Dip

Prep time: 15 minutes | Cook time: 25 minutes | Serves 4 to 6

4 ounces cream cheese, softened
½ cup shredded Parmesan cheese, plus ½ cup extra for topping (optional) ⅓ cup mayonnaise
¼ cup sour cream
1 tablespoon chopped fresh parsley
2 teaspoons fresh lemon juice
1½ teaspoons Sriracha sauce
½ teaspoon garlic powder
8 ounces fresh lump crabmeat
Salt and pepper

1. Preheat the oven to 375°F. 2. Combine all the ingredients except for the crabmeat in a mixing bowl and use a hand mixer to blend until smooth. 3. Put the crabmeat in a separate bowl, check for shells, and rinse with cold water, if needed. Pat dry or allow to rest in a strainer until most of the water has drained. 4. Add the crabmeat to the bowl with the cream cheese mixture and gently fold to combine. Taste for seasoning and add salt and pepper to taste, if needed. Pour into an 8-inch round or square baking dish and bake for 25 minutes, until the cheese has melted and the dip is warm throughout. 5. If desired, top the dip with another ½ cup of Parmesan cheese and broil for 2 to 3 minutes, until the cheese has melted and browned slightly.

Per Serving:
calories: 275 | fat: 23g | protein: 16g | carbs: 1g | net carbs: 1g | fiber: 0g

Sausage Balls

Prep time: 5 minutes | Cook time: 25 minutes | Makes 2 dozen

1 pound (454 g) bulk Italian sausage (not sweet)
1 cup almond flour
1½ cups finely shredded Cheddar cheese
1 large egg
2 teaspoons baking powder
1 teaspoon onion powder
1 teaspoon fennel seed (optional)
½ teaspoon cayenne pepper (optional)

1. Preheat the oven to 350°F (180°C) and line a rimmed baking sheet with aluminum foil. 2. In a large bowl, combine all the ingredients. Use a fork to mix until well blended. 3. Form the sausage mixture into 1½-inch balls and place 1 inch apart on the prepared baking sheet. 4. Bake for 20 to 25 minutes, or until browned and cooked through.

Per Serving:
calories: 241 | fat: 21g | protein: 11g | carbs: 3g | net carbs: 2g | fiber: 1g

Greens Chips with Curried Yogurt Sauce

Prep time: 10 minutes | Cook time: 5 to 6 minutes | Serves 4

1 cup low-fat Greek yogurt
1 tablespoon freshly squeezed lemon juice
1 tablespoon curry powder
½ bunch curly kale, stemmed, ribs removed and discarded, leaves cut into 2- to 3-inch pieces
½ bunch chard, stemmed, ribs removed and discarded, leaves cut into 2- to 3-inch pieces
1½ teaspoons olive oil

1. In a small bowl, stir together the yogurt, lemon juice, and curry powder. Set aside. 2. In a large bowl, toss the kale and chard with the olive oil, working the oil into the leaves with your hands. This helps break up the fibers in the leaves so the chips are tender. 3. Air fry the greens in batches at 390°F (199°C) for 5 to 6 minutes, until crisp, shaking the basket once during cooking. Serve with the yogurt sauce.

Per Serving:
calories: 76 | fat: 2g | protein: 6g | carbs: 11g | net carbs: 10g | fiber: 2g

Salmon-Stuffed Cucumbers

Prep time: 10 minutes | Cook time: 0 minutes | Serves 4

2 large cucumbers, peeled
1 (4 ounces / 113 g) can red salmon
1 medium very ripe avocado, peeled, pitted, and mashed
1 tablespoon extra-virgin olive oil
Zest and juice of 1 lime
3 tablespoons chopped fresh cilantro
½ teaspoon salt
¼ teaspoon freshly ground black pepper

1. Slice the cucumber into 1-inch-thick segments and using a spoon, scrape seeds out of center of each segment and stand up on a plate. 2. In a medium bowl, combine the salmon, avocado, olive oil, lime zest and juice, cilantro, salt, and pepper and mix until creamy. 3. Spoon the salmon mixture into the center of each cucumber segment and serve chilled.

Per Serving:

calories: 174 | fat: 12g | protein: 10g | carbs: 9g | net carbs: 6g | fiber: 3g

Walnut Herb-Crusted Goat Cheese

Prep time: 10 minutes | Cook time: 0 minutes | Serves 4

6 ounces chopped walnuts
1 tablespoon chopped oregano
1 tablespoon chopped parsley
1 teaspoon chopped fresh thyme
¼ teaspoon freshly ground black pepper
1 (8 ounces) log goat cheese

1. Place the walnuts, oregano, parsley, thyme, and pepper in a food processor and pulse until finely chopped. 2. Pour the walnut mixture onto a plate and roll the goat cheese log in the nut mixture, pressing so the cheese is covered and the walnut mixture sticks to the log. 3. Wrap the cheese in plastic and store in the refrigerator for up to 1 week. 4. Slice and enjoy!

Per Serving:

calories: 304 | fat: 28g | protein: 12g | carbs: 4g | net carbs: 2g | fiber: 2g

Macadamia Nut Cream Cheese Log

Prep time: 10 minutes | Cook time: 0 minutes | Serves 8

1 (8-ounce / 227-g) brick cream cheese, cold
1 cup finely chopped macadamia nuts

1. Place the cream cheese on a piece of parchment paper or wax paper. 2. Roll the paper around the cream cheese, then roll the wrapped cream cheese with the palm of your hands lengthwise on the cream cheese, using the paper to help you roll the cream cheese into an 8-inch log. 3. Open the paper and sprinkle the macadamia nuts all over the top and sides of the cream cheese until the log is entirely covered in nuts. 4. Chill in the refrigerator for 30 minutes before serving. 5. Serve on a small plate, cut into 8 even slices.

Per Serving:

calories: 285 | fat: 29g | protein: 4g | carbs: 4g | net carbs: 3g | fiber: 1g

Sarah's Expert Crackers

Prep time: 15 minutes | Cook time: 40 minutes | Serves 10

1 cup blanched almond flour
2 tablespoons hemp hearts
2 tablespoons flaxseed meal
2 tablespoons psyllium husk powder
2 tablespoons chia seeds
2 tablespoons shelled pumpkin seeds
2 tablespoons Everything and More seasoning
½ tablespoon salt
1½ cups water
1 squirt liquid stevia

1. Preheat oven to 350°F. 2. In a medium mixing bowl, combine dry ingredients. 3. Add water and liquid stevia and mix together until a thick dough is formed. 4. Place dough between two pieces of parchment paper and roll out to desired cracker thickness. 5. Remove top piece of parchment paper and use a pizza cutter to cut dough into desired cracker shapes. 6. While cracker shapes are still on bottom piece of parchment paper, put on a baking sheet and into oven. 7. Bake 30–40 minutes until centers of crackers are hard. 8. Let cool 5 minutes, then serve.

Per Serving:

calories: 111| fat: 6g | protein: 5g | carbs: 7g | net carbs: 5g | fiber: 2g

Crab Salad–Stuffed Avocado

Prep time: 20 minutes | Cook time: 0 minutes | Serves 2

1 avocado, peeled, halved lengthwise, and pitted
½ teaspoon freshly squeezed lemon juice
4½ ounces Dungeness crabmeat
½ cup cream cheese
¼ cup chopped red bell pepper
¼ cup chopped, peeled English cucumber
½ scallion, chopped
1 teaspoon chopped cilantro
Pinch sea salt
Freshly ground black pepper

1. Brush the cut edges of the avocado with the lemon juice and set the halves aside on a plate. 2. In a medium bowl, stir together the crabmeat, cream cheese, red pepper, cucumber, scallion, cilantro, salt, and pepper until well mixed. 3. Divide the crab mixture between the avocado halves and store them, covered with plastic wrap, in the refrigerator until you want to serve them, up to 2 days.

Per Serving:

calories: 389 | fat: 31g | protein: 19g | carbs: 10g | net carbs: 5g | fiber: 5g

Cheesy Sausage Balls

Prep time: 10 minutes | Cook time: 25 minutes | serves 6

1 pound bulk breakfast sausage
1½ cups shredded sharp cheddar cheese
1 cup finely ground blanched almond flour
1 tablespoon baking powder

1. Preheat the oven to 375°F. Line a sheet pan with parchment paper. 2. Place all the ingredients in a large bowl. Using your hands, mix everything together until well combined but not overmixed. 3. Using a tablespoon or small cookie scoop, form the mixture into 1-inch balls and place on the lined sheet pan. Bake for 20 to 25 minutes, until the sausage balls are crispy around the edges and golden brown on top. Leftovers can be stored in an airtight container in the refrigerator for up to 5 days.

Per Serving:
calories: 527 | fat: 45g | protein: 22g | carbs: 6g | net carbs: 3g | fiber: 3g

Bacon-Cheddar Dip Stuffed Mushrooms

Prep time: 10 minutes | Cook time: 35 minutes | Serves 12

24 ounces (680 g) baby portobello mushrooms
2 tablespoons avocado oil
3 ounces (85 g) cream cheese
¼ cup sour cream
2 cloves garlic, minced
1 tablespoon chopped fresh dill
1 tablespoon chopped fresh parsley
¾ cup (3 ounces / 85 g) shredded Cheddar cheese
⅓ cup cooked bacon bits
3 tablespoons sliced green onions

1. Preheat the oven to 400ºF (205ºC). Line a sheet pan with foil or parchment paper and grease lightly. 2. Remove the stems from the mushrooms and place cavity side up on the baking sheet. Drizzle with the avocado oil. 3. Roast the mushrooms for 15 to 20 minutes, until soft. 4. Meanwhile, in a microwave-safe bowl or a saucepan, melt the cream cheese in the microwave or over low heat on the stove until it's soft and easy to stir. Remove from the heat. 5. Stir the sour cream, garlic, dill, and parsley into the cream cheese. Stir in the Cheddar, bacon, and green onions. 6. When the mushrooms are soft, remove from the oven but leave the oven on. Drain any liquid from the pan and from inside the mushrooms. Pat the cavities dry with paper towels. Use a small cookie scoop or spoon to fill them with the dip mixture. 7. Bake the stuffed mushrooms for 10 to 15 minutes, until hot.

Per Serving:
calories: 107 | fat: 8g | protein: 4g | carbs: 3g | net carbs: 3g | fiber: 0g

Buffalo Chicken Meatballs

Prep time: 5 minutes | Cook time: 10 minutes | Serves 4

1 pound (454 g) ground chicken
½ cup almond flour
2 tablespoons cream cheese
1 packet dry ranch dressing mix
½ teaspoon salt
¼ teaspoon pepper
¼ teaspoon garlic powder
1 cup water
2 tablespoons butter, melted
⅓ cup hot sauce
¼ cup crumbled feta cheese
¼ cup sliced green onion

1. In large bowl, mix ground chicken, almond flour, cream cheese, ranch, salt, pepper, and garlic powder. Roll mixture into 16 balls. 2. Place meatballs on steam rack and add 1 cup water to Instant Pot. Click lid closed. Press the Meat/Stew button and set time for 10 minutes. 3. Combine butter and hot sauce. When timer beeps, remove meatballs and place in clean large bowl. Toss in hot sauce mixture. Top with sprinkled feta and green onions to serve.

Per Serving:
calories: 367 | fat: 25g | protein: 25g | carbs: 9g | net carbs: 7g | fiber: 2g

Salami Chips with Buffalo Chicken Dip

Prep time: 10 minutes | Cook time: 10 minutes | Serves 6

8 ounces (227 g) salami, cut crosswise into 24 slices
Buffalo Chicken Dip:
1 cup full-fat coconut milk
¾ cup shredded cooked chicken
⅓ cup nutritional yeast
1 tablespoon coconut aminos
1 tablespoon hot sauce
2 teaspoons onion powder
1½ teaspoons garlic powder
1 teaspoon turmeric powder
½ teaspoon finely ground sea salt
¼ teaspoon ground black pepper
¼ cup roughly chopped fresh parsley

1. Preheat the oven to 400ºF (205ºC). Line 2 rimmed baking sheets with parchment paper or silicone baking mats. 2. Set the salami slices on the lined baking sheets. Bake for 8 to 10 minutes, until the centers look crisp and the edges are just slightly turned up. Meanwhile, make the dip: 1. Place the dip ingredients in a small saucepan. Bring to a simmer over medium-high heat, then reduce the heat to medium-low and cook, uncovered, for 6 minutes, or until thickened, stirring often. 2. Transfer the salami chips to a serving plate and the dip to a serving bowl. Stir the parsley into the dip and dig in! Storage: Store in an airtight container in the fridge for up to 3 days or in the freezer for up to 3 months.

Per Serving:
calories: 294 | fat: 21g | protein: 20g | carbs: 7g | net carbs: 5g | fiber: 2g

Keto Trail Mix

Prep time: 5 minutes | Cook time: 0 minutes | Serves 4

¼ cup pumpkin seeds
¼ cup salted almonds
¼ cup salted macadamia nuts
¼ cup salted walnuts
1 cup crunchy cheese snack
¼ cup sugar-free chocolate chips

1. In a resealable 1-quart plastic bag, combine the pumpkin seeds, almonds, macadamia nuts, walnuts, cheese snack, and chocolate chips. Seal the bag and shake to mix.

Per Serving:

calories: 253 | fat: 23g | protein: 7g | carbs: 5g | net carbs: 2g | fiber: 3g

Burrata Caprese Stack

Prep time: 5 minutes | Cook time: 0 minutes | Serves 4

1 large organic tomato, preferably heirloom
½ teaspoon salt
¼ teaspoon freshly ground black pepper
1 (4 ounces / 113 g) ball burrata cheese
8 fresh basil leaves, thinly sliced
2 tablespoons extra-virgin olive oil
1 tablespoon red wine or balsamic vinegar

1. Slice the tomato into 4 thick slices, removing any tough center core and sprinkle with salt and pepper. Place the tomatoes, seasoned-side up, on a plate. 2. On a separate rimmed plate, slice the burrata into 4 thick slices and place one slice on top of each tomato slice. Top each with one-quarter of the basil and pour any reserved burrata cream from the rimmed plate over top. 3. Drizzle with olive oil and vinegar and serve with a fork and knife.

Per Serving:

calories: 118 | fat: 11g | protein: 4g | carbs: 4g | net carbs: 4g | fiber: 1g

Cheesy Spinach Puffs

Prep time: 10 minutes | Cook time: 10 minutes | Serves 8

16 ounces (454 g) frozen spinach, thawed, drained, and squeezed of as much excess liquid as possible
1 cup almond flour
4 tablespoons butter, melted, plus more for the baking sheet
2 eggs
¼ cup grated Parmesan cheese
¼ cup cream cheese
3 tablespoons heavy (whipping) cream
1 tablespoon onion powder
1 teaspoon garlic powder
Salt and freshly ground black pepper, to taste

1. In a food processor, combine the spinach, almond flour, butter, eggs, Parmesan, cream cheese, cream, onion powder, and garlic powder. Season with salt and pepper. Blend until smooth. Transfer to the refrigerator and chill for 10 to 15 minutes. 2. Preheat the oven to 350ºF (180ºC). 3. Grease a baking sheet with butter. 4. Scoop the spinach mixture in heaping tablespoons and roll into balls. Place on the prepared baking sheet and bake for about 10 minutes until set. When tapped with your finger, they should not still be soft. Enjoy warm (best!) or cold. Refrigerate in an airtight container for up to 4 days.

Per Serving:

calories: 159 | fat: 14g | protein: 6g | carbs: 3g | net carbs: 1g | fiber: 2g

Roasted Garlic Bulbs

Prep time: 2 minutes | Cook time: 25 minutes | Serves 4

4 bulbs garlic
1 tablespoon avocado oil
1 teaspoon salt
Pinch of black pepper
1 cup water

1. Slice the pointy tops off the bulbs of garlic to expose the cloves. 2. Drizzle the avocado oil on top of the garlic and sprinkle with the salt and pepper. 3. Place the bulbs in the steamer basket, cut-side up. Alternatively, you may place them on a piece of aluminum foil with the sides pulled up and resting on top of the trivet. Place the steamer basket in the pot. 4. Close the lid and seal the vent. Cook on High Pressure for 25 minutes. Quick release the steam. 5. Let the garlic cool completely before removing the bulbs from the pot. 6. Hold the stem end (bottom) of the bulb and squeeze out all the garlic. Mash the cloves with a fork to make a paste.

Per Serving:

calories: 44 | fat: 5g | protein: 0g | carbs: 1g | net carbs: 1g | fiber: 0g

Herbed Shrimp

Prep time: 5 minutes | Cook time: 5 minutes | Serves 4

2 tablespoons olive oil
¾ pound (340 g) shrimp, peeled and deveined
1 teaspoon paprika
1 teaspoon garlic powder
1 teaspoon onion powder
1 teaspoon dried parsley flakes
½ teaspoon dried oregano
½ teaspoon dried thyme
½ teaspoon dried basil
½ teaspoon dried rosemary
¼ teaspoon red pepper flakes
Coarse sea salt and ground black pepper, to taste
1 cup chicken broth

1. Set your Instant Pot to Sauté and heat the olive oil. 2. Add the shrimp and sauté for 2 to 3 minutes. 3. Add the remaining ingredients to the Instant Pot and stir to combine. 4. Secure the lid. Select the Manual mode and set the cooking time for 2 minutes at Low Pressure. 5. When the timer beeps, perform a quick pressure release. Carefully remove the lid. 6. Transfer the shrimp to a plate and serve.

Per Serving:

calories: 146 | fat: 8g | protein: 19g | carbs: 3g | net carbs: 2g | fiber: 1g

Salsa Shrimp-Stuffed Avocados

Prep time: 10 minutes | Cook time: 15 minutes | Serves 4

2 avocados, halved and pitted
12 large precooked shrimp, peeled and deveined
3 tablespoons salsa
¼ cup shredded Mexican cheese blend
Finely chopped fresh cilantro, for garnish (optional)
Sour cream, for garnish (optional)

1 Preheat the oven to 350°F. Line a rimmed baking sheet with parchment paper. 2 Rinse the shrimp and halve lengthwise. Place in a bowl and top with the salsa. Stir to coat the shrimp evenly with the salsa. 3 Place the avocado halves cut side up on the lined baking sheet. Fill each half with salsa-coated shrimp and top with the cheese. 4 Bake for 15 minutes, until the cheese is melted. 5 Serve garnished with cilantro and/or topped with sour cream, if desired.

Per Serving:

calories: 185 | fat: 13g | protein: 11g | carbs: 7g | net carbs: 6g | fiber: 1g

Cucumber Finger Sandwiches

Prep time: 10 minutes | Cook time: 0 minutes | serves 4

1 medium English cucumber
2 ounces cream cheese (¼ cup), softened
2 to 3 slices sharp cheddar cheese, cut into 1-inch pieces
4 slices bacon, cooked and cut crosswise into 1-inch pieces

1. Slice the cucumber crosswise into rounds about ¼ inch thick. Spread the cream cheese on half of the cucumber slices, then top each with a piece of cheese and a piece of bacon. Place the remainder of the cucumber slices on top to make sandwiches. Serve immediately or cover and refrigerate before serving. These sandwiches should be eaten the day they are made or they will become soggy.

Per Serving:

calories: 187 | fat: 14g | protein: 10g | carbs: 3g | net carbs: 3g | fiber: 0g

Pizza Bites

Prep time: 5 minutes | Cook time: 10 minutes | Makes 12 pizza bites

12 large pepperoni slices
2 tablespoons tomato paste
12 mini Mozzarella balls (approximately 8 ounces / 227 g)
12 fresh basil leaves (optional)

1. Preheat the oven to 400ºF (205ºC). 2. Line each of 12 cups of a mini muffin pan with one pepperoni slice. To make them sit better, use kitchen shears to make three or four small cuts toward the center of the slice, but do not cut too far in—leave the center intact. 3. Bake 5 minutes, remove from the oven, and allow to cool in the pan for 5 to 10 minutes, until somewhat crisp. Keep the oven turned on. 4. Spoon ½ teaspoon of tomato paste into each pepperoni cup and gently spread to coat the bottom. Place a Mozzarella ball and a basil leaf, if using, in each cup. Return muffin pan to the oven and cook another 3 to 5 minutes, until the cheese is melting. 5. Remove pan from the oven and allow the bites to cool for 5 to 10 minutes before serving.

Per Serving:

calories: 193 | fat: 15g | protein: 11g | carbs: 2g | net carbs: 2g | fiber: 0g

Cheese Stuffed Mushrooms

Prep time: 15 minutes | Cook time: 8 minutes | Serves 4

1 cup cremini mushroom caps
1 tablespoon chopped scallions
1 tablespoon chopped chives
1 teaspoon cream cheese
1 teaspoon sour cream
1 ounce (28 g) Monterey Jack cheese, shredded
1 teaspoon butter, softened
½ teaspoon smoked paprika
1 cup water, for cooking

1. Trim the mushroom caps if needed and wash them well. 2. After this, in the mixing bowl, mix up scallions, chives, cream cheese, sour cream, butter, and smoked paprika. 3. Then fill the mushroom caps with the cream cheese mixture and top with shredded Monterey Jack cheese. 4. Pour water and insert the trivet in the instant pot. 5. Arrange the stuffed mushrooms caps on the trivet and close the lid. 6. Cook the meal on Manual (High Pressure) for 8 minutes. 7. Then make a quick pressure release.

Per Serving:

calories: 45 | fat: 4g | protein: 3g | carbs: 1g | net carbs: 1g | fiber: 0g

English Cucumber Tea Sandwiches

Prep time: 10 minutes | Cook time: 0 minutes | Makes 12 snacks

1 large cucumber, peeled (approximately 10 ounces / 283 g)
4 ounces (113 g) cream cheese, softened
2 tablespoons finely chopped fresh dill
Freshly ground black pepper, to taste

1. Slice the cucumbers into 24 rounds approximately ¼ inch (6 mm) thick. Place in a single layer between two kitchen towels. Put a cutting board on top. Allow to sit about 5 minutes. 2. Mix the cream cheese and dill. 3. Spread 2 teaspoons cream cheese on half the cucumber slices. Grind black pepper over the cheese. Place another slice of cucumber on top of each and secure with a toothpick, if desired.

Per Serving:

calories: 96 | fat: 8g | protein: 3g | carbs: 3g | net carbs: 1g | fiber: 2g

Cauliflower Popcorn

Prep time: 5 minutes | Cook time: 40 minutes | Serves 2 to 3

Nonstick avocado oil cooking spray, for greasing
1 small to medium head cauliflower, florets with stems chopped into bite-size pieces
½ cup avocado oil
½ cup neutral-flavored grass-fed collagen protein powder (optional)
Popcorn seasonings of choice: salt, freshly ground black pepper, garlic powder, onion powder, dried oregano, dried sage, and/or nutritional yeast

1. Preheat the oven to 400°F (205°C). Coat a broiling pan with nonstick avocado oil spray. (If you have an air fryer, you can make your Cauliflower Popcorn in there instead; just coat the fryer basket with nonstick spray.) 2. Put the cauliflower in a mixing bowl. Pour the avocado oil over the top and sprinkle in the protein powder. Add the seasonings of your choice to the bowl. Stir all together to evenly coat the cauliflower. 3. Spread the cauliflower in an even layer on the prepared pan and place in the oven (or pour into your air fryer). Cook for roughly 40 minutes, checking periodically and stirring every 10 minutes or so (same goes for the air fryer, if using). 4. Remove from the oven (or air fryer) and serve.

Per Serving:
calories: 389 | fat: 37g | protein: 4g | carbs: 10g | net carbs: 5g | fiber: 5g

Low-Carb Granola Bars

Prep time: 10 minutes | Cook time: 15 to 20 minutes | Makes about 12 bars

1 cup almonds
1 cup hazelnuts
1 cup unsweetened coconut flakes
1 egg
¼ cup coconut oil, melted
¼ cup unsweetened peanut butter
½ cup dark chocolate chips
1 tablespoon vanilla extract
1 tablespoon ground cinnamon
Pinch salt

1. Preheat the oven to 350°F (180°C). 2. In a food processor, pulse together the almonds and macadamia nuts for 1 to 2 minutes until roughly chopped. (You want them pretty fine but not turning into nut butter.) Transfer them to a large bowl. 3. Stir in the coconut, egg, coconut oil, peanut butter, chocolate chips, vanilla, cinnamon, and salt. Transfer the mixture to an 8- or 9-inch square baking dish and gently press into an even layer. Bake for 15 to 20 minutes or until golden brown. Cool and cut into 12 bars. Refrigerate in an airtight container for up to 2 weeks.

Per Serving:
1 bar: calories: 588 | fat: 58g | protein: 11g | carbs: 6g | net carbs: 5g | fiber: 1g

Sautéed Asparagus with Lemon-Tahini Sauce

Prep time: 5 minutes | Cook time: 10 minutes | Serves 4

16 asparagus spears, woody ends snapped off
2 tablespoons avocado oil
Lemon-Tahini Sauce:
2 tablespoons tahini
1 tablespoon avocado oil
2½ teaspoons lemon juice
1 small clove garlic, minced
1/16 teaspoon finely ground sea salt
Pinch of ground black pepper
1 to 1½ tablespoons water

1. Place the asparagus and oil in a large frying pan over medium heat. Cook, tossing the spears in the oil every once in a while, until the spears begin to brown slightly, about 10 minutes. 2. Meanwhile, make the sauce: Place the tahini, oil, lemon juice, garlic, salt, pepper, and 1 tablespoon of water in a medium-sized bowl. Whisk until incorporated. If the dressing is too thick, add the additional ½ tablespoon of water and whisk again. 3. Place the cooked asparagus on a serving plate and drizzle with the lemon tahini sauce.

Per Serving:
calories: 106 | fat: 8g | protein: 4g | carbs: 6g | net carbs: 3g | fiber: 3g

Avocado Feta Dip

Prep time: 15 minutes | Cook time: 0 minutes | Serves 8

2 avocados, diced
2 Roma tomatoes, chopped
¼ medium red onion, finely chopped (about ½ cup)
2 garlic cloves, minced
2 tablespoons chopped fresh parsley (or cilantro)
2 tablespoons olive oil or avocado oil
2 tablespoons red wine vinegar
1 tablespoon freshly squeezed lemon or lime juice
½ teaspoon sea salt
¼ teaspoon freshly ground black pepper
8 ounces (227 g) feta cheese, crumbled

1. In a large bowl, gently stir together the avocados, tomatoes, onion, garlic, and parsley. 2. In a small bowl, whisk together the oil, vinegar, lemon juice, salt, and pepper. Pour the mixture over the avocado mixture. Fold in the cheese. 3. Cover and let chill in the refrigerator for 1 to 2 hours before serving.

Per Serving:
½ cup: calories: 190 | fat: 16g | protein: 6g | carbs: 6g | net carbs: 3g | fiber: 3g

Hot Chard Artichoke Dip

Prep time: 10 minutes | Cook time: 20 minutes | Serves 4

4 ounces cream cheese, at room temperature
½ cup coconut milk
½ cup grated Asiago cheese
½ cup shredded Cheddar cheese
1 teaspoon minced garlic
Dash hot sauce (optional)
2 cups chopped Swiss chard
½ cup roughly chopped artichoke hearts (packed in brine, not oil)

1. Preheat the oven. Set the oven temperature to 450°F. 2. Mix the ingredients. In a large bowl, stir together the cream cheese, coconut milk, Asiago, Cheddar, garlic, and hot sauce (if using), until everything is well mixed. Stir in the chard and the artichoke hearts and mix until they're well incorporated. Note: You've got to use artichokes packed in brine rather than oil because the extra oil will come out of the dip when you heat it, which will mess up the texture. 3. Bake. Spoon the mixture into a 1-quart baking dish, and bake it for 15 to 20 minutes until it's bubbly and lightly golden. 4. Serve. Cut up low-carb veggies to serve with this creamy, rich dip.

Per Serving:
calories: 280 | fat: 25g | protein: 11g | carbs: 5g | net carbs: 4g | fiber: 1g

Pancetta Pizza Dip

Prep time: 10 minutes | Cook time: 4 minutes | Serves 10

10 ounces (283 g) Pepper Jack cheese
10 ounces (283 g) cream cheese
10 ounces (283 g) pancetta, chopped
1 pound (454 g) tomatoes, puréed
1 cup green olives, pitted and halved
1 teaspoon dried oregano
½ teaspoon garlic powder
1 cup chicken broth
4 ounces (113 g) Mozzarella cheese, thinly sliced

1. Mix together the Pepper Jack cheese, cream cheese, pancetta, tomatoes, olives, oregano, and garlic powder in the Instant Pot. Pour in the chicken broth. 2. Lock the lid. Select the Manual mode and set the cooking time for 4 minutes at High Pressure. 3. When the timer beeps, perform a quick pressure release. Carefully remove the lid. 4. Scatter the Mozzarella cheese on top. Cover and allow to sit in the residual heat. Serve warm.

Per Serving:
calories: 287 | fat: 21g | protein: 21g | carbs: 3g | net carbs: 2g | fiber: 1g

Smoked Salmon Cream Cheese Rollups with Arugula and Truffle Oil Drizzle

Prep time: 10 minutes | Cook time: 0 minutes | Serves 4

½ cup cream cheese
¼ cup plain Greek-style yogurt
2 teaspoons chopped fresh dill
12 slices (½ pound) smoked salmon
¾ cup arugula
Truffle oil, for garnish

1. Mix the filling. In a small bowl, blend together the cream cheese, yogurt, and dill until the mixture is smooth. 2. Make the rollups. Spread the cream cheese mixture onto the smoked salmon slices, dividing it evenly. Place several arugula leaves at one end of each slice and roll them up. Secure them with a toothpick if they're starting to unroll. 3. Serve. Drizzle the rolls with truffle oil and place three rolls on each of four plates.

Per Serving:
calories: 234 | fat: 20g | protein: 13g | carbs: 2g | net carbs: 2g | fiber: 0g

Chocolate Soft-Serve Ice Cream

Prep time: 10 minutes | Cook time: 0 minutes | Serves 4

1 (13½ ounces/400 ml) can full-fat coconut milk
¼ cup (40 g) collagen peptides or protein powder (optional)
¼ cup (25 g) unflavored MCT oil powder (optional)
2 tablespoons smooth unsweetened almond butter
2 tablespoons cocoa powder
3 drops liquid stevia, or 1 tablespoon erythritol
1 teaspoon vanilla extract

1. Place all the ingredients in a blender or food processor. Blend until smooth and fully incorporated. 2. Divide the mixture among 4 freezer-safe serving bowls and place in the freezer for 30 minutes. At the 30 minutes mark, remove from the freezer and mash with a fork until the ice cream is smooth. If it's still too runny and doesn't develop the consistency of soft-serve as you mash it, freeze for another 15 minutes, then mash with a fork again. 3. Enjoy immediately.

Per Serving:
calories: 478 | fat: 47g | protein: 6g | carbs: 9g | net carbs: 4g | fiber: 5g

Chapter 7 Vegetarian Mains

Three-Cheese Zucchini Boats

Prep time: 15 minutes | Cook time: 20 minutes | Serves 2

2 medium zucchini
1 tablespoon avocado oil
¼ cup low-carb, no-sugar-added pasta sauce
¼ cup full-fat ricotta cheese
¼ cup shredded Mozzarella cheese
¼ teaspoon dried oregano
¼ teaspoon garlic powder
½ teaspoon dried parsley
2 tablespoons grated vegetarian Parmesan cheese

1. Cut off 1 inch from the top and bottom of each zucchini. Slice zucchini in half lengthwise and use a spoon to scoop out a bit of the inside, making room for filling. Brush with oil and spoon 2 tablespoons pasta sauce into each shell. 2. In a medium bowl, mix ricotta, Mozzarella, oregano, garlic powder, and parsley. Spoon the mixture into each zucchini shell. Place stuffed zucchini shells into the air fryer basket. 3. Adjust the temperature to 350°F (177°C) and air fry for 20 minutes. 4. To remove from the basket, use tongs or a spatula and carefully lift out. Top with Parmesan. Serve immediately.

Per Serving:
calories: 245 | fat: 18g | protein: 12g | carbs: 9g | net carbs: 7g | fiber: 2g

Crispy Eggplant Rounds

Prep time: 15 minutes | Cook time: 10 minutes | Serves 4

1 large eggplant, ends trimmed, cut into ½-inch slices
½ teaspoon salt
2 ounces (57 g) Parmesan 100% cheese crisps, finely ground
½ teaspoon paprika
¼ teaspoon garlic powder
1 large egg

1. Sprinkle eggplant rounds with salt. Place rounds on a kitchen towel for 30 minutes to draw out excess water. Pat rounds dry. 2. In a medium bowl, mix cheese crisps, paprika, and garlic powder. In a separate medium bowl, whisk egg. Dip each eggplant round in egg, then gently press into cheese crisps to coat both sides. 3. Place eggplant rounds into ungreased air fryer basket. Adjust the temperature to 400°F (204°C) and air fry for 10 minutes, turning rounds halfway through cooking. Eggplant will be golden and crispy when done. Serve warm.

Per Serving:
calories: 133 | fat: 8g | protein: 10g | carbs: 6g | net carbs: 4g | fiber: 3g

Crustless Spinach Cheese Pie

Prep time: 10 minutes | Cook time: 20 minutes | Serves 4

6 large eggs
¼ cup heavy whipping cream
1 cup frozen chopped spinach, drained
1 cup shredded sharp Cheddar cheese
¼ cup diced yellow onion

1. In a medium bowl, whisk eggs and add cream. Add remaining ingredients to bowl. 2. Pour into a round baking dish. Place into the air fryer basket. 3. Adjust the temperature to 320°F (160°C) and bake for 20 minutes. 4. Eggs will be firm and slightly browned when cooked. Serve immediately.

Per Serving:
calories: 317 | fat: 24g | protein: 21g | carbs: 4g | net carbs: 3g | fiber: 1g

Broccoli-Cheese Fritters

Prep time: 5 minutes | Cook time: 20 to 25 minutes | Serves 4

1 cup broccoli florets
1 cup shredded Mozzarella cheese
¾ cup almond flour
½ cup flaxseed meal, divided
2 teaspoons baking powder
1 teaspoon garlic powder
Salt and freshly ground black pepper, to taste
2 eggs, lightly beaten
½ cup ranch dressing

1. Preheat the air fryer to 400°F (204°C). 2. In a food processor fitted with a metal blade, pulse the broccoli until very finely chopped. 3. Transfer the broccoli to a large bowl and add the Mozzarella, almond flour, ¼ cup of the flaxseed meal, baking powder, and garlic powder. Stir until thoroughly combined. Season to taste with salt and black pepper. Add the eggs and stir again to form a sticky dough. Shape the dough into 1¼-inch fritters. 4. Place the remaining ¼ cup flaxseed meal in a shallow bowl and roll the fritters in the meal to form an even coating. 5. Working in batches if necessary, arrange the fritters in a single layer in the basket of the air fryer and spray generously with olive oil. Pausing halfway through the cooking time to shake the basket, air fry for 20 to 25 minutes until the fritters are golden brown and crispy. Serve with the ranch dressing for dipping.

Per Serving:
calories: 638 | fat: 54g | protein: 28g | carbs: 16g | net carbs: 9g | fiber: 7g

Cauliflower Steak with Gremolata

Prep time: 15 minutes | Cook time: 25 minutes | Serves 4

2 tablespoons olive oil
1 tablespoon Italian seasoning
1 large head cauliflower, outer leaves removed and sliced lengthwise through the core into thick "steaks"
Salt and freshly ground black pepper, to taste
¼ cup Parmesan cheese

Gremolata:
1 bunch Italian parsley (about 1 cup packed)
2 cloves garlic
Zest of 1 small lemon, plus 1 to 2 teaspoons lemon juice
½ cup olive oil
Salt and pepper, to taste

1. Preheat the air fryer to 400ºF (204ºC). 2. In a small bowl, combine the olive oil and Italian seasoning. Brush both sides of each cauliflower "steak" generously with the oil. Season to taste with salt and black pepper. 3. Working in batches if necessary, arrange the cauliflower in a single layer in the air fryer basket. Pausing halfway through the cooking time to turn the "steaks," air fry for 15 to 20 minutes until the cauliflower is tender and the edges begin to brown. Sprinkle with the Parmesan and air fry for 5 minutes longer. 4. To make the gremolata: In a food processor fitted with a metal blade, combine the parsley, garlic, and lemon zest and juice. With the motor running, add the olive oil in a steady stream until the mixture forms a bright green sauce. Season to taste with salt and black pepper. Serve the cauliflower steaks with the gremolata spooned over the top.

Per Serving:

calories: 257 | fat: 23g | protein: 6g | carbs: 9g | net carbs: 7g | fiber: 4g

Eggplant Parmesan

Prep time: 15 minutes | Cook time: 17 minutes | Serves 4

1 medium eggplant, ends trimmed, sliced into ½-inch rounds
¼ teaspoon salt
2 tablespoons coconut oil
½ cup grated Parmesan cheese

1 ounce (28 g) 100% cheese crisps, finely crushed
½ cup low-carb marinara sauce
½ cup shredded Mozzarella cheese

1. Sprinkle eggplant rounds with salt on both sides and wrap in a kitchen towel for 30 minutes. Press to remove excess water, then drizzle rounds with coconut oil on both sides. 2. In a medium bowl, mix Parmesan and cheese crisps. Press each eggplant slice into mixture to coat both sides. 3. Place rounds into ungreased air fryer basket. Adjust the temperature to 350ºF (177ºC) and air fry for 15 minutes, turning rounds halfway through cooking. They will be crispy around the edges when done. 4. Spoon marinara over rounds and sprinkle with Mozzarella. Continue cooking an additional 2 minutes at 350ºF (177ºC) until cheese is melted. Serve warm.

Per Serving:

calories: 330 | fat: 24g | protein: 18g | carbs: 13g | net carbs: 9g | fiber: 4g

Broccoli with Garlic Sauce

Prep time: 19 minutes | Cook time: 15 minutes | Serves 4

2 tablespoons olive oil
Kosher salt and freshly ground black pepper, to taste
1 pound (454 g) broccoli florets
Dipping Sauce:
2 teaspoons dried rosemary, crushed
3 garlic cloves, minced
⅓ teaspoon dried marjoram, crushed
¼ cup sour cream
⅓ cup mayonnaise

1. Lightly grease your broccoli with a thin layer of olive oil. Season with salt and ground black pepper. 2. Arrange the seasoned broccoli in the air fryer basket. Bake at 395ºF (202ºC) for 15 minutes, shaking once or twice. In the meantime, prepare the dipping sauce by mixing all the sauce ingredients. Serve warm broccoli with the dipping sauce and enjoy!

Per Serving:

calories: 250 | fat: 23g | protein: 3g | carbs: 10g | net carbs: 9g | fiber: 1g

Zucchini-Ricotta Tart

Prep time: 15 minutes | Cook time: 60 minutes | Serves 6

½ cup grated Parmesan cheese, divided
1½ cups almond flour
1 tablespoon coconut flour
½ teaspoon garlic powder
¾ teaspoon salt, divided
¼ cup unsalted butter, melted

1 zucchini, thinly sliced (about 2 cups)
1 cup ricotta cheese
3 eggs
2 tablespoons heavy cream
2 cloves garlic, minced
½ teaspoon dried tarragon

1. Preheat the air fryer to 330ºF (166ºC). Coat a round pan with olive oil and set aside. 2. In a large bowl, whisk ¼ cup of the Parmesan with the almond flour, coconut flour, garlic powder, and ¼ teaspoon of the salt. Stir in the melted butter until the dough resembles coarse crumbs. Press the dough firmly into the bottom and up the sides of the prepared pan. Air fry for 12 to 15 minutes until the crust begins to brown. Let cool to room temperature. 3. Meanwhile, place the zucchini in a colander and sprinkle with the remaining ½ teaspoon salt. Toss gently to distribute the salt and let sit for 30 minutes. Use paper towels to pat the zucchini dry. 4. In a large bowl, whisk together the ricotta, eggs, heavy cream, garlic, and tarragon. Gently stir in the zucchini slices. Pour the cheese mixture into the cooled crust and sprinkle with the remaining ¼ cup Parmesan. 5. Increase the air fryer to 350ºF (177ºC). Place the pan in the air fryer basket and air fry for 45 to 50 minutes, or until set and a tester inserted into the center of the tart comes out clean. Serve warm or at room temperature.

Per Serving:

calories: 530 | fat: 43g | protein: 24g | carbs: 11g | net carbs: 5g | fiber: 6g

Vegetable Burgers

Prep time: 10 minutes | Cook time: 12 minutes | Serves 4

8 ounces (227 g) cremini mushrooms
2 large egg yolks
½ medium zucchini, trimmed and chopped
¼ cup peeled and chopped yellow onion
1 clove garlic, peeled and finely minced
½ teaspoon salt
¼ teaspoon ground black pepper

1. Place all ingredients into a food processor and pulse twenty times until finely chopped and combined. 2. Separate mixture into four equal sections and press each into a burger shape. Place burgers into ungreased air fryer basket. Adjust the temperature to 375°F (191°C) and air fry for 12 minutes, turning burgers halfway through cooking. Burgers will be browned and firm when done. 3. Place burgers on a large plate and let cool 5 minutes before serving.

Per Serving:
calories: 63 | fat: 3g | protein: 4g | carbs: 6g | net carbs: 5g | fiber: 1g

Fettuccine Alfredo (2 Variations)

Prep time: 5 minutes | Cook time: 10 minutes | Serves 4 to 6

For Both Variations:
2 (7 ounces / 198 g) packages shirataki noodles or 5 cups spaghetti squash or hearts of palm noodles
1 tablespoon chopped fresh parsley, chives, or basil, for serving (optional)
For the Dairy Variation:
2 tablespoons grass-fed butter or ghee
2 teaspoons garlic powder or 2 small garlic cloves, minced
1½ cups grass-fed heavy (whipping) cream
1 cup grated Parmesan cheese
Salt and freshly ground black pepper, to taste
For the Vegan Variation:
2 tablespoons butter-flavored coconut oil
2 teaspoons garlic powder or 2 small garlic cloves, minced
1½ cups heavy coconut cream (shake the can well before measuring)
4 tablespoons nutritional yeast
Salt and freshly ground black pepper, to taste

1. If you're making the dairy version, melt the butter in a skillet over medium heat, add the garlic, and stir together. Add the cream and cheese, season with salt and pepper, and whisk everything together. Cook for about 10 minutes, or until the cheese is melted. 2. If you're making the vegan version, melt the coconut oil in a skillet over medium heat, add the garlic, and stir together. Add the coconut cream and nutritional yeast, season with salt and pepper, and whisk everything together. Cook for about 10 minutes. 3. Add the noodles to the skillet and cook, stirring, for 1 minute to coat in the sauce. 4. Dish up in bowls and sprinkle with chopped parsley, chives, or basil, if desired.

Per Serving:
calories: 510 | fat: 46g | protein: 12g | carbs: 12g | net carbs: 10g | fiber: 2g

Cauliflower Tikka Masala

Prep time: 10 minutes | Cook time: 20 minutes | Serves 4

For The Cauliflower
1 head cauliflower, cut into small florets
1 tablespoon coconut oil, melted
1 teaspoon ground cumin
½ teaspoon ground coriander
For The Sauce
2 tablespoons coconut oil
½ onion, chopped
1 tablespoon minced garlic
1 tablespoon grated ginger
2 tablespoons garam masala
1 tablespoon tomato paste
½ teaspoon salt
1 cup crushed tomatoes
1 cup heavy (whipping) cream
1 tablespoon chopped fresh cilantro

Make The Cauliflower: 1. Preheat the oven. Set the oven temperature to 425°F. Line a baking sheet with aluminum foil. 2. Prepare the cauliflower. In a large bowl, toss the cauliflower with the coconut oil, cumin, and coriander. Spread the cauliflower on the baking sheet in a single layer and bake it for 20 minutes, until the cauliflower is tender. Make The Sauce: 1. Sauté the vegetables. While the cauliflower is baking, in a large skillet over medium-high heat, warm the coconut oil. Add the onion, garlic, and ginger and sauté until they've softened, about 3 minutes. 2. Finish the sauce. Stir in the garam masala, tomato paste, and salt until the vegetables are coated. Stir in the crushed tomatoes and bring to a boil, then reduce the heat to low and simmer the sauce for 10 minutes, stirring it often. Remove the skillet from the heat and stir in the cream and cilantro. 3. Assemble and serve. Add the cauliflower to the sauce, stirring to combine everything. Divide the mixture between four bowls and serve it hot.

Per Serving:
calories: 372 | fat: 32g | protein: 8g | carbs: 17g | net carbs: 10g | fiber: 7g

Pesto Vegetable Skewers

Prep time: 30 minutes | Cook time: 8 minutes | Makes 8 skewers

1 medium zucchini, trimmed and cut into ½-inch slices
½ medium yellow onion, peeled and cut into 1-inch squares
1 medium red bell pepper, seeded and cut into 1-inch squares
16 whole cremini mushrooms
⅓ cup basil pesto
½ teaspoon salt
¼ teaspoon ground black pepper

1. Divide zucchini slices, onion, and bell pepper into eight even portions. Place on 6-inch skewers for a total of eight kebabs. Add 2 mushrooms to each skewer and brush kebabs generously with pesto. 2. Sprinkle each kebab with salt and black pepper on all sides, then place into ungreased air fryer basket. Adjust the temperature to 375°F (191°C) and air fry for 8 minutes, turning kebabs halfway through cooking. Vegetables will be browned at the edges and tender-crisp when done. Serve warm.

Per Serving:
calories: 50 | fat: 4g | protein: 2g | carbs: 4g | net carbs: 3g | fiber: 1g

Greek Vegetable Briam

Prep time: 10 minutes | Cook time: 30 minutes | Serves 4

⅓ cup good-quality olive oil, divided
1 onion, thinly sliced
1 tablespoon minced garlic
¾ small eggplant, diced
2 zucchini, diced
2 cups chopped cauliflower
1 red bell pepper, diced
2 cups diced tomatoes
2 tablespoons chopped fresh parsley
2 tablespoons chopped fresh oregano
Sea salt, for seasoning
Freshly ground black pepper, for seasoning
1½ cups crumbled feta cheese
¼ cup pumpkin seeds

1. Preheat the oven. Set the oven to broil and lightly grease a 9-by-13-inch casserole dish with olive oil. 2. Sauté the aromatics. In a medium stockpot over medium heat, warm 3 tablespoons of the olive oil. Add the onion and garlic and sauté until they've softened, about 3 minutes. 3. Sauté the vegetables. Stir in the eggplant and cook for 5 minutes, stirring occasionally. Add the zucchini, cauliflower, and red bell pepper and cook for 5 minutes. Stir in the tomatoes, parsley, and oregano and cook, giving it a stir from time to time, until the vegetables are tender, about 10 minutes. Season it with salt and pepper. 4. Broil. Transfer the vegetable mixture to the casserole dish and top with the crumbled feta. Broil for about 4 minutes until the cheese is golden. 5. Serve. Divide the casserole between four plates and top it with the pumpkin seeds. Drizzle with the remaining olive oil.

Per Serving:
calories: 356 | fat: 28g | protein: 11g | carbs: 18g | net carbs: 11g | fiber: 7g

Buffalo Cauliflower Bites with Blue Cheese

Prep time: 10 minutes | Cook time: 8 to 10 minutes | Serves 4

1 large head cauliflower, chopped into florets
1 tablespoon olive oil
Salt and freshly ground black pepper, to taste
¼ cup unsalted butter, melted
¼ cup hot sauce
Garlic Blue Cheese Dip:
½ cup mayonnaise
¼ cup sour cream
2 tablespoons heavy cream
1 tablespoon fresh lemon juice
1 clove garlic, minced
¼ cup crumbled blue cheese
Salt and freshly ground black pepper, to taste

1. Preheat the air fryer to 400°F (204°C). 2. In a large bowl, combine the cauliflower and olive oil. Season to taste with salt and black pepper. Toss until the vegetables are thoroughly coated. 3. Working in batches, place half of the cauliflower in the air fryer basket. Pausing halfway through the cooking time to shake the basket, air fry for 8 to 10 minutes until the cauliflower is evenly browned. Transfer to a large bowl and repeat with the remaining cauliflower. 4. In a small bowl, whisk together the melted butter and hot sauce. 5. To make the dip: In a small bowl, combine the mayonnaise, sour cream, heavy cream, lemon juice, garlic, and blue cheese. Season to taste with salt and freshly ground black pepper. 6. Just before serving, pour the butter mixture over the cauliflower and toss gently until thoroughly coated. Serve with the dip on the side.

Per Serving:
calories: 420 | fat: 39g | protein: 9g | carbs: 14g | net carbs: 11g | fiber: 3g

Cheesy Broccoli Casserole

Prep time: 10 minutes | Cook time: 35 minutes | Serves 4

2 tablespoons butter
¼ white onion, diced
1 garlic clove, minced
1 pound (454 g) broccoli florets, roughly chopped
Salt, to taste
Freshly ground black pepper, to taste
4 ounces (113 g) cream cheese, at room temperature
1 cup shredded Cheddar cheese, divided
½ cup heavy (whipping) cream
2 eggs

1. Preheat the oven to 350°F (180°C). 2. In a large skillet over medium heat, melt the butter. 3. Add the onion and garlic. Sauté for 5 to 7 minutes until the onion is softened and translucent. 4. Add the broccoli. Season with salt and pepper. Cook for 4 to 5 minutes until just softened. Transfer to a 7-by-11-inch baking dish. 5. In a medium bowl, stir together the cream cheese, ½ cup of Cheddar, the cream, and eggs. Pour over the broccoli. Season with more salt and pepper, and top with the remaining ½ cup of Cheddar. Bake for 20 minutes. Refrigerate leftovers in an airtight container for up to 1 week.

Per Serving:
calories: 440 | fat: 39g | protein: 16g | carbs: 11g | net carbs: 8g | fiber: 3g

Sweet Pepper Nachos

Prep time: 10 minutes | Cook time: 5 minutes | Serves 2

6 mini sweet peppers, seeded and sliced in half
¾ cup shredded Colby jack cheese
¼ cup sliced pickled jalapeños
½ medium avocado, peeled, pitted, and diced
2 tablespoons sour cream

1. Place peppers into an ungreased round nonstick baking dish. Sprinkle with Colby and top with jalapeños. 2. Place dish into air fryer basket. Adjust the temperature to 350°F (177°C) and bake for 5 minutes. Cheese will be melted and bubbly when done. 3. Remove dish from air fryer and top with avocado. Drizzle with sour cream. Serve warm.

Per Serving:
calories: 255 | fat: 21g | protein: 11g | carbs: 9g | net carbs: 5g | fiber: 4g

Green Vegetable Stir-Fry with Tofu

Prep time: 15 minutes | Cook time: 15 minutes | Serves 2

3 tablespoons avocado oil, divided
1 cup Brussels sprouts, halved
½ onion, diced
½ leek, white and light green parts diced
½ head green cabbage, diced
¼ cup water, plus more if needed
½ cup kale, coarsely chopped
1 cup spinach, coarsely chopped
8 ounces (227 g) tofu, diced
2 teaspoons garlic powder
Salt and freshly ground black pepper, to taste
½ avocado, pitted, peeled, and diced
MCT oil (optional)

1. In a large skillet with a lid (or a wok if you have one), heat 2 tablespoons of avocado oil over medium-high heat. Add the Brussels sprouts, onion, leek, and cabbage and stir together. Add the water, cover, lower the heat to medium, and cook for about 5 minutes. 2. Toss in the kale and spinach and cook for 3 minutes, stirring constantly, until the onion, leek, and cabbage are caramelized. 3. Add the tofu to the stir-fry, then season with the garlic, salt, pepper, and the remaining tablespoon of avocado oil. 4. Turn the heat back up to medium-high and cook for about 10 minutes, stirring constantly, until the tofu is nice and caramelized on all sides. If you experience any burning, turn down the heat and add 2 to 3 tablespoons of water. 5. Divide the stir-fry between two plates and sprinkle with diced avocado. Feel free to drizzle algae oil or MCT oil over the top for a little extra fat.

Per Serving:
calories: 473 | fat: 33g | protein: 17g | carbs: 27g | net carbs: 15g | fiber: 12g

Herbed Ricotta–Stuffed Mushrooms

Prep time: 10 minutes | Cook time: 30 minutes | Serves 4

6 tablespoons extra-virgin olive oil, divided
4 portobello mushroom caps, cleaned and gills removed
1 cup whole-milk ricotta cheese
⅓ cup chopped fresh herbs
(such as basil, parsley, rosemary, oregano, or thyme)
2 garlic cloves, finely minced
½ teaspoon salt
¼ teaspoon freshly ground black pepper

1. Preheat the oven to 400°F (205°C). 2. Line a baking sheet with parchment or foil and drizzle with 2 tablespoons olive oil, spreading evenly. Place the mushroom caps on the baking sheet, gill-side up. 3. In a medium bowl, mix together the ricotta, herbs, 2 tablespoons olive oil, garlic, salt, and pepper. Stuff each mushroom cap with one-quarter of the cheese mixture, pressing down if needed. Drizzle with remaining 2 tablespoons olive oil and bake until golden brown and the mushrooms are soft, 30 to 35 minutes, depending on the size of the mushrooms.

Per Serving:
calories: 400 | fat: 36g | protein: 12g | carbs: 7g | net carbs: 6g | fiber: 1g

Stuffed Eggplant

Prep time: 20 minutes | Cook time: 1 hour | Serves 2 to 4

1 small eggplant, halved lengthwise
3 tablespoons olive, avocado, or macadamia nut oil
1 onion, diced
12 asparagus spears or green beans, diced
1 red bell pepper, diced
1 large tomato, chopped
2 garlic cloves, minced
½ block (8 ounces / 227 g) extra-firm tofu (optional)
3 tablespoons chopped fresh basil leaves
Salt and freshly ground black pepper, to taste
¼ cup water
2 eggs
Chopped fresh parsley, for garnish (optional)
Shredded cheese, for garnish (optional)

1. Preheat the oven to 350°F (180°C). 2. Scoop out the flesh from the halved eggplant and chop it into cubes. Reserve the eggplant skin. 3. In a sauté pan with a lid, heat the oil over medium-high heat. Add the eggplant, onion, asparagus, bell pepper, tomato, garlic, and tofu (if using) and stir. Stir in the basil, season with salt and pepper, and cook for about 5 minutes. 4. Add the water, cover the pan, reduce the heat to medium, and cook for about 15 minutes longer. 5. Put the eggplant "boats" (the reserved skin) on a baking sheet. Scoop some of the cooked eggplant mixture into each boat (you may have some filling left over, which is fine—you can roast it alongside the eggplant). 6. Crack an egg into each eggplant boat, on top of the filling, then bake for about 40 minutes, or until desired doneness. 7. Remove the eggplant from the oven and, if desired, sprinkle parsley and cheese over the top. Let the cheese melt and cool for about 5 minutes, then serve them up!

Per Serving:
calories: 380 | fat: 26g | protein: 12g | carbs: 25g | net carbs: 15g | fiber: 10g

Mediterranean Pan Pizza

Prep time: 5 minutes | Cook time: 8 minutes | Serves 2

1 cup shredded Mozzarella cheese
¼ medium red bell pepper, seeded and chopped
½ cup chopped fresh spinach leaves
2 tablespoons chopped black olives
2 tablespoons crumbled feta cheese

1. Sprinkle Mozzarella into an ungreased round nonstick baking dish in an even layer. Add remaining ingredients on top. 2. Place dish into air fryer basket. Adjust the temperature to 350°F (177°C) and bake for 8 minutes, checking halfway through to avoid burning. Top of pizza will be golden brown and the cheese melted when done. 3. Remove dish from fryer and let cool 5 minutes before slicing and serving.

Per Serving:
calories: 239 | fat: 17g | protein: 17g | carbs: 6g | net carbs: 5g | fiber: 1g

Vegetarian Chili with Avocado and Sour Cream

Prep time: 10 minutes | Cook time: 25 minutes | Serves 8

2 tablespoons good-quality olive oil
½ onion, finely chopped
1 red bell pepper, diced
2 jalapeño peppers, chopped
1 tablespoon minced garlic
2 tablespoons chili powder
1 teaspoon ground cumin
4 cups canned diced tomatoes
2 cups pecans, chopped
1 cup sour cream
1 avocado, diced
2 tablespoons chopped fresh cilantro

1. Sauté the vegetables. In a large pot over medium-high heat, warm the olive oil. Add the onion, red bell pepper, jalapeño peppers, and garlic and sauté until they've softened, about 4 minutes. Stir in the chili powder and cumin, stirring to coat the vegetables with the spices. 2. Cook the chili. Stir in the tomatoes and pecans and bring the chili to a boil, then reduce the heat to low and simmer until the vegetables are soft and the flavors mellow, about 20 minutes. 3. Serve. Ladle the chili into bowls and serve it with the sour cream, avocado, and cilantro.

Per Serving:

calories: 332 | fat: 32g | protein: 5g | carbs: 11g | net carbs: 5g | fiber: 6g

Zucchini Lasagna

Prep time: 15 minutes | Cook time: 1 hour | Serves 8

½ cup extra-virgin olive oil, divided
4 to 5 medium zucchini squash
1 teaspoon salt
8 ounces (227 g) frozen spinach, thawed and well drained (about 1 cup)
2 cups whole-milk ricotta cheese
¼ cup chopped fresh basil or 2 teaspoons dried basil
1 teaspoon garlic powder
½ teaspoon freshly ground black pepper
2 cups shredded fresh whole-milk mozzarella cheese
1¾ cups shredded Parmesan cheese
½ (24 ounces / 680 g) jar low-sugar marinara sauce (less than 5 grams sugar)

1. Preheat the oven to 425°F (220°C). 2. Line two baking sheets with parchment paper or aluminum foil and drizzle each with 2 tablespoons olive oil, spreading evenly. 3. Slice the zucchini lengthwise into ¼-inch-thick long slices and place on the prepared baking sheet in a single layer. Sprinkle with ½ teaspoon salt per sheet. Bake until softened, but not mushy, 15 to 18 minutes. Remove from the oven and allow to cool slightly before assembling the lasagna. 4. Reduce the oven temperature to 375°F (190°C). 5. While the zucchini cooks, prep the filling. In a large bowl, combine the spinach, ricotta, basil, garlic powder, and pepper. In a small bowl, mix together the mozzarella and Parmesan cheeses. In a medium bowl, combine the marinara sauce and remaining ¼ cup olive oil and stir to fully incorporate the oil into sauce. 6. To assemble the lasagna, spoon a third of the marinara sauce mixture into the bottom of a 9-by-13-inch glass baking dish and spread evenly. Place 1 layer of softened zucchini slices to fully cover the sauce, then add a third of the ricotta-spinach mixture and spread evenly on top of the zucchini. Sprinkle a third of the mozzarella-Parmesan mixture on top of the ricotta. Repeat with 2 more cycles of these layers: marinara, zucchini, ricotta-spinach, then cheese blend. 7. Bake until the cheese is bubbly and melted, 30 to 35 minutes. Turn the broiler to low and broil until the top is golden brown, about 5 minutes. Remove from the oven and allow to cool slightly before slicing.

Per Serving:

calories: 520 | fat: 43g | protein: 26g | carbs: 10g | net carbs: 7g | fiber: 3g

Eggplant and Zucchini Bites

Prep time: 30 minutes | Cook time: 30 minutes | Serves 8

2 teaspoons fresh mint leaves, chopped
1½ teaspoons red pepper chili flakes
2 tablespoons melted butter
1 pound (454 g) eggplant, peeled and cubed
1 pound (454 g) zucchini, peeled and cubed
3 tablespoons olive oil

1. Toss all the above ingredients in a large-sized mixing dish. 2. Roast the eggplant and zucchini bites for 30 minutes at 325°F (163°C) in your air fryer, turning once or twice. 3. Serve with a homemade dipping sauce.

Per Serving:

calories: 140 | fat: 12g | protein: 2g | carbs: 8g | net carbs: 6g | fiber: 2g

Parmesan Artichokes

Prep time: 10 minutes | Cook time: 10 minutes | Serves 4

2 medium artichokes, trimmed and quartered, center removed
2 tablespoons coconut oil
1 large egg, beaten
½ cup grated vegetarian Parmesan cheese
¼ cup blanched finely ground almond flour
½ teaspoon crushed red pepper flakes

1. In a large bowl, toss artichokes in coconut oil and then dip each piece into the egg. 2. Mix the Parmesan and almond flour in a large bowl. Add artichoke pieces and toss to cover as completely as possible, sprinkle with pepper flakes. Place into the air fryer basket. 3. Adjust the temperature to 400°F (204°C) and air fry for 10 minutes. 4. Toss the basket two times during cooking. Serve warm.

Per Serving:

calories: 220 | fat: 18g | protein: 10g | carbs: 9g | net carbs: 4g | fiber: 5g

Cheesy Garden Veggie Crustless Quiche

Prep time: 5 minutes | Cook time: 25 minutes | Serves 4

1 tablespoon grass-fed butter, divided
6 eggs
¾ cup heavy (whipping) cream
3 ounces goat cheese, divided
½ cup sliced mushrooms, chopped
1 scallion, white and green parts, chopped
1 cup shredded fresh spinach
10 cherry tomatoes, cut in half

1. Preheat the oven. Set the oven temperature to 350°F. Grease a 9-inch pie plate with ½ teaspoon of the butter and set it aside. 2. Mix the quiche base. In a medium bowl, whisk the eggs, cream, and 2 ounces of the cheese until it's all well blended. Set it aside. 3. Sauté the vegetables. In a small skillet over medium-high heat, melt the remaining butter. Add the mushrooms and scallion and sauté them until they've softened, about 2 minutes. Add the spinach and sauté until it's wilted, about 2 minutes. 4. Assemble and bake. Spread the vegetable mixture in the bottom of the pie plate and pour the egg-and-cream mixture over the vegetables. Scatter the cherry tomatoes and the remaining 1 ounce of goat cheese on top. Bake for 20 to 25 minutes until the quiche is cooked through, puffed, and lightly browned. 5. Serve. Cut the quiche into wedges and divide it between four plates. Serve it warm or cold.

Per Serving:
calories: 355 | fat: 30g | protein: 18g | carbs: 5g | net carbs: 4g | fiber: 1g

Zucchini Roll Manicotti

Prep time: 15 minutes | Cook time: 30 minutes | Serves 4

Olive oil cooking spray
4 zucchini
2 tablespoons good-quality olive oil
1 red bell pepper, diced
½ onion, minced
2 teaspoons minced garlic
1 cup goat cheese
1 cup shredded mozzarella cheese
1 tablespoon chopped fresh oregano
Sea salt, for seasoning
Freshly ground black pepper, for seasoning
2 cups low-carb marinara sauce, divided
½ cup grated Parmesan cheese

1. Preheat the oven. Set the oven temperature to 375°F. Lightly grease a 9-by-13-inch baking dish with olive oil cooking spray. 2. Prepare the zucchini. Cut the zucchini lengthwise into ⅛-inch-thick slices and set them aside. 3. Make the filling. In a medium skillet over medium-high heat, warm the olive oil. Add the red bell pepper, onion, and garlic and sauté until they've softened, about 4 minutes. Remove the skillet from the heat and transfer the vegetables to a medium bowl. Stir the goat cheese, mozzarella, and oregano into the vegetables. Season it all with salt and pepper. 4. Assemble the manicotti. Spread 1 cup of the marinara sauce in the bottom of the baking dish. Lay a zucchini slice on a clean cutting board and place a couple tablespoons of filling at one end. Roll the slice up and place it in the baking dish, seam-side down. Repeat with the remaining zucchini slices. Spoon the remaining sauce over the rolls and top with the Parmesan. 5. Bake. Bake the rolls for 30 to 35 minutes until the zucchini is tender and the cheese is golden. 6. Serve. Spoon the rolls onto four plates and serve them hot.

Per Serving:
calories: 342 | fat: 24g | protein: 20g | carbs: 14g | net carbs: 11g | fiber: 3g

Mediterranean Filling Stuffed Portobello Mushrooms

Prep time: 10 minutes | Cook time: 35 minutes | Serves 4

4 large portobello mushroom caps
3 tablespoons good-quality olive oil, divided
1 cup chopped fresh spinach
1 red bell pepper, chopped
1 celery stalk, chopped
½ cup chopped sun-dried tomato
¼ onion, chopped
2 teaspoons minced garlic
1 teaspoon chopped fresh oregano
2 cups chopped pecans
¼ cup balsamic vinaigrette
Sea salt, for seasoning
Freshly ground black pepper, for seasoning

1. Preheat the oven. Set the oven temperature to 350°F. Line a baking sheet with parchment paper. 2. Prepare the mushrooms. Use a spoon to scoop the black gills out of the mushrooms. Massage 2 tablespoons of the olive oil all over the mushroom caps and place the mushrooms on the prepared baking sheet. Set them aside. 3. Prepare the filling. In a large skillet over medium-high heat, warm the remaining 1 tablespoon of olive oil. Add the spinach, red bell pepper, celery, sun-dried tomato, onion, garlic, and oregano and sauté until the vegetables are tender, about 10 minutes. Stir in the pecans and balsamic vinaigrette and season the mixture with salt and pepper. 4. Assemble and bake. Stuff the mushroom caps with the filling and bake for 20 to 25 minutes until they're tender and golden. 5. Serve. Place one stuffed mushroom on each of four plates and serve them hot.

Per Serving:
calories: 595 | fat: 56g | protein: 10g | carbs: 18g | net carbs: 9g | fiber: 9g

Greek Stuffed Eggplant

Prep time: 15 minutes | Cook time: 20 minutes | Serves 2

1 large eggplant
2 tablespoons unsalted butter
¼ medium yellow onion, diced
¼ cup chopped artichoke hearts
1 cup fresh spinach
2 tablespoons diced red bell pepper
½ cup crumbled feta

1. Slice eggplant in half lengthwise and scoop out flesh, leaving enough inside for shell to remain intact. Take eggplant that was scooped out, chop it, and set aside. 2. In a medium skillet over medium heat, add butter and onion. Sauté until onions begin to soften, about 3 to 5 minutes. Add chopped eggplant, artichokes, spinach, and bell pepper. Continue cooking 5 minutes until peppers soften and spinach wilts. Remove from the heat and gently fold in the feta. 3. Place filling into each eggplant shell and place into the air fryer basket. 4. Adjust the temperature to 320°F (160°C) and air fry for 20 minutes. 5. Eggplant will be tender when done. Serve warm.

Per Serving:
calories: 275 | fat: 20g | protein: 9g | carbs: 17g | net carbs: 13g | fiber: 4g

Chapter 8 Stews and Soups

Beef and Cauliflower Soup

Prep time: 10 minutes | Cook time: 14 minutes | Serves 4

1 cup ground beef
½ cup cauliflower, shredded
1 teaspoon unsweetened tomato purée
¼ cup coconut milk
1 teaspoon minced garlic
1 teaspoon dried oregano
½ teaspoon salt
4 cups water

1. Put all ingredients in the Instant Pot and stir well. 2. Close the lid. Select Manual mode and set cooking time for 14 minutes on High Pressure. 3. When timer beeps, make a quick pressure release and open the lid. 4. Blend with an immersion blender until smooth. 5. Serve warm.

Per Serving:
calories: 106 | fat: 8g | protein: 7g | carbs: 2g | net carbs: 1g | fiber: 1g

Chicken Enchilada Soup

Prep time: 10 minutes | Cook time: 40 minutes | Serves 6

2 (6-ounce / 170-g) boneless, skinless chicken breasts
½ tablespoon chili powder
½ teaspoon salt
½ teaspoon garlic powder
¼ teaspoon pepper
½ cup red enchilada sauce
½ medium onion, diced
1 (4-ounce / 113-g) can green chilies
2 cups chicken broth
⅛ cup pickled jalapeños
4 ounces (113 g) cream cheese
1 cup uncooked cauliflower rice
1 avocado, diced
1 cup shredded mild Cheddar cheese
½ cup sour cream

1. Sprinkle seasoning over chicken breasts and set aside. Pour enchilada sauce into Instant Pot and place chicken on top. 2. Add onion, chilies, broth, and jalapeños to the pot, then place cream cheese on top of chicken breasts. Click lid closed. Adjust time for 25 minutes. When timer beeps, quick-release the pressure and shred chicken with forks. 3. Mix soup together and add cauliflower rice, with pot on Keep Warm setting. Replace lid and let pot sit for 15 minutes, still on Keep Warm. This will cook cauliflower rice. Serve with avocado, Cheddar, and sour cream.

Per Serving:
calories: 318 | fat: 19g | protein: 21g | carbs: 10g | net carbs: 7g | fiber: 3g

Coconut Curry Broccoli Soup

Prep time: 10 minutes | Cook time: 20 minutes | Serves 4

4 tablespoons butter
1 celery stalk, diced
1 carrot, diced
½ onion, diced
1 garlic clove, minced
2 tablespoons curry powder
1 teaspoon red pepper flakes
3 cups chicken broth
2 cups broccoli florets
1 cup canned coconut cream
Salt and freshly ground black pepper, to taste

1. In a large saucepan over medium heat, melt the butter. 2. Add the celery, carrot, onion, garlic, curry powder, and red pepper flakes. Stir to combine. Sauté for 5 to 7 minutes until the vegetables soften. 3. Stir in the chicken broth and bring to a simmer. 4. Add the broccoli and simmer for 5 to 7 minutes. 5. Stir in the coconut cream and simmer for 5 to 10 minutes more until the broccoli is cooked. Season well with salt and pepper and serve hot. Refrigerate leftovers in an airtight container for up to 1 week.

Per Serving:
calories: 274 | fat: 25g | protein: 7g | carbs: 11g | net carbs: 8g | fiber: 3g

Garlicky Chicken Soup

Prep time: 5 minutes | Cook time: 20 minutes | Serves 6

10 roasted garlic cloves
½ medium onion, diced
4 tablespoons butter
4 cups chicken broth
½ teaspoon salt
¼ teaspoon pepper
1 teaspoon thyme
1 pound (454 g) boneless, skinless chicken thighs, cubed
½ cup heavy cream
2 ounces (57 g) cream cheese

1. In small bowl, mash roasted garlic into paste. Press the Sauté button and add garlic, onion, and butter to Instant Pot. Sauté for 2 to 3 minutes until onion begins to soften. Press the Cancel button. 2. Add Chicken Broth, salt, pepper, thyme, and chicken to Instant Pot. Click lid closed. Press the Manual button and adjust time for 20 minutes. 3. When timer beeps, quick-release the pressure. Stir in heavy cream and cream cheese until smooth. Serve warm.

Per Serving:
calories: 291 | fat: 21g | protein: 17g | carbs: 4g | net carbs: 3g | fiber: 1g

Slow Cooker Beer Soup with Cheddar & Sausage

Prep time: 15 minutes | Cook time: 8 hours | Serves 8

1 cup heavy cream
10 ounces sausages, sliced
1 cup celery, chopped
1 cup carrots, chopped
4 garlic cloves, minced
8 ounces cream cheese
1 teaspoon red pepper flakes
6 ounces beer
16 ounces beef stock
1 onion, diced
1 cup cheddar cheese, grated
Salt and black pepper, to taste
Fresh cilantro, chopped, to garnish

1. Turn on the slow cooker. Add beef stock, beer, sausages, carrots, onion, garlic, celery, salt, red pepper flakes, and black pepper, and stir to combine. Pour in enough water to cover all the ingredients by roughly 2 inches. Close the lid and cook for 6 hours on Low. 2. Open the lid and stir in the heavy cream, cheddar, and cream cheese, and cook for 2 more hours. Ladle the soup into bowls and garnish with cilantro before serving. Yummy!

Per Serving:

calories: 387| fat: 28g | protein: 24g | carbs: 12g | net carbs: 9g | fiber: 2g

Cioppino Seafood Soup

Prep time: 10 minutes | Cook time: 30 minutes | Serves 6

2 tablespoons olive oil
½ onion, chopped
2 celery stalks, sliced
1 red bell pepper, chopped
1 tablespoon minced garlic
2 cups fish stock
1 (15-ounce) can coconut milk
1 cup crushed tomatoes
2 tablespoons tomato paste
1 tablespoon chopped fresh basil
2 teaspoons chopped fresh oregano
½ teaspoon sea salt
½ teaspoon freshly ground black pepper
¼ teaspoon red pepper flakes
10 ounces salmon, cut into 1-inch pieces
½ pound shrimp, peeled and deveined
12 clams or mussels, cleaned and debearded but in the shell

1. Sauté the vegetables. In a large stockpot over medium-high heat, warm the olive oil. Add the onion, celery, red bell pepper, and garlic and sauté until they've softened, about 4 minutes. 2. Make the soup base. Stir in the fish stock, coconut milk, crushed tomatoes, tomato paste, basil, oregano, salt, pepper, and red pepper flakes. Bring the soup to a boil, then reduce the heat to low and simmer the soup for 10 minutes. 3. Add the seafood. Stir in the salmon and simmer until it goes opaque, about 5 minutes. Add the shrimp and simmer until they're almost cooked through, about 3 minutes. Add the mussels and let them simmer until they open, about 3 minutes. Throw out any mussels that don't open. 4. Serve. Ladle the soup into bowls and serve it hot.

Per Serving:

calories: 377 | fat: 29g | protein: 24g | carbs: 9g | net carbs: 7g | fiber: 2g

Broccoli Ginger Soup

Prep time: 5 minutes | Cook time: 25 minutes | Serves 4

3 tablespoons coconut oil or avocado oil
1 small white onion, sliced
2 cloves garlic, minced
5 cups (420 g) broccoli florets
1 (13½ ounces/400 ml) can full-fat coconut milk
1½ cups (355 ml) chicken bone broth
1 (2-in/5 cm) piece fresh ginger root, peeled and minced
1½ teaspoons turmeric powder
¾ teaspoon finely ground sea salt
⅓ cup (55 g) collagen peptides (optional)
¼ cup (40 g) sesame seeds

1. Melt the oil in a large frying pan over medium heat. Add the onion and garlic and cook until translucent, about 10 minutes. 2. Add the broccoli, coconut milk, broth, ginger, turmeric, and salt. Cover and cook for 15 minutes, or until the broccoli is tender. 3. Transfer the broccoli mixture to a blender or food processor. Add the collagen, if using, and blend until smooth. 4. Divide among 4 bowls, top each bowl with 1 tablespoon of sesame seeds, and enjoy!

Per Serving:

calories: 344 | fat: 26g | protein: 13g | carbs: 12g | net carbs: 7g | fiber: 5g

Tuscan Kale Soup

Prep time: 10 minutes | Cook time: 25 minutes | serves 8

¼ cup cold-pressed olive oil
½ cup finely diced yellow onion
2 garlic cloves, chopped
2 tablespoons dried oregano
8 cups vegetable broth
¼ cup hemp hearts
3 cups lacinato kale, stems removed, and leaves cut into thin ribbons
1 cup chopped fresh parsley, plus a few sprigs for garnish
½ cup diced rutabaga
⅓ cup diced sun-dried tomatoes
⅓ cup diced carrot
Juice of 1 lemon
Sea salt

1. In a large stockpot over medium heat, heat the olive oil. 2. Add the onion, garlic, and oregano and cook, stirring frequently to prevent sticking, until the onion is tender and the garlic is fragrant, about 5 minutes. 3. Pour the broth into the pot and turn the heat to low. 4. After the broth has been simmering for about 5 minutes, toss in the hemp hearts and simmer for another 15 minutes. 5. Add the kale, parsley, rutabaga, sun-dried tomatoes, and carrot and simmer for another 5 minutes until the carrots are tender. 6. Remove the pot from the heat and squeeze in the lemon juice, then throw in the entire lemon peel to allow the oils from the skin to get into the broth. Season with salt. 7. Garnish the soup with parsley sprigs and serve hot.

Per Serving:

calories: 130 | fat: 9g | protein: 3g | carbs: 9g | net carbs: 5g | fiber: 4g

Beef and Mushroom Stew

Prep time: 15 minutes | Cook time: 30 minutes | Serves 4

- 2 tablespoons coconut oil
- 1 pound (454 g) cubed chuck roast
- 1 cup sliced button mushrooms
- ½ medium onion, chopped
- 2 cups beef broth
- ½ cup chopped celery
- 1 tablespoon sugar-free tomato paste
- 1 teaspoon thyme
- 2 garlic cloves, minced
- ½ teaspoon xanthan gum

1. Press the Sauté button and add coconut oil to Instant Pot. Brown cubes of chuck roast until golden, working in batches if necessary. (If the pan is overcrowded, they will not brown properly.) Set aside after browning is completed. 2. Add mushrooms and onions to pot. Sauté until mushrooms begin to brown and onions are translucent. Press the Cancel button. 3. Add broth to Instant Pot. Use wooden spoon to scrape bits from bottom if necessary. Add celery, tomato paste, thyme, and garlic. Click lid closed. Press the Manual button and adjust time for 35 minutes. When timer beeps, allow a natural release. 4. When pressure valve drops, stir in xanthan gum and allow to thicken. Serve warm.

Per Serving:

calories: 354 | fat: 25g | protein: 24g | carbs: 4g | net carbs: 2g | fiber: 2g

Chilled Cilantro and Avocado Soup

Prep time: 10 minutes | Cook time: 7 minutes | Serves 6

- 2 to 3 tablespoons olive oil
- 1 large white onion, diced
- 3 garlic cloves, crushed
- 1 serrano chile, seeded and diced
- Salt and freshly ground black pepper, to taste
- 4 or 5 ripe avocados, peeled, halved, and pitted
- 4 cups chicken broth, or vegetable broth
- 2 cups water
- Juice of 1 lemon
- ¼ cup chopped fresh cilantro, plus more for garnish
- ½ cup sour cream

1. In a large pan over medium heat, heat the olive oil. 2. Add the onion and garlic. Sauté for 5 to 7 minutes until the onion is softened and translucent. 3. Add the serrano, season with salt and pepper, and remove from the heat. 4. In a blender, combine the avocados, chicken broth, water, lemon juice, cilantro, and onion-garlic-chile mixture. Purée until smooth (you may have to do this in batches), strain through a fine-mesh sieve, and season with more salt and pepper. Refrigerate, covered, for about 3 hours or until chilled through. 5. To serve, top with sour cream and a sprinkle of chopped cilantro. Refrigerate leftovers in an airtight container for up to 1 week.

Per Serving:

calories: 513 | fat: 45g | protein: 7g | carbs: 20g | net carbs: 8g | fiber: 12g

Broc Obama Cheese Soup

Prep time: 25 minutes | Cook time: 25 minutes | Serves 8

- 8 cups chicken broth
- 2 large heads broccoli, chopped into bite-sized florets
- 1 clove garlic, peeled and minced
- ¼ cup heavy whipping cream
- ¼ cup shredded Cheddar cheese
- ⅛ teaspoon salt
- ⅛ teaspoon black pepper

1 In a medium pot over medium heat, add broth and bring to boil (about 5 minutes). Add broccoli and garlic. Reduce heat to low, cover pot, and simmer until vegetables are fully softened, about 15 minutes. 2 Remove from heat and blend using a hand immersion blender to desired consistency while still in pot. Leave some chunks of varying sizes for variety. 3 Return pot to medium heat and add cream and cheese. Stir 3 to 5 minutes until fully blended. Add salt and pepper. 4 Remove from heat, let cool 10 minutes, and serve.

Per Serving:

calories: 82 | fat: 4g | protein: 5g | carbs: 8g | net carbs: 5g | fiber: 3g

Cauliflower Rice and Chicken Thigh Soup

Prep time: 15 minutes | Cook time: 13 minutes | Serves 5

- 2 cups cauliflower florets
- 1 pound (454 g) boneless, skinless chicken thighs
- 4½ cups chicken broth
- ½ yellow onion, chopped
- 2 garlic cloves, minced
- 1 tablespoon unflavored gelatin powder
- 2 teaspoons sea salt
- ½ teaspoon ground black pepper
- ½ cup sliced zucchini
- ⅓ cup sliced turnips
- 1 teaspoon dried parsley
- 3 celery stalks, chopped
- 1 teaspoon ground turmeric
- ½ teaspoon dried marjoram
- 1 teaspoon dried thyme
- ½ teaspoon dried oregano

1. Add the cauliflower florets to a food processor and pulse until a ricelike consistency is achieved. Set aside. 2. Add the chicken thighs, chicken broth, onions, garlic, gelatin powder, sea salt, and black pepper to the pot. Gently stir to combine. 3. Lock the lid. Select Manual mode and set cooking time for 10 minutes on High Pressure. 4. When cooking is complete, quick release the pressure and open the lid. 5. Transfer the chicken thighs to a cutting board. Chop the chicken into bite-sized pieces and then return the chopped chicken to the pot. 6. Add the cauliflower rice, zucchini, turnips, parsley, celery, turmeric, marjoram, thyme, and oregano to the pot. Stir to combine. 7. Lock the lid. Select Manual mode and set cooking time for 3 minutes on High Pressure. 8. When cooking is complete, quick release the pressure. 9. Open the lid. Ladle the soup into serving bowls. Serve hot.

Per Serving:

calories: 247 | fat: 10g | protein: 30g | carbs: 8g | net carbs: 6g | fiber: 2g

Broccoli Cheddar Pancetta Soup

Prep time: 15 minutes | Cook time: 30 minutes | Serves 6

2 ounces (57 g) pancetta, diced
2 tablespoons butter or ghee
¼ medium onion, finely chopped (about ½ cup)
3 garlic cloves, minced
3 cups bone broth
½ cup heavy (whipping) cream
2 cups broccoli florets, chopped into bite-size pieces
1 teaspoon garlic powder
1 teaspoon onion powder
1 teaspoon paprika
1 teaspoon salt
½ teaspoon freshly ground black pepper
Pinch cayenne pepper
½ tablespoon gelatin (or ½ teaspoon xanthan or guar gum), for thickening
2 cups shredded sharp Cheddar cheese

1. In a large pot over medium heat, cook the pancetta, stirring often, until crisp. Remove the pancetta pieces to a paper towel using a slotted spoon, leaving as much grease as possible in the pot. 2. Add the butter, onion, and garlic to the pot and sauté for 5 minutes. 3. Add the bone broth, cream, broccoli, garlic, onion, paprika, salt, pepper, and cayenne to the pot and stir well. Sprinkle in the gelatin and stir until well incorporated. Bring to a boil. 4. Once boiling, reduce the heat to low and simmer for 10 to 15 minutes, stirring occasionally. 5. Then, with the heat on low, gradually add the cheese, ½ cup at a time, stirring constantly. Once all of the cheese has been added, remove the pot from the heat. Sprinkle the pancetta pieces over the top and serve. 6. To store, divide the soup into glass jars and freeze for easy meals throughout the coming weeks and months. Make sure to only fill the jars three-quarters full because the liquid will expand as it freezes.

Per Serving:
1½ cups: calories: 311 | fat: 29g | protein: 17g | carbs: 5g | net carbs: 4g | fiber: 1g

Power Green Soup

Prep time: 10 minutes | Cook time: 15 minutes | Serves 6

1 broccoli head, chopped
1 cup spinach
1 onion, chopped
2 garlic cloves, minced
½ cup watercress
5 cups veggie stock
1 cup coconut milk
1 tablespoon ghee
1 bay leaf
Salt and black pepper, to taste

1. Melt the ghee in a large pot over medium heat. Add onion and garlic, and cook for 3 minutes. Add broccoli and cook for an additional 5 minutes. Pour the stock over and add the bay leaf. Close the lid, bring to a boil, and reduce the heat. Simmer for about 3 minutes. 2. At the end, add spinach and watercress, and cook for 3 more minutes. Stir in the coconut cream, salt and black pepper. Discard the bay leaf, and blend the soup with a hand blender.

Per Serving:
calories: 392 | fat: 38g | protein: 5g | carbs: 7g | net carbs: 6g | fiber: 1g

Creamy Mushroom Soup

Prep time: 10 minutes | Cook time: 30 minutes | Serves 4

2 slices bacon, cut into ¼-inch dice
2 tablespoons minced shallots or onions
1 teaspoon minced garlic
1 pound (454 g) button mushrooms, cleaned and quartered or sliced
1 teaspoon dried thyme leaves
2 cups chicken bone broth, homemade or store-bought
1 teaspoon fine sea salt
½ teaspoon freshly ground black pepper
2 large eggs
2 tablespoons lemon juice
For Garnish:
Fresh thyme leaves
MCT oil or extra-virgin olive oil, for drizzling

1. Place the diced bacon in a stockpot and sauté over medium heat until crispy, about 3 minutes. Remove the bacon from the pan, but leave the drippings. Add the shallots and garlic to the pan with the drippings and sauté over medium heat for about 3 minutes, until softened and aromatic. 2. Add the mushrooms and dried thyme and sauté over medium heat until the mushrooms are golden brown, about 10 minutes. Add the broth, salt, and pepper and bring to boil. 3. Whisk the eggs and lemon juice in a medium bowl. While whisking, very slowly pour in ½ cup of the hot soup (if you add the hot soup too quickly, the eggs will curdle). Slowly whisk another cup of the hot soup into the egg mixture. 4. Pour the hot egg mixture into the pot while stirring. Add the cooked bacon, then reduce the heat and simmer for 10 minutes, stirring constantly. The soup will thicken slightly as it cooks. Remove from the heat. Garnish with fresh thyme and drizzle with MCT oil before serving. 5. This soup is best served fresh but can be stored in an airtight container in the fridge for up to 3 days. To reheat, place in a saucepan over medium-low heat until warmed, stirring constantly to keep the eggs from curdling.

Per Serving:
calories: 185 | fat: 13g | protein: 11g | carbs: 6g | net carbs: 4g | fiber: 2g

Miso Magic

Prep time: 5 minutes | Cook time: 10 minutes | serves 8

8 cups water
6 to 7 tablespoons miso paste
3 sheets dried seaweed
2 cups thinly sliced shiitake mushrooms
1 cup drained and cubed sprouted tofu
1 cup chopped scallions
1 teaspoon sesame oil

1. In a large stockpot over medium heat, add the miso paste and seaweed to the water and bring to a low boil. 2. Toss in the mushrooms, tofu, scallions, and sesame oil. 3. Allow to simmer for about 5 minutes and serve.

Per Serving:
calories: 80 | fat: 2g | protein: 4g | carbs: 12g | net carbs: 10g | fiber: 2g

Green Garden Soup

Prep time: 20 minutes | Cook time: 29 minutes | Serves 5

1 tablespoon olive oil
1 garlic clove, diced
½ cup cauliflower florets
1 cup kale, chopped
2 tablespoons chives, chopped
1 teaspoon sea salt
6 cups beef broth

1. Heat the olive oil in the Instant Pot on Sauté mode for 2 minutes and add the garlic. Sauté for 2 minutes or until fragrant. 2. Add cauliflower, kale, chives, sea salt, and beef broth. 3. Close the lid. Select Manual mode and set cooking time for 5 minutes on High Pressure. 4. When timer beeps, use a quick pressure release and open the lid. 5. Ladle the soup into the bowls. Serve warm.

Per Serving:
calories: 80 | fat: 5g | protein: 7g | carbs: 2g | net carbs: 2g | fiber: 1g

Venison and Tomato Stew

Prep time: 12 minutes | Cook time: 42 minutes | Serves 8

1 tablespoon unsalted butter
1 cup diced onions
2 cups button mushrooms, sliced in half
2 large stalks celery, cut into ¼-inch pieces
Cloves squeezed from 2 heads roasted garlic or 4 cloves garlic, minced
2 pounds (907 g) boneless venison or beef roast, cut into 4 large pieces
5 cups beef broth
1 (14½-ounce / 411-g) can diced tomatoes
1 teaspoon fine sea salt
1 teaspoon ground black pepper
½ teaspoon dried rosemary, or 1 teaspoon fresh rosemary, finely chopped
½ teaspoon dried thyme leaves, or 1 teaspoon fresh thyme leaves, finely chopped
½ head cauliflower, cut into large florets
Fresh thyme leaves, for garnish

1. Place the butter in the Instant Pot and press Sauté. Once melted, add the onions and sauté for 4 minutes, or until soft. 2. Add the mushrooms, celery, and garlic and sauté for another 3 minutes, or until the mushrooms are golden brown. Press Cancel to stop the Sauté. Add the roast, broth, tomatoes, salt, pepper, rosemary, and thyme. 3. Seal the lid, press Manual, and set the timer for 30 minutes. Once finished, turn the valve to venting for a quick release. 4. Add the cauliflower. Seal the lid, press Manual, and set the timer for 5 minutes. Once finished, let the pressure release naturally. 5. Remove the lid and shred the meat with two forks. Taste the liquid and add more salt, if needed. Ladle the stew into bowls. Garnish with thyme leaves.

Per Serving:
calories: 359 | fat: 21g | protein: 32g | carbs: 9g | net carbs: 6g | fiber: 3g

Chili-Infused Lamb Soup

Prep time: 5 minutes | Cook time: 25 minutes | Serves 6

1 tablespoon coconut oil
¾ pound ground lamb
2 cups shredded cabbage
½ onion, chopped
2 teaspoons minced garlic
4 cups chicken broth
2 cups coconut milk
1½ tablespoons red chili paste or as much as you want
Zest and juice of 1 lime
1 cup shredded kale

1. Cook the lamb. In a medium stockpot over medium-high heat, warm the coconut oil. Add the lamb and cook it, stirring it often, until it has browned, about 6 minutes. 2. Cook the vegetables. Add the cabbage, onion, and garlic and sauté until they've softened, about 5 minutes. 3. Simmer the soup. Stir in the chicken broth, coconut milk, red chili paste, lime zest, and lime juice. Bring it to a boil, then reduce the heat to low and simmer until the cabbage is tender, about 10 minutes. 4. Add the kale. Stir in the kale and simmer the soup for 3 more minutes. 5. Serve. Spoon the soup into six bowls and serve.

Per Serving:
calories: 380 | fat: 32g | protein: 17g | carbs: 7g | net carbs: 6g | fiber: 1g

Chicken Zucchini Soup

Prep time: 8 minutes | Cook time: 14 minutes | Serves 6

¼ cup coconut oil or unsalted butter
1 cup chopped celery
¼ cup chopped onions
2 cloves garlic, minced
1 pound (454 g) boneless, skinless chicken breasts, cut into 1-inch cubes
6 cups chicken broth
1 tablespoon dried parsley
1 teaspoon fine sea salt
½ teaspoon dried marjoram
½ teaspoon ground black pepper
1 bay leaf
2 cups zucchini noodles

1. Place the coconut oil in the Instant Pot and press Sauté. Once melted, add the celery, onions, and garlic and cook, stirring occasionally, for 4 minutes, or until the onions are soft. Press Cancel to stop the Sauté. 2. Add the cubed chicken, broth, parsley, salt, marjoram, pepper, and bay leaf. Seal the lid, press Manual, and set the timer for 10 minutes. Once finished, let the pressure release naturally. 3. Remove the lid and stir well. Place the noodles in bowls, using ⅓ cup per bowl. Ladle the soup over the noodles and serve immediately; if it sits too long, the noodles will get too soft.

Per Serving:
calories: 253 | fat: 15g | protein: 21g | carbs: 11g | net carbs: 10g | fiber: 1g

Thai Shrimp and Mushroom Soup

Prep time: 15 minutes | Cook time: 10 minutes | Serves 6

2 tablespoons unsalted butter, divided
½ pound (227 g) medium uncooked shrimp, shelled and deveined
½ medium yellow onion, diced
2 cloves garlic, minced
1 cup sliced fresh white mushrooms
1 tablespoon freshly grated ginger root
4 cups chicken broth
2 tablespoons fish sauce
2½ teaspoons red curry paste
2 tablespoons lime juice
1 stalk lemongrass, outer stalk removed, crushed, and finely chopped
2 tablespoons coconut aminos
1 teaspoon sea salt
½ teaspoon ground black pepper
13.5 ounces (383 g) can unsweetened, full-fat coconut milk
3 tablespoons chopped fresh cilantro

1. Select the Instant Pot on Sauté mode. Add 1 tablespoon butter. 2. Once the butter is melted, add the shrimp and sauté for 3 minutes or until opaque. Transfer the shrimp to a medium bowl. Set aside. 3. Add the remaining butter to the pot. Once the butter is melted, add the onions and garlic and sauté for 2 minutes or until the garlic is fragrant and the onions are softened. 4. Add the mushrooms, ginger root, chicken broth, fish sauce, red curry paste, lime juice, lemongrass, coconut aminos, sea salt, and black pepper to the pot. Stir to combine. 5. Lock the lid. Select Manual mode and set cooking time for 5 minutes on High Pressure. 6. When cooking is complete, allow the pressure to release naturally for 5 minutes, then release the remaining pressure. 7. Open the lid. Stir in the cooked shrimp and coconut milk. 8. Select Sauté mode. Bring the soup to a boil and then press Keep Warm / Cancel. Let the soup rest in the pot for 2 minutes. 9. Ladle the soup into bowls and sprinkle the cilantro over top. Serve hot.

Per Serving:
calories: 237 | fat: 20g | protein: 9g | carbs: 9g | net carbs: 6g | fiber: 2g

Avocado and Serrano Chile Soup

Prep time: 10 minutes | Cook time: 7 minutes | Serves 4

2 avocados
1 small fresh tomatillo, quartered
2 cups chicken broth
2 tablespoons avocado oil
1 tablespoon butter
2 tablespoons finely minced onion
1 clove garlic, minced
½ Serrano chile, deseeded and ribs removed, minced, plus thin slices for garnish
¼ teaspoon sea salt
Pinch of ground white pepper
½ cup full-fat coconut milk
Fresh cilantro sprigs, for garnish

1. Scoop the avocado flesh into a food processor. Add the tomatillo and chicken broth and purée until smooth. Set aside. 2. Set the Instant Pot to Sauté mode and add the avocado oil and butter. When the butter melts, add the onion and garlic and sauté for a minute or until softened. Add the Serrano chile and sauté for 1 minute more. 3. Pour the puréed avocado mixture into the pot, add the salt and pepper, and stir to combine. 4. Secure the lid. Press the Manual button and set cooking time for 5 minutes on High Pressure. 5. When timer beeps, use a quick pressure release. Open the lid and stir in the coconut milk. 6. Serve hot topped with thin slices of Serrano chile, and cilantro sprigs.

Per Serving:
calories: 333 | fat: 32g | protein: 4g | carbs: 15g | net carbs: 7g | fiber: 8g

Pancetta and Jalapeño Soup

Prep time: 10 minutes | Cook time: 10 minutes | Serves 4

3 ounces (85 g) pancetta, chopped
1 teaspoon coconut oil
2 jalapeño peppers, sliced
½ teaspoon garlic powder
½ teaspoon smoked paprika
½ cup heavy cream
2 cups water
½ cup Monterey Jack cheese, shredded

1. Toss the pancetta in the Instant Pot, then add the coconut oil and cook for 4 minutes on Sauté mode. Stir constantly. 2. Add the sliced jalapeños, garlic powder, and smoked paprika. Sauté for 1 more minute. 3. Pour in the heavy cream and water. Add the Monterey Jack cheese and stir to mix well. 4. Close the lid and select Manual mode and set cooking time on High Pressure. 5. When timer beeps, make a quick pressure release. Open the lid. 6. Serve warm.

Per Serving:
calories: 234 | fat: 20g | protein: 12g | carbs: 2g | net carbs: 1g | fiber: 0g

Mushroom Pizza Soup

Prep time: 10 minutes | Cook time: 22 minutes | Serves 3

1 teaspoon coconut oil
¼ cup cremini mushrooms, sliced
5 ounces (142 g) Italian sausages, chopped
½ jalapeño pepper, sliced
½ teaspoon Italian seasoning
1 teaspoon unsweetened tomato purée
1 cup water
4 ounces (113 g) Mozzarella, shredded

1. Melt the coconut oil in the Instant Pot on Sauté mode. 2. Add the mushrooms and cook for 10 minutes. 3. Add the chopped sausages, sliced jalapeño, Italian seasoning, and unsweetened tomato purée. Pour in the water and stir to mix well. 4. Close the lid and select Manual mode. Set cooking time for 12 minutes on High Pressure. 5. When timer beeps, use a quick pressure release and open the lid. 6. Ladle the soup in the bowls. Top it with Mozzarella. Serve warm.

Per Serving:
calories: 289 | fat: 23g | protein: 18g | carbs: 3g | net carbs: 2g | fiber: 0g

Shrimp Chowder

Prep time: 10 minutes | Cook time: 40 minutes | Serves 6

- ¼ cup (60 ml) refined avocado oil or melted ghee (if tolerated)
- 1⅔ cups (140 g) diced mushrooms
- ⅓ cup (55 g) diced yellow onions
- 10½ ounces (300 g) small raw shrimp, shelled and deveined
- 1 can (13½-ounce/400-ml) full-fat coconut milk
- ⅓ cup (80 ml) chicken bone broth
- 2 tablespoons apple cider vinegar
- 1 teaspoon onion powder
- 1 teaspoon paprika
- 1 bay leaf
- ¾ teaspoon finely ground gray sea salt
- ½ teaspoon dried oregano leaves
- ¼ teaspoon ground black pepper
- 12 radishes (about 6 ounces/170 g), cubed
- 1 medium zucchini (about 7 ounces/200 g), cubed

1. Heat the avocado oil in a large saucepan on medium for a couple of minutes, then add the mushrooms and onions. Sauté for 8 to 10 minutes, until the onions are translucent and mushrooms are beginning to brown. 2. Add the remaining ingredients, except the radishes and zucchini. Cover and bring to a boil, then reduce the heat to low and simmer for 20 minutes. 3. After 20 minutes, add the radishes and zucchini. Continue to cook for 10 minutes, until the vegetables are fork-tender. 4. Remove the bay leaf, divide among 6 small soup bowls, and enjoy.

Per Serving:

calories: 301 | fat: 23g | protein: 14g | carbs: 7g | net carbs: 5g | fiber: 2g

Tomato-Basil Parmesan Soup

Prep time: 5 minutes | Cook time: 12 minutes | Serves 12

- 2 tablespoons unsalted butter or coconut oil
- ½ cup finely diced onions
- Cloves squeezed from 1 head roasted garlic, or 2 cloves garlic, minced
- 1 tablespoon dried basil leaves
- 1 teaspoon dried oregano leaves
- 1 (8 ounces / 227 g) package cream cheese, softened
- 4 cups chicken broth
- 2 (14½ ounces / 411 g) cans diced tomatoes
- 1 cup shredded Parmesan cheese, plus more for garnish
- 1 teaspoon fine sea salt
- ¼ teaspoon ground black pepper
- Fresh basil leaves, for garnish

1. Place the butter in the Instant Pot and press Sauté. Once melted, add the onions, garlic, basil, and oregano and cook, stirring often, for 4 minutes, or until the onions are soft. Press Cancel to stop the Sauté. 2. Add the cream cheese and whisk to loosen. (If you don't use a whisk to loosen the cream cheese, you will end up with clumps in your soup.) Slowly whisk in the broth. Add the tomatoes, Parmesan, salt, and pepper and stir to combine. 3. Seal the lid, press Manual, and set the timer for 8 minutes. Once finished, turn the valve to venting for a quick release. 4. Remove the lid and purée the soup with a stick blender, or transfer the soup to a regular blender or food processor and process until smooth. If using a regular blender, you may need to blend the soup in two batches; if you overfill the blender jar, the soup will not purée properly. 5. Season with salt and pepper to taste, if desired. Ladle the soup into bowls and garnish with more Parmesan and basil leaves.

Per Serving:

calories: 146 | fat: 10g | protein: 8g | carbs: 4g | net carbs: 3g | fiber: 1g

Loaded Fauxtato Soup

Prep time: 5 minutes | Cook time: 20 minutes | serves 4

- 3 tablespoons salted butter
- ½ cup chopped white onions
- 2 cloves garlic, minced
- 1 (16 ounces) bag frozen cauliflower florets
- 2 cups vegetable broth
- 2 cups shredded sharp cheddar cheese, plus extra for garnish
- 1 cup heavy whipping cream
- Salt and ground black pepper
- 8 slices bacon, cooked and cut into small pieces, for garnish

1. Melt the butter in a stockpot over medium heat. Sauté the onions and garlic in the butter until the onions are tender and translucent. 2. Add the cauliflower and broth to the pot. Bring to a gentle boil over high heat, then reduce the heat to maintain a simmer and continue cooking until the cauliflower is tender, stirring occasionally, about 15 minutes. 3. Turn the heat down to the lowest setting and add the cheese and cream to the pot. Stir until the cheese is melted and well combined with the rest of the soup. 4. Season to taste with salt and pepper. Serve garnished with extra cheese and bacon pieces. Leftovers can be stored in an airtight container in the refrigerator for up to 5 days.

Per Serving:

calories: 560 | fat: 45g | protein: 5g | carbs: 9g | net carbs: 6g | fiber: 3g

Cauliflower Soup

Prep time: 10 minutes | Cook time: 6 minutes | Serves 4

- 2 cups chopped cauliflower
- 2 tablespoons fresh cilantro
- 1 cup coconut cream
- 2 cups beef broth
- 3 ounces (85 g) Provolone cheese, chopped

1. Put cauliflower, cilantro, coconut cream, beef broth, and cheese in the Instant Pot. Stir to mix well. 2. Select Manual mode and set cooking time for 6 minutes on High Pressure. 3. When timer beeps, allow a natural pressure release for 4 minutes, then release any remaining pressure. Open the lid. 4. Blend the soup and ladle in bowls to serve.

Per Serving:

calories: 244 | fat: 21g | protein: 10g | carbs: 7g | net carbs: 4g | fiber: 3g

Chicken Soup

Prep time: 15 minutes | Cook time: 45 minutes | Serves 4

3 tablespoons olive oil
1 (14 ounces / 397 g) bag frozen peppers and onions
1 pound (454 g) chicken thigh meat, diced
1 tablespoon dried thyme
½ tablespoon garlic powder
1 teaspoon salt
1 teaspoon freshly ground black pepper
1 (32 ounces / 907 g) container chicken or vegetable broth, or bone broth
½ pound (227 g) spinach
1 teaspoon dried basil (optional)

1. Heat the oil in a large pot over medium heat. 2. Add the peppers and onions and cook until no longer frozen, 8 to 10 minutes. 3. Add the chicken and cook, stirring occasionally. 4. Stir in the thyme, garlic powder, salt, and pepper. Add the broth and cook for about 25 minutes. 5. Add the spinach and cook for another 5 minutes. 6. Serve the soup in bowls, sprinkled with the basil (if using).

Per Serving:
calories: 323 | fat: 19g | protein: 28g | carbs: 10g | net carbs: 7g | fiber: 3g

Curried Chicken Soup

Prep time: 10 minutes | Cook time: 10 minutes | Serves 6

1 pound (454 g) boneless, skinless chicken thighs
1½ cups unsweetened coconut milk
½ onion, finely diced
3 or 4 garlic cloves, crushed
1 (2-inch) piece ginger, finely chopped
1 cup sliced mushrooms, such as cremini and shiitake
4 ounces (113 g) baby spinach
1 teaspoon salt
½ teaspoon ground turmeric
½ teaspoon cayenne
1 teaspoon garam masala
¼ cup chopped fresh cilantro

1. In the inner cooking pot of your Instant Pot, add the chicken, coconut milk, onion, garlic, ginger, mushrooms, spinach, salt, turmeric, cayenne, garam masala, and cilantro. 2. Lock the lid into place. Select Manual and adjust the pressure to High. Cook for 10 minutes. When the cooking is complete, let the pressure release naturally. Unlock the lid. 3. Use tongs to transfer the chicken to a bowl. Shred the chicken, then stir it back into the soup. 4. Eat and rejoice.

Per Serving:
calories: 378 | fat: 26g | protein: 26g | carbs: 6g | net carbs: 2g | fiber: 4g

Chapter 9 Desserts

Creamy Banana Fat Bombs

Prep time: 10 minutes | Cook time: 0 minutes | Makes 12 fat bombs

1¼ cups cream cheese, at room temperature
¾ cup heavy (whipping) cream
1 tablespoon pure banana extract
6 drops liquid stevia

1. Line a baking sheet with parchment paper and set aside. 2. In a medium bowl, beat together the cream cheese, heavy cream, banana extract, and stevia until smooth and very thick, about 5 minutes. 3. Gently spoon the mixture onto the baking sheet in mounds, leaving some space between each mound, and place the baking sheet in the refrigerator until firm, about 1 hour. 4. Store the fat bombs in an airtight container in the refrigerator for up to 1 week.

Per Serving:
calories: 134 | fat: 12g | protein: 3g | carbs: 1g | net carbs: 1g | fiber: 0g

Chocolate Cheesecake with Toasted Almond Crust

Prep time: 15 minutes | Cook time: 1 hour 20 minutes | Serves 10

For The Crust
1½ cups almond flour
4 tablespoons monk fruit sweetener, granulated form
1 tablespoon cocoa powder
⅓ cup melted grass-fed butter
For The Filling
1½ pounds cream cheese, softened
¾ cup monk fruit sweetener, granulated form
3 eggs, beaten
1 teaspoon vanilla extract
½ teaspoon almond extract (optional)
5 ounces keto-friendly chocolate chips like Lily's Dark Chocolate Chips, melted and cooled
1 cup sour cream

Make The Crust: 1. Preheat the oven. Set the oven temperature to 350°F. 2. Mix the crust ingredients. In a medium bowl, stir together the almond flour, sweetener, cocoa powder, and melted butter until the ingredients hold together when pressed. Press the crumbs into the bottom of a 10-inch springform pan and 1 inch up the sides. 3. Chill and bake. Chill the crust in the freezer for 10 minutes. Transfer it to the oven and bake it for 10 minutes. Cool the crust completely before filling. Make The Filling: 1. Change the oven temperature. Reduce the oven temperature to 275°F. 2. Mix the cheesecake base. In a large bowl, beat the cream cheese until very light and fluffy, scraping down the sides with a spatula at least once. Beat in the sweetener until the mixture is smooth, scraping down the sides of the bowl. 3. Add the eggs. Beat in the eggs one at a time, scraping down the sides of the bowl occasionally and then beat in the vanilla extract and almond extract (if using). 4. Add the remaining ingredients. Beat in the melted chocolate and sour cream until the filling is well blended, scraping down the sides of the bowl. 5. Bake. Pour the filling into the prebaked crust and bake it for 1 hour and 10 minutes. Turn off the oven and cool the cheesecake in the closed oven until it reaches room temperature. 6. Chill. Chill the cheesecake in the refrigerator for at least 4 to 6 hours. 7. Serve. Cut the cheesecake into 10 slices and serve.

Per Serving:
calories: 408 | fat: 40g | protein: 8g | carbs: 4g | net carbs: 4g | fiber: 0g

Strawberry Shortcakes

Prep time: 10 minutes | Cook time: 15 minutes | serves 6

1½ cups fresh strawberries
¾ cup finely ground blanched almond flour
1 teaspoon baking powder
⅛ teaspoon salt
1 large egg
⅓ cup granular erythritol
2 tablespoons heavy whipping cream
2 tablespoons salted butter, melted but not hot
½ teaspoon vanilla extract
1½ cups whipped cream, for serving

1. Preheat the oven to 375°F. Line a baking sheet with parchment paper. 2. Hull and slice the strawberries and set aside. 3. In a small bowl, whisk together the almond flour, baking powder, and salt. 4. In a medium-sized mixing bowl, whisk the egg, then stir in the erythritol, cream, melted butter, and vanilla extract. While stirring, slowly add the dry ingredients; continue stirring until well blended. 5. Drop spoonfuls of the batter onto the prepared baking sheet, spacing the shortcakes 2 inches apart, to make a total of 6 shortcakes. Bake for 13 to 15 minutes, until the shortcakes are golden brown on the tops and a toothpick or tester inserted in the middle of a shortcake comes out clean. Allow to completely cool on the pan. 6. To serve, top the shortcakes with whipped cream and the sliced strawberries. Leftover shortcakes can be stored in an airtight container in the refrigerator for up to 5 days.

Per Serving:
calories: 154 | fat: 13g | protein: 4g | carbs: 5g | net carbs: 3g | fiber: 2g

Birthday Mug Cakes

Prep time: 5 minutes | Cook time: 2 minutes | Serves 2

Frosting:
2 ounces (57 g) full-fat cream cheese, at room temperature
1 tablespoon butter, at room temperature
2 teaspoons granulated erythritol
¼ teaspoon vanilla extract

Cake:
⅓ cup almond flour
2 tablespoons granulated erythritol
½ teaspoon baking powder
1 large egg
¼ teaspoon vanilla extract

1. To make the frosting: In a small bowl, combine the cream cheese, butter, erythritol, and vanilla. Whisk well, then place in the refrigerator to chill. 2. To make the cake: In a 12-ounce (340-g) coffee mug, combine the almond flour, erythritol, and baking powder. Using a fork, break up any clumps and mix the ingredients well. 3. Add the egg and vanilla, then beat well. Make sure you scrape the bottom edges for any unmixed flour. 4. Microwave on high power for 70 seconds. 5. Let the cake cool for 5 to 10 minutes. 6. Flip the mug onto a plate, then tap a few times. (Alternately, you can skip this step and eat it directly from the mug.). Cut the cake in half crosswise, for 2 cupcakes. 7. Frost the cupcakes before serving.

Per Serving:

calories: 279 | fat: 26g | protein: 8g | carbs: 5g | net carbs: 3g | fiber: 2g

Ultimate Chocolate Cheesecake

Prep time: 10 minutes | Cook time: 50 minutes | Serves 12

2 cups pecans
2 tablespoons butter
16 ounces (454 g) cream cheese, softened
1 cup powdered erythritol
¼ cup sour cream
2 tablespoons cocoa powder
2 teaspoons vanilla extract
2 cups low-carb chocolate chips
1 tablespoon coconut oil
2 eggs
2 cups water

1. Preheat oven to 400°F (205°C). Place pecans and butter into food processor. Pulse until dough-like consistency. Press into bottom of 7-inch springform pan. Bake for 10 minutes then set aside to cool. 2. While crust bakes, mix cream cheese, erythritol, sour cream, cocoa powder, and vanilla together in large bowl using a rubber spatula. Set aside. 3. In medium bowl, combine chocolate chips and coconut oil. Microwave in 20-second increments until chocolate begins to melt and then stir until smooth. Gently fold chocolate mixture into cheesecake mixture. 4. Add eggs and gently fold in, careful not to overmix. Pour mixture over cooled pecan crust. Cover with foil. 5. Pour water into Instant Pot and place steam rack on bottom. Place cheesecake on steam rack and click lid closed. Press the Manual button and adjust time for 40 minutes. When timer beeps, allow a natural release. Carefully remove and let cool completely. Serve chilled.

Per Serving:

calories: 461 | fat: 40g | protein: 5g | carbs: 20g | net carbs: 15g | fiber: 5g

Giant Skillet Cookie for Two

Prep time: 10 minutes | Cook time: 20 minutes | Makes 6-inch cookie

½ cup blanched almond flour
1 teaspoon unflavored beef gelatin powder
½ teaspoon baking powder
¼ teaspoon pink Himalayan salt
2 tablespoons unsalted butter
1 tablespoon cream cheese
2 tablespoons heavy whipping cream
1 large egg yolk
½ teaspoon vanilla extract
½ teaspoon liquid stevia
2 tablespoons sugar-free chocolate chips, divided

1. Preheat the oven to 350°F and grease a 6-inch oven-safe skillet with coconut oil spray. 2. In a small bowl, combine the almond flour, gelatin, baking powder, and salt using a fork. Set aside. 3. Put the butter and cream cheese in a small microwave-safe bowl that's large enough to accommodate the beaters of a hand mixer. Microwave for 20 to 30 seconds, just until soft. Combine using a hand mixer. Add the cream, egg yolk, vanilla extract, and stevia and mix to combine. 4. Add the dry mixture to the wet mixture and combine using the mixer until uniform. Fold in 1½ tablespoons of the chocolate chips using a rubber spatula. 5. Pour the mixture into the greased skillet and spread evenly with the spatula. Top the cookie with the remaining ½ tablespoon of chocolate chips. Bake for 20 minutes, or until golden brown. 6. Allow to rest in the skillet for 15 minutes prior to serving, or dig in immediately with spoons, if desired.

Per Serving:

calories: 406 | fat: 39g | protein: 10g | carbs: 11g | net carbs: 6g | fiber: 5g

Mini Cheesecake

Prep time: 10 minutes | Cook time: 15 minutes | Serves 2

½ cup walnuts
2 tablespoons salted butter
2 tablespoons granular erythritol
4 ounces (113 g) full-fat cream cheese, softened
1 large egg
½ teaspoon vanilla extract
⅛ cup powdered erythritol

1. Place walnuts, butter, and granular erythritol in a food processor. Pulse until ingredients stick together and a dough forms. 2. Press dough into a springform pan then place the pan into the air fryer basket. 3. Adjust the temperature to 400°F (204°C) and bake for 5 minutes. 4. When done, remove the crust and let cool. 5. In a medium bowl, mix cream cheese with egg, vanilla extract, and powdered erythritol until smooth. 6. Spoon mixture on top of baked walnut crust and place into the air fryer basket. 7. Adjust the temperature to 300°F (149°C) and bake for 10 minutes. 8. Once done, chill for 2 hours before serving.

Per Serving:

calories: 699 | fat: 68g | protein: 15g | carbs: 12g | net carbs: 6g | fiber: 3g

Strawberry-Lime Ice Pops

Prep time: 5 minutes | Cook time: 0 minutes | Serves 4

½ (13.5-ounce) can coconut cream, ¾ cup unsweetened full-fat coconut milk, or ¾ cup heavy (whipping) cream
2 teaspoons Swerve natural sweetener or 2 drops liquid stevia
1 tablespoon freshly squeezed lime juice
¼ cup hulled and sliced strawberries (fresh or frozen)

1. In a food processor (or blender), mix together the coconut cream, sweetener, and lime juice. 2. Add the strawberries, and pulse just a few times so the strawberries retain their texture. 3. Pour into ice pop molds, and freeze for at least 2 hours before serving.

Per Serving:

calories: 166 | fat: 17g | protein: 1g | carbs: 5g | net carbs: 3g | fiber: 1g

Cookies-and-Cream Fat Bomb

Prep time: 10 minutes | Cook time: 1 to 3 minutes | Serves 2

1¾ ounces (50 g) cacao butter
4 teaspoons powdered erythritol
4 teaspoons heavy cream powder
Pinch of pink Himalayan sea salt
2 teaspoons cacao nibs

1. In a small microwave-safe bowl, heat the cacao butter on high power in 30-second increments until it is liquid. Make sure to stir between intervals of microwaving. 2. Add the powdered erythritol, heavy cream powder, and salt to the cacao butter. Whisk until the mixture is well combined. 3. Line 2 cups of a muffin pan with paper cupcake liners. Split the liquid between the cups. 4. Pour 1 teaspoon of cacao nibs into each cup, then place the muffin pan in the refrigerator to cool for about 1 hour. (The cups can be stored in the refrigerator until ready to enjoy.)

Per Serving:

calories: 242 | fat: 24g | protein: 1g | carbs: 5g | net carbs: 4g | fiber: 1g

Electrolyte Gummies

Prep time: 5 minutes | Cook time: 0 minutes | Makes 10 gummies

1 cup cold water
2 tablespoons unflavored gelatin
2 packets/scoops flavored electrolyte powder

Stovetop Directions: 1. In a small saucepan, whisk together the water and gelatin until dissolved. Heat over medium heat for about 5 minutes until it just begins to simmer. Add your flavoring of choice and whisk until well combined. 2. Pour the mixture into silicone molds and refrigerate for 30 to 40 minutes or until set. 3. Pop the gummies out of the molds and enjoy! Microwave Directions: 1. Pour the water into a small microwavable bowl or measuring cup (preferably with a spout). 2. Whisk in the gelatin until dissolved and then microwave for 2 minutes or until just starting to bubble. 3. Add your flavoring of choice and whisk until well combined. 4. Pour the mixture into silicone molds and refrigerate for 30 to 40 minutes or until set. 5. Pop the gummies out of the molds and enjoy! Store in an airtight container in the refrigerator for up to 3 weeks.

Per Serving:

1 gummy: calories: 4 | fat: 0g | protein: 1g | carbs: 0g | net carbs: 0g | fiber: 0g

Pecan Butter Cookies

Prep time: 5 minutes | Cook time: 24 minutes | Makes 12 cookies

1 cup chopped pecans
½ cup salted butter, melted
½ cup coconut flour
¾ cup erythritol, divided
1 teaspoon vanilla extract

1. In a food processor, blend together pecans, butter, flour, ½ cup erythritol, and vanilla 1 minute until a dough forms. 2. Form dough into twelve individual cookie balls, about 1 tablespoon each. 3. Cut three pieces of parchment to fit air fryer basket. Place four cookies on each ungreased parchment and place one piece parchment with cookies into air fryer basket. Adjust air fryer temperature to 325°F (163°C) and set the timer for 8 minutes. Repeat cooking with remaining batches. 4. When the timer goes off, allow cookies to cool 5 minutes on a large serving plate until cool enough to handle. While still warm, dust cookies with remaining erythritol. Allow to cool completely, about 15 minutes, before serving.

Per Serving:

calories: 121 | fat: 13g | protein: 1g | carbs: 2g | net carbs: 1g | fiber: 1g

Fresh Cream-Filled Strawberries

Prep time: 10 minutes | Cook time: 0 minutes | Serves 6

1 cup heavy (whipping) cream
Sweetener of choice (optional)
12 large strawberries, hulled and hollowed out

1. In a large bowl, whisk the cream and sweetener (if using) until thickened into whipped cream, about 5 minutes. 2. Spoon the whipped cream into the hollowed strawberries or use a pastry tube to pipe it inside. Serve immediately. 3. Optional garnishes could include lime zest, finely chopped mint, or shaved dark chocolate.

Per Serving:

calories: 153 | fat: 15g | protein: 1g | carbs: 3g | net carbs: 3g | fiber: 0g

Snickerdoodle Cream Cheesecake

Prep time: 5 minutes | Cook time: 90 minutes | Serves 1

Filling:
1 tablespoon cream cheese, room temperature
1 teaspoon powdered erythritol
1 teaspoon ground cinnamon
Cake:
1½ tablespoons coconut flour
1 tablespoon golden flax meal
¼ teaspoon baking powder
⅛ teaspoon cream of tartar

2 tablespoons unsalted butter, melted but not hot
1 large egg
½ teaspoon vanilla extract
¼ teaspoon plus 15 drops of liquid stevia
For Garnish (Optional):
Ground cinnamon
Powdered erythritol

1. Make the filling: Place a piece of plastic wrap in a small bowl and put the cream cheese, erythritol, and cinnamon in the center. Use a spoon to combine the ingredients, then wrap the plastic wrap around the mixture to enclose it securely. Using your hands, form the filling into a small disc, 1 inch in diameter and ½ inch thick. Place in the freezer for 30 minutes. 2. Make the cake: In a small bowl, use a fork to whisk together the coconut flour, flax meal, baking powder, and cream of tartar. In another small bowl, whisk together the melted butter, egg, vanilla extract, and stevia. 3. Slowly add the dry mixture to the wet mixture and whisk together until it has a thick batterlike consistency. 4. Grease a 4- or 5-ounce microwave-safe ramekin with coconut oil spray. Pour half of the batter into the ramekin. Remove the cream cheese disc from the freezer, unwrap, and place in the center of the ramekin. Gently press it down, but do not let it hit the bottom. Pour the rest of the batter on top of the filling and spread, fully covering the disc and creating an even surface. 5. Microwave for 90 seconds. Flip the cake over onto a plate and, if desired, dust with ground cinnamon and powdered erythritol. Enjoy!

Per Serving:

calories: 403 | fat: 36g | protein: 11g | carbs: 12g | net carbs: 5g | fiber: 7g

Fudge Pops

Prep time: 5 minutes | Cook time: 0 minutes | serves 4

1 (14-ounce) can full-fat coconut cream
3 avocados, peeled, pitted, and chopped
⅓ cup cacao powder

5 or 6 drops liquid stevia
⅓ cup freshly grated orange zest
Sea salt

1. In a high-powered blender, combine the coconut cream with the avocados, cacao powder, and stevia. 2. Whip the mixture in the blender for 5 minutes until it becomes airy. 3. Stir in the orange zest and salt and pour the mixture into popsicle molds. 4. Place the molds in the freezer overnight to set. 5. To serve, run warm water over the popsicle molds to loosen the fudge pops.

Per Serving:

calories: 434 | fat: 40g | protein: 4g | carbs: 21g | net carbs: 9g | fiber: 12g

Blueberry Fat Bombs

Prep time: 10 minutes | Cook time: 0 minutes | Makes 12 fat bombs

½ cup coconut oil, at room temperature
½ cup cream cheese, at room temperature

½ cup blueberries, mashed with a fork
6 drops liquid stevia
Pinch ground nutmeg

1. Line a mini muffin tin with paper liners and set aside. 2. In a medium bowl, stir together the coconut oil and cream cheese until well blended. 3. Stir in the blueberries, stevia, and nutmeg until combined. 4. Divide the blueberry mixture into the muffin cups and place the tray in the freezer until set, about 3 hours. 5. Place the fat bombs in an airtight container and store in the freezer until you wish to eat them.

Per Serving:

calories: 115 | fat: 12g | protein: 1g | carbs: 1g | net carbs: 1g | fiber: 0g

Glazed Pumpkin Bundt Cake

Prep time: 7 minutes | Cook time: 35 minutes | Serves 12

Cake:
3 cups blanched almond flour
1 teaspoon baking soda
½ teaspoon fine sea salt
2 teaspoons ground cinnamon
1 teaspoon ground nutmeg
1 teaspoon ginger powder
¼ teaspoon ground cloves
6 large eggs
2 cups pumpkin purée

1 cup Swerve
¼ cup (½ stick) unsalted butter (or coconut oil for dairy-free), softened
Glaze:
1 cup (2 sticks) unsalted butter (or coconut oil for dairy-free), melted
½ cup Swerve

1. In a large bowl, stir together the almond flour, baking soda, salt, and spices. In another large bowl, add the eggs, pumpkin, sweetener, and butter and stir until smooth. Pour the wet ingredients into the dry ingredients and stir well. 2. Grease a 6-cup Bundt pan. Pour the batter into the prepared pan and cover with a paper towel and then with aluminum foil. 3. Place a trivet in the bottom of the Instant Pot and pour in 2 cups of cold water. Place the Bundt pan on the trivet. 4. Lock the lid. Select the Manual mode and set the cooking time for 35 minutes at High Pressure. 5. When the timer beeps, use a natural pressure release for 10 minutes. Carefully remove the lid. 6. Let the cake cool in the pot for 10 minutes before removing. 7. While the cake is cooling, make the glaze: In a small bowl, mix the butter and sweetener together. Spoon the glaze over the warm cake. 8. Allow to cool for 5 minutes before slicing and serving.

Per Serving:

calories: 332 | fat: 22g | protein: 7g | carbs: 27g | net carbs: 26g | fiber: 1g

Chocolate Mousse

Prep time: 10 minutes | Cook time: 0 minutes | Serves 2

1½ tablespoons heavy (whipping) cream
4 tablespoons butter, at room temperature
1 tablespoon unsweetened cocoa powder
4 tablespoons cream cheese, at room temperature
1 tablespoon Swerve natural sweetener

1. In a medium chilled bowl, use a whisk or fork to whip the cream. Refrigerate to keep cold. 2. In a separate medium bowl, use a hand mixer to beat the butter, cocoa powder, cream cheese, and sweetener until thoroughly combined. 3. Take the whipped cream out of the refrigerator. Gently fold the whipped cream into the chocolate mixture with a rubber scraper. 4. Divide the pudding between two dessert bowls. 5. Cover and chill for 1 hour before serving.

Per Serving:

calories: 486 | fat: 50g | protein: 4g | carbs: 5g | net carbs: 4g | fiber: 1g

Blackberry "Cheesecake" Bites

Prep time: 5 minutes | Cook time: 0 minutes | serves 4

1½ cups almonds, soaked overnight
1 cup blackberries
⅓ cup coconut oil, melted
¼ cup full-fat coconut cream
⅓ cup monk fruit sweetener
¼ cup freshly squeezed lemon juice

1. Prepare a muffin tin by lining the cups with cupcake liners. Set aside. 2. In a high-powered blender, combine the soaked almonds, blackberries, melted coconut oil, coconut cream, monk fruit sweetener, and lemon juice. 3. Blend on high until the mixture is whipped and fluffy. 4. Divide the mixture equally among the muffin cups. 5. Place the muffin tin in the freezer for 90 minutes to allow the cheesecake bites to set.

Per Serving:

calories: 514 | fat: 48g | protein: 12g | carbs: 18g | net carbs: 9g | fiber: 9g

Pumpkin Pie Spice Pots De Crème

Prep time: 5 minutes | Cook time: 7 minutes | Serves 4

2 cups heavy cream (or full-fat coconut milk for dairy-free)
4 large egg yolks
¼ cup Swerve, or more to taste
2 teaspoons pumpkin pie spice
1 teaspoon vanilla extract
Pinch of fine sea salt
1 cup cold water

1. Heat the cream in a pan over medium-high heat until hot, about 2 minutes. 2. Place the remaining ingredients except the water in a medium bowl and stir until smooth. 3. Slowly pour in the hot cream while stirring. Taste and adjust the sweetness to your liking. Scoop the mixture into four ramekins with a spatula. Cover the ramekins with aluminum foil. 4. Place a trivet in the Instant Pot and pour in the water. Place the ramekins on the trivet. 5. Lock the lid. Select the Manual mode and set the cooking time for 5 minutes at High Pressure. 6. When the timer beeps, use a quick pressure release. Carefully remove the lid. 7. Remove the foil and set the foil aside. Let the pots de crème cool for 15 minutes. Cover the ramekins with the foil again and place in the refrigerator to chill completely, about 2 hours. 8. Serve.

Per Serving:

calories: 289 | fat: 27g | protein: 8g | carbs: 4g | net carbs: 4g | fiber: 0g

Protein Powder Doughnut Holes

Prep time: 25 minutes | Cook time: 6 minutes | Makes 12 holes

½ cup blanched finely ground almond flour
½ cup low-carb vanilla protein powder
½ cup granular erythritol
½ teaspoon baking powder
1 large egg
5 tablespoons unsalted butter, melted
½ teaspoon vanilla extract

1. Mix all ingredients in a large bowl. Place into the freezer for 20 minutes. 2. Wet your hands with water and roll the dough into twelve balls. 3. Cut a piece of parchment to fit your air fryer basket. Working in batches as necessary, place doughnut holes into the air fryer basket on top of parchment. 4. Adjust the temperature to 380°F (193°C) and air fry for 6 minutes. 5. Flip doughnut holes halfway through the cooking time. 6. Let cool completely before serving.

Per Serving:

1 hole: calories: 89 | fat: 7g | protein: 5g | carbs: 2g | net carbs: 1g | fiber: 1g

Pecan Bars

Prep time: 5 minutes | Cook time: 40 minutes | Serves 12

2 cups coconut flour
5 tablespoons erythritol
4 tablespoons coconut oil, softened
½ cup heavy cream
1 egg, beaten
4 pecans, chopped

1. Mix coconut flour, erythritol, coconut oil, heavy cream, and egg. 2. Pour the batter in the air fryer basket and flatten well. 3. Top the mixture with pecans and cook the meal at 350°F (177°C) for 40 minutes. 4. Cut the cooked meal into the bars.

Per Serving:

calories: 261 | fat: 20g | protein: 7g | carbs: 14g | net carbs: 3g | fiber: 11g

Crustless Cheesecake Bites

Prep time: 10 minutes | Cook time: 30 minutes | Serves 4

4 ounces cream cheese, at room temperature
¼ cup sour cream
2 large eggs
⅓ cup Swerve natural sweetener
¼ teaspoon vanilla extract

1. Preheat the oven to 350°F. 2. In a medium mixing bowl, use a hand mixer to beat the cream cheese, sour cream, eggs, sweetener, and vanilla until well mixed. 3. Place silicone liners (or cupcake paper liners) in the cups of a muffin tin. 4. Pour the cheesecake batter into the liners, and bake for 30 minutes. 5. Refrigerate until completely cooled before serving, about 3 hours. Store extra cheesecake bites in a zip-top bag in the freezer for up to 3 months.

Per Serving:

calories: 169 | fat: 15g | protein: 5g | carbs: 18g | net carbs: 2g | fiber: 0g

Almond Chai Truffles

Prep time: 200 minutes | Cook time: 0 minutes | Serves 10

½ cup (140 g) unsweetened smooth almond butter
¼ cup plus 2 tablespoons (90 g) cacao butter, melted
1 tablespoon plus 1 teaspoon chai spice (recipe below)
1 tablespoon confectioners'-style erythritol or 2 to 4 drops liquid stevia
½ teaspoon vanilla extract or powder
Pinch of finely ground gray sea salt
3 tablespoons almonds, roasted
Special Equipment:
10 mini paper liners (optional)

1. Combine the almond butter, cacao butter, chai spice, erythritol, vanilla, and salt in a medium-sized bowl and stir to combine. Place in the fridge to set for 30 to 45 minutes, until firm yet still pliable. 2. Meanwhile, put the roasted almonds in a small baggie, seal, and cover with a kitchen towel. Bash with a mallet or the bottom of a mug until the pieces are no larger than ⅛ inch (3 mm). Pour the pieces into a small bowl. 3. Line a rimmed baking sheet with parchment paper or a silicone baking mat. 4. Remove the truffle mixture from the fridge and break it up with a fork until no clumps larger than a pencil eraser remain. Scoop up a tablespoon of the mixture and roll it quickly between your palms, then place it in the bowl with the roasted almond pieces and toss to coat. Once coated, transfer to the prepared baking sheet. Clean your hands so as not to transfer the almond pieces to the truffle mixture. Repeat with the remaining dough, making 10 truffles total. 5. Serve the truffles in mini paper liners, if desired. They are best when consumed at room temperature.

Per Serving:

calories: 196 | fat: 18g | protein: 4g | carbs: 4g | net carbs: 2g | fiber: 2g

Daikon and Almond Cake

Prep time: 10 minutes | Cook time: 45 minutes | Serves 12

5 eggs, beaten
½ cup heavy cream
1 cup almond flour
1 daikon, diced
1 teaspoon ground cinnamon
2 tablespoon erythritol
1 tablespoon butter, melted
1 cup water

1. In the mixing bowl, mix up eggs, heavy cream, almond flour, ground cinnamon, and erythritol. 2. When the mixture is smooth, add daikon and stir it carefully with the help of the spatula. 3. Pour the mixture in the cake pan. 4. Then pour water and insert the trivet in the instant pot. 5. Place the cake in the instant pot. 6. Set the lid in place. Select the Manual mode and set the cooking time for 45 minutes on High Pressure. When the timer goes off, do a quick pressure release. Carefully open the lid. 7. Serve immediately.

Per Serving:

calories: 66 | fat: 6g | protein: 3g | carbs: 4g | net carbs: 3g | fiber: 1g

Mint–Chocolate Chip Ice Cream

Prep time: 10 minutes | Cook time: 30 minutes | Serves 2

½ tablespoon butter
1 tablespoon Swerve natural sweetener
10 tablespoons heavy (whipping) cream, divided
¼ teaspoon peppermint extract
2 tablespoons sugar-free chocolate chips (I use Lily's)

1. Put a medium metal bowl and your hand-mixer beaters in the freezer to chill. 2. In a small, heavy saucepan over medium heat, melt the butter. Whisk in the sweetener and 5 tablespoons of cream. 3. Turn the heat up to medium-high and bring the mixture to a boil, stirring constantly. Turn the heat down to low and simmer, stirring occasionally, for about 30 minutes. You want the mixture to be thick, so it sticks to the back of a spoon. 4. Stir in the peppermint extract. 5. Pour the thickened mixture into a medium bowl and refrigerate to cool. 6. Remove the metal bowl and the mixer beaters from the freezer. Pour the remaining 5 tablespoons of cream into the bowl. With the electric beater, whip the cream until it is thick and fluffy and forms peaks. Don't overbeat, or the cream will turn to butter. Take the cream mixture out of the refrigerator. 7. Using a rubber scraper, gently fold the whipped cream into the cooled mixture. 8. Transfer the mixture to a small metal container that can go in the freezer (I use a mini loaf pan since I only make enough for two). 9. Mix in the chocolate chips, and cover the container with foil or plastic wrap. 10. Freeze the ice cream for 4 to 5 hours before serving, stirring it twice during that time.

Per Serving:

calories: 325 | fat: 33g | protein: 3g | carbs: 17g | net carbs: 4g | fiber: 4g

Lime Muffins

Prep time: 10 minutes | Cook time: 15 minutes | Serves 6

- 1 teaspoon lime zest
- 1 tablespoon lemon juice
- 1 teaspoon baking powder
- 1 cup almond flour
- 2 eggs, beaten
- 1 tablespoon Swerve
- ¼ cup heavy cream
- 1 cup water, for cooking

1. In the mixing bowl, mix up lemon juice, baking powder, almond flour, eggs, Swerve, and heavy cream. 2. When the muffin batter is smooth, add lime zest and mix it up. 3. Fill the muffin molds with batter. 4. Then pour water and insert the rack in the instant pot. 5. Place the muffins on the rack. Close and seal the lid. 6. Cook the muffins on Manual (High Pressure) for 15 minutes. 7. Then allow the natural pressure release.

Per Serving:

calories: 153 | fat: 12g | protein: 6g | carbs: 5g | net carbs: 3g | fiber: 2g

Lemon Vanilla Cheesecake

Prep time: 15 minutes | Cook time: 20 minutes | Serves 6

- 2 teaspoons freshly squeezed lemon juice
- 2 teaspoons vanilla extract or almond extract
- ½ cup sour cream, divided, at room temperature
- ½ cup plus 2 teaspoons Swerve
- 8 ounces (227 g) cream cheese, at room temperature
- 2 eggs, at room temperature

1. Pour 2 cups of water into the inner cooking pot of the Instant Pot, then place a trivet (preferably with handles) in the pot. Line the sides of a 6-inch springform pan with parchment paper. 2. In a food processor, put the lemon juice, vanilla, ¼ cup of sour cream, ½ cup of Swerve, and the cream cheese. 3. Gently but thoroughly blend all the ingredients, scraping down the sides of the bowl as needed. 4. Add the eggs and blend only as long as you need to in order to get them well incorporated, 20 to 30 seconds. Your mixture will be pourable by now. 5. Pour the mixture into the prepared pan. Cover the pan with aluminum foil and place on the trivet. (If your trivet doesn't have handles, you may wish to use a foil sling to make removing the pan easier.) 6. Lock the lid into place. Select Manual and adjust the pressure to High. Cook for 20 minutes. When the cooking is complete, let the pressure release naturally. Unlock the lid. 7. Meanwhile, in a small bowl, mix together the remaining ¼ cup of sour cream and 2 teaspoons of Swerve for the topping. 8. Take out the cheesecake and remove the foil. Spread the topping over the top. Doing this while the cheesecake is still hot helps melt the topping into the cheesecake. 9. Put the cheesecake in the refrigerator and leave it alone. Seriously. Leave it alone and let it chill for at least 6 to 8 hours. It won't taste right hot. 10. When you're ready to serve, open the sides of the pan and peel off the parchment paper. Slice and serve.

Per Serving:

calories: 207 | fat: 19g | protein: 5g | carbs: 4g | net carbs: 4g | fiber: 0g

Cheesecake

Prep time: 10 minutes | Cook time: 40 minutes | Serves 4

Crust:
- ⅔ cup almond flour
- 2 teaspoons granulated erythritol
- ¼ teaspoon psyllium husk powder
- ⅛ teaspoon ground cinnamon
- 2 tablespoons butter, melted
- 1½ teaspoons heavy (whipping) cream

Filling:
- 8 ounces (227 g) full-fat cream cheese, at room temperature
- 1 large egg
- 2 tablespoons granulated erythritol
- 2 tablespoons sour cream
- ¼ teaspoon freshly squeezed lemon juice
- ½ teaspoon liquid stevia
- Pinch of pink Himalayan sea salt

1. Preheat the oven to 325°F (163°C). 2. To make the crust: In a small bowl, combine the almond flour, erythritol, psyllium husk powder, and cinnamon. 3. Add the butter and cream and combine with a fork. 4. Transfer the mixture to a 7-inch springform pan. 5. Using a fork or your hands, pack the mixture against the bottom of the pan to form a crust. Do not put crust up the sides. 6. To make the filling: In a large mixing bowl, using a whisk or hand mixer on medium-high speed, combine the cream cheese, egg, erythritol, sour cream, lemon juice, stevia, and salt. 7. Pour the filling directly over the crust. 8. Bake for 38 to 40 minutes, until the very edges have a hint of brown. 9. Remove cheesecake from the oven and let cool for 1 hour. Release the springform pan and transfer the cheesecake to the refrigerator to chill for at least 1 hour. 10. Cut the cheesecake into 4 pieces and serve.

Per Serving:

calories: 373 | fat: 36g | protein: 9g | carbs: 6g | net carbs: 4g | fiber: 2g

"Frosty" Chocolate Shake

Prep time: 10 minutes | Cook time: 0 minutes | Serves 2

- ¾ cup heavy (whipping) cream
- 4 ounces coconut milk
- 1 tablespoon Swerve natural sweetener
- ¼ teaspoon vanilla extract
- 2 tablespoons unsweetened cocoa powder

1. Pour the cream into a medium cold metal bowl, and with your hand mixer and cold beaters, beat the cream just until it forms peaks. 2. Slowly pour in the coconut milk, and gently stir it into the cream. Add the sweetener, vanilla, and cocoa powder, and beat until fully combined. 3. Pour into two tall glasses, and chill in the freezer for 1 hour before serving. I usually stir the shakes twice during this time.

Per Serving:

calories: 444 | fat: 47g | protein: 4g | carbs: 15g | net carbs: 7g | fiber: 2g

Keto Macaroons

Prep time: 5 minutes | Cook time: 20 minutes | Makes 10 macaroons

3 large egg whites
¼ teaspoon salt
4 tablespoons almond flour
½ teaspoon powdered stevia
1 teaspoon vanilla extract
2 cups unsweetened coconut flakes, roughly chopped if very large
½ ounce (14 g) 80% or higher cacao dark chocolate (optional)
¼ teaspoon coconut oil (optional)

1. Preheat the oven to 350°F (180°C). Line a baking sheet with parchment paper. 2. Beat the egg whites until peaks form. In a separate bowl, combine the salt, almond flour, stevia, vanilla, and coconut flakes. Gently fold the egg whites into the coconut mixture. 3. Scoop heaping tablespoons of the mixture onto the baking sheet. Try to make the portions uniform in size and shape. (A cookie scoop is the ideal tool if you have one, but a rounded measuring spoon works as well.) 4. Bake for 20 minutes, or until lightly golden on the edges. Remove from oven and allow to cool completely. 5. If using, melt the chocolate and coconut oil together in a small microwave-safe bowl. Use a spoon to drizzle a few lines of chocolate across the top of each macaroon. Allow the chocolate to cool before serving.

Per Serving:
calories: 59 | fat: 5g | protein: 2g | carbs: 2g | net carbs: 1g | fiber: 1g

Coconut Whipped Cream

Prep time: 5 minutes | Cook time: 0 minutes | Serves 7

1 (13½-ounce/400-ml) can coconut cream, chilled, or cream from 2 (13½-ounce/400-ml) cans full-fat coconut milk, chilled for at least 12 hours (see Tip below)

Optional Additions:
1 tablespoon confectioners'-style erythritol
1 teaspoon vanilla extract
2 tablespoons cacao powder

1. Place the coconut cream in a blender or the bowl of a stand mixer fitted with the whisk attachment. If using a blender, cover, turn the speed to low, and slowly increase the speed until you reach medium. Stay at medium speed until the coconut milk has thickened to the consistency of whipped cream, about 30 seconds if using a high-powered blender. If using a stand mixer, whisk for 30 seconds, or until fluffy. Stop here if you want your whipped cream plain and unsweetened. Continue to Step 2 for a sweetened and flavored option. 2. To make sweetened, vanilla-flavored whipped cream, add the erythritol and vanilla. To make sweetened, chocolate-flavored whipped cream, add the erythritol, vanilla, and cacao powder. Cover and blend for another 10 seconds, until the ingredients are thoroughly combined.

Per Serving:
calories: 116 | fat: 12g | protein: 1g | carbs: 2g | net carbs: 2g | fiber: 0g

Zucchini Bread

Prep time: 10 minutes | Cook time: 40 minutes | Serves 12

2 cups coconut flour
2 teaspoons baking powder
¾ cup erythritol
½ cup coconut oil, melted
1 teaspoon apple cider vinegar
1 teaspoon vanilla extract
3 eggs, beaten
1 zucchini, grated
1 teaspoon ground cinnamon

1. In the mixing bowl, mix coconut flour with baking powder, erythritol, coconut oil, apple cider vinegar, vanilla extract, eggs, zucchini, and ground cinnamon. 2. Transfer the mixture into the air fryer basket and flatten it in the shape of the bread. 3. Cook the bread at 350°F (177°C) for 40 minutes.

Per Serving:
calories: 135 | fat: 14g | protein: 2g | carbs: 4g | net carbs: 3g | fiber: 1g

Strawberry Shake

Prep time: 10 minutes | Cook time: 0 minutes | Serves 2

¾ cup heavy (whipping) cream
2 ounces cream cheese, at room temperature
1 tablespoon Swerve natural sweetener
¼ teaspoon vanilla extract
6 strawberries, sliced
6 ice cubes

1. In a food processor (or blender), combine the heavy cream, cream cheese, sweetener, and vanilla. Mix on high to fully combine. 2. Add the strawberries and ice, and blend until smooth. 3. Pour into two tall glasses and serve.

Per Serving:
calories: 407 | fat: 42g | protein: 4g | carbs: 13g | net carbs: 6g | fiber: 1g

Appendix 1: Measurement Conversion Chart

MEASUREMENT CONVERSION CHART

VOLUME EQUIVALENTS(DRY)

US STANDARD	METRIC (APPROXIMATE)
1/8 teaspoon	0.5 mL
1/4 teaspoon	1 mL
1/2 teaspoon	2 mL
3/4 teaspoon	4 mL
1 teaspoon	5 mL
1 tablespoon	15 mL
1/4 cup	59 mL
1/2 cup	118 mL
3/4 cup	177 mL
1 cup	235 mL
2 cups	475 mL
3 cups	700 mL
4 cups	1 L

VOLUME EQUIVALENTS(LIQUID)

US STANDARD	US STANDARD (OUNCES)	METRIC (APPROXIMATE)
2 tablespoons	1 fl.oz.	30 mL
1/4 cup	2 fl.oz.	60 mL
1/2 cup	4 fl.oz.	120 mL
1 cup	8 fl.oz.	240 mL
1 1/2 cup	12 fl.oz.	355 mL
2 cups or 1 pint	16 fl.oz.	475 mL
4 cups or 1 quart	32 fl.oz.	1 L
1 gallon	128 fl.oz.	4 L

TEMPERATURES EQUIVALENTS

FAHRENHEIT(F)	CELSIUS(C) (APPROXIMATE)
225 °F	107 °C
250 °F	120 °C
275 °F	135 °C
300 °F	150 °C
325 °F	160 °C
350 °F	180 °C
375 °F	190 °C
400 °F	205 °C
425 °F	220 °C
450 °F	235 °C
475 °F	245 °C
500 °F	260 °C

WEIGHT EQUIVALENTS

US STANDARD	METRIC (APPROXIMATE)
1 ounce	28 g
2 ounces	57 g
5 ounces	142 g
10 ounces	284 g
15 ounces	425 g
16 ounces (1 pound)	455 g
1.5 pounds	680 g
2 pounds	907 g

Appendix 2: The Dirty Dozen and Clean Fifteen

The Dirty Dozen and Clean Fifteen

The Environmental Working Group (EWG) is a nonprofit, nonpartisan organization dedicated to protecting human health and the environment Its mission is to empower people to live healthier lives in a healthier environment. This organization publishes an annual list of the twelve kinds of produce, in sequence, that have the highest amount of pesticide residue-the Dirty Dozen-as well as a list of the fifteen kinds of produce that have the least amount of pesticide residue-the Clean Fifteen.

THE DIRTY DOZEN

- The 2016 Dirty Dozen includes the following produce. These are considered among the year's most important produce to buy organic:

Strawberries	Spinach
Apples	Tomatoes
Nectarines	Bell peppers
Peaches	Cherry tomatoes
Celery	Cucumbers
Grapes	Kale/collard greens
Cherries	Hot peppers

- The Dirty Dozen list contains two additional items kale/collard greens and hot peppers-because they tend to contain trace levels of highly hazardous pesticides.

THE CLEAN FIFTEEN

- The least critical to buy organically are the Clean Fifteen list. The following are on the 2016 list:

Avocados	Papayas
Corn	Kiw
Pineapples	Eggplant
Cabbage	Honeydew
Sweet peas	Grapefruit
Onions	Cantaloupe
Asparagus	Cauliflower
Mangos	

- Some of the sweet corn sold in the United States are made from genetically engineered (GE) seedstock. Buy organic varieties of these crops to avoid GE produce.

Made in the USA
Monee, IL
18 August 2023